Genocide, State Crime and the Law

D1610816

Genocide, State Crime and the Law critically explores the use and role of law in the perpetration, redress and prevention of mass harm by the state. In this broad ranging book, Jennifer Balint charts the place of law in the perpetration of genocide and other crimes of the state together with its role in redress and in the process of reconstruction and reconciliation, considering law in its social and political context. The book argues for a new approach to these crimes perpetrated 'in the name of the state' – that we understand them as state crimes against humanity with particular institutional dimensions that law must address to be effective in accountability and as a basis for restoration.

Focusing on seven instances of state crime – the genocide of the Armenians by the Ottoman state, the Holocaust and Nazi Germany, Cambodia under the Khmer Rouge, apartheid South Africa, Ethiopia under Mengistu and the Dergue, the genocide in Rwanda, and the conflict in the former Yugoslavia – and drawing on others, the book shows how law is companion and collaborator in these acts of nation-building by the state, and the limits and potentials of law's constitutive role in post-conflict reconstruction. It considers how law can be a partner in destruction yet also provide a space for justice.

An important, and indeed vital, contribution to the growing interest and literature in the area of genocide and post-conflict studies, *Genocide, State Crime and the Law* will be of considerable value to those concerned with law's ability to be a force for good in the wake of harm and atrocity.

Jennifer Balint is Lecturer in Socio-Legal Studies at the School of Social and Political Sciences, the University of Melbourne, Australia. Her research interests lie primarily in the area of access to justice and the constitutive role of law, with a focus on genocide and other forms of state crime.

LIVERPOOL JMU LIBRARY

3 1111 01423 8107

WITHDRAWN

Genocide, State Crime and the Law

In the Name of the State

Jennifer Balint

 Routledge
Taylor & Francis Group

a GlassHouse book

First published 2012
by Routledge
2 Park Square, Milton Park, Abingdon, Oxon OX14 4RN

Simultaneously published in the USA and Canada
by Routledge
711 Third Avenue, New York, NY 10017

A GlassHouse Book

Routledge is an imprint of the Taylor & Francis Group, an Informa business

© 2012 Jennifer Balint

The right of Jennifer Balint to be identified as author of this work has been
asserted by him/her in accordance with sections 77 and 78 of the Copyright,
Designs and Patents Act 1988.

All rights reserved. No part of this book may be reprinted or reproduced or
utilised in any form or by any electronic, mechanical, or other means, now
known or hereafter invented, including photocopying and recording, or in any
information storage or retrieval system, without permission in writing from
the publishers.

Trademark notice: Product or corporate names may be trademarks or
registered trademarks, and are used only for identification and explanation
without intent to infringe.

British Library Cataloguing in Publication Data
A catalogue record for this book is available from the British Library

Library of Congress Cataloguing in Publication Data
Balint, Jennifer.
  Genocide, state crime and the law / In the Name of the State Jennifer Balint.
     p. cm.
  1. Genocide. 2. State crimes. 3. Crimes against humanity. 4. Political crimes
and offenses. 5. Atrocities. I. Title.
  K5302.B35 2011
  345'.0251–dc22
                  2011005699

ISBN13: 978-0-415-68027-1 (pbk)
ISBN13: 978-0-203-80627-2 (ebk)

Typeset in Times New Roman
by Taylor & Francis Books

To my family

Contents

List of illustrations

Table

Figure

Box

Acknowledgements

This book owes a number of debts, some stretching back, some recent. To Israel Charny, for reminding me about prevention and treating seriously my early work. To Colin Tatz, who taught me first about the wider concept of genocide, and showed me a way to pursue my questions. To John Braithwaite, who allowed me to follow my ideas and who guided me generously in bringing them all together, to him in particular my deep gratitude. M. Cherif Bassiouni, who showed me the broader picture of law and state crime. Workshops held at the Oñati International Institute for the Sociology of Law hosted by Adam Podgórecki and Adam Czarnota were important in the development of ideas. My colleagues in Criminology at Melbourne University who have been readers and collaborators, and particularly Nesam McMillan for her generosity. Ruth Balint for her critical reading.

I was fortunate to observe many of the proceedings I discuss in the book. I am grateful to the many individuals and organizations around the world who spoke with me and allowed me to ask my questions, who hosted me in their homes and who supported my work. For their support of earlier work that provided the foundation for this book and for a stimulating intellectual environment, my deep thanks to the Research School of Social Sciences at the Australian National University, and colleagues there, and to the Evans Grawemeyer Scholarship of the Australian Department of Foreign Affairs and Trade that supported necessary fieldwork. My thanks as well to the Collegium Budapest where some of the earlier work was completed. This publication is supported by a grant from the Research and Research Training Committee, Faculty of Arts, The University of Melbourne. My thanks to Colin Perrin of GlassHouse Books for his interest in publishing the book. Earlier versions of some sections of chapters 4 and 5 were published as 'Dealing with International Crimes: Towards a Conceptual Model of Accountability and Justice' in A.L. Smeulers and R.H. Haveman (eds), *Supranational Criminology: Towards a Criminology of International Crimes*, Antwerp: Intersentia, 2008, pp. 311–34, and 'Law's Constitutive Possibilities: Reconstruction and Reconciliation in the Wake of Genocide and State Crime', in Emilios Christodoulidis and Scott Veitch (eds), *Lethe's Law.*

Justice, Law and Ethics in Reconciliation, Oxford: Hart Publishing, 2001, pp. 129–49.

Friends and broader family have supported in many important ways. Deep thanks to my parents, John and Susan, my in-laws Reg and Barbara, and brother Peter and family. To my partner Dave and our daughter Alice, thank you.

Introduction

When my grandfather gained refuge in Australia during the Second World War, together with my grandmother and their first born son, after the war had ended he put in a reparations claim for possessions they and their families had lost – a list that runs to pages of household possessions, of carpets, jewellery, furniture, crockery, linen, as well as two rural properties. These were articles belonging to his and my grandmother's families. As his reparations claim reads, the items had mostly been taken from secure places by the Hungarian Arrow Cross or the Nazi Gestapo, some had been destroyed in the siege of Budapest, and the land had been taken and titles transferred to 'unknown persons' towards the end of the war.

This was not his first attempt to claim reparations. Earlier he had made a claim through the Reparations Office in Budapest of which he heard nothing. This second attempt was made through a legal process that came out of the 1947 Peace Treaty signed with Hungary after the end of the Second World War, according to which Hungary was to return, or compensate, all property taken as a result of the war 'to the extent of two-thirds of the sum necessary, at the date of payment, to purchase similar property or to make good the loss suffered' (Treaty of Peace with Hungary 1947, Art. 26.4.a). Yet this claim, like the first, also came to nothing, stymied by the political changes in Hungary in its effective occupation by the Soviet Union.

Both claims were attempts to use the law to put on record the harm he and his family had suffered, and were his only recourse against the Hungarian state. In his pursuing a reparations claim in the wake of fleeing the country my grandfather had glimpsed law's potentially enabling effects, how law may still be a site for justice and for hearing injustice. Yet his interaction with the law also demonstrated its limits and its exclusions.

This process was the only one available to my grandfather, the only way that the loss he and my grandmother had suffered could be officially acknowledged. The loss was a far greater loss of course than any items of furniture or jewellery. He and my grandmother had lost close members of their families and dear friends, murdered in Europe in the Holocaust, and had been forced to flee Hungary themselves as refugees.

These failed reparations claims were not his first experience of the exclusionary powers of law. In his youth, he had been directly affected by the Hungarian *numerus clausus* law, the first introduced in Europe, that set limits on the number of Jewish Hungarians permitted to enter university. As he was to write later, it was only through the intervention of a high-placed official in the Education Department known to the family that he was able to get admission to university to study Civil Engineering. Despite graduating with Honours, he was later confronted with the unofficial laws of exclusion functioning in Hungarian society and faced prejudice in finding work. This was despite a family that included two Members of Parliament, and whose family home could be found in the tree-lined exclusive Alkotmány utca, the boulevard that ran straight to the Hungarian Parliament in Budapest.

As a member of a group banned from attending university, he had experienced the exclusionary powers of law. Being blocked from obtaining work further demonstrated his position in Hungarian society, and as a result of this and what the state and its society through law had communicated, he made plans to leave. In 1938 he managed to find work in Turkey, and, as he would tell it, joined other émigrés at the international café spinning a globe, trying to find a place that may take them in. He was fortunate to get a visa to Australia just before the outbreak of the Second World War, arriving in Melbourne with his family in 1939.

Letters written at the time between my grandmother and grandfather, while my grandmother was still in Budapest and my grandfather in Istanbul, show they knew the importance of gaining the right papers, the critical power of law as the imprint of the state. Legal papers, as Hannah Arendt was later to confirm, are all that matters, they are what makes an individual's humanity respected (Arendt 1959: 302).[1]

My grandfather's experiences with the law, both formal and informal, had demonstrated law's social and political embeddedness, and its powers of inclusion and exclusion, of defining the citizen. The *numerus clausus* law was mitigated through fortuitous family connections, the anti-Semitism institutionalized in Hungary had forced him to leave, and the reparations claims process was cut short due to the Soviet occupation. While the reparations process showed the possibility of law as justice, his experiences in Hungary had showed him the nature of law's exclusions.

The reparations claim through the Treaty of Peace was a chance to demonstrate what had been lost and to have this acknowledged, in however small a way. A process existed, to 'make good the loss suffered'. In this 1947 Treaty of Peace we see rights written down, codified in law, that give recognition to loss. Yet the fulfilment of these laws was dependent on the state – which ultimately failed to recognize this loss.

It was right that the process for my grandfather's reparations be through Hungary, that it be the state that was required to compensate, and to organize the return of that which had been stolen. These were state crimes. The state had a responsibility to make good. In legal redress that comes from the state we also see a statement of inclusion, of who belongs, whose harms are considered worthy of redress and are seen in fact as a crime. It points to who is considered a full citizen. Conversely, when these harms are not recognized, or when law is absent, it points to who is not.

This book is interested in how it is that law can address crimes of the state. How it is that law can encapsulate the dimensions of state crime. How law can cope with the largest of crimes. We know, for the victims, that the ability to 'make good' is limited. Yet if we are interested in how law can create a world, how law can provide redress, then how does law do this for state crime, for what Judith Shklar called the 'organized corporate enterprise'? (Shklar 1964: 192). These are acts perpetrated 'in the name of the state'. They are committed in the process of building a nation. The parameters of state crime are quite different to ordinary crime and require a particular approach.

Genocide, State Crime and the Law seeks to place genocide and other mass harms perpetrated by the state as *state* crime. It asks that we consider these acts by states or 'states to be' as particular crimes that require a considered redress. It questions the extent to which law is able to encompass the scope of these crimes and what, in law's role as *companion* to state crime and law's attempt to provide redress, this may tell us about the potentials, and limitations, of law. It considers law as both state law, and also what has been considered 'living' law, the normative orders that exist alongside and sometimes compete with official state law. It suggests that an analysis of the nature of genocide and state crime is crucial in order to understand the impact of political-legal processes to address mass harms perpetrated by the state.

These are acts, drawing on the genesis of the international legal concept of crimes against humanity that came out of the Paris Peace Conference of 1919, which offend the 'laws of humanity'.[2] Perpetrated in the 'name of the state' they include genocide, apartheid, and other forms of systematic state oppression and state murder. These are crimes that are committed as terrible programmes of nation-building – the Nazi *Weltanschauung* that sought a greater Germany, a 'Jew-less' Reich and one that also excluded Romani, the Hutu Power of the genocide in Rwanda that sought to 'reclaim' the nation without Tutsis, the new 'State of the people' of Pol Pot and the Khmer Rouge that was a violent oppression of all deemed to be 'non-Khmer', the apartheid vision of the South African state that led to the disenfranchisement and dispossession of black and other 'non-white' South Africans, the 'historic revolution' of Mengistu and the Dergue's 'Ethiopia Tikdem' (Ethiopia First), the 'Greater Serbia' of Milosevic and the Serbian state to be, the 'Greater Turkey' of the Ottoman Empire that had no room for Christian Armenians or Pontiac Greeks or Assyrians.

There are increasing expectations of law, that in the wake of state crime it will reconstitute, reconstruct and reconcile a society. We increasingly see this expectation in legal mandates to address state crime. The Rwandan criminal trials are to 'achieve reconciliation and justice' (Organic Law 1996, Preamble). The El Salvador Commission on the Truth is to 'contribute to the reconciliation of Salvadorian society' (Mexico Peace Agreements 1991, Preamble). The Act establishing the Truth and Reconciliation Commission in Sierra Leone states as one of its objectives and functions, to 'promote healing and reconciliation and to prevent a repetition of the violations and abuses suffered' and to 'promote reconciliation' (Truth and Reconciliation Commission Act 2000, Part III 1, 2b). The United Nations agreement on trials of the Khmer Rouge notes the 'pursuit of justice and national reconciliation' (Agreement Between the United Nations and the Royal Government of Cambodia 2003, Preamble). The book considers what makes this possible and how indeed law can address the institutional and state dimensions of genocide and other state crime, together with playing a reconstructive role in societies coming out of state crime.

The increasing use of law

Law may of course not always occupy a central place, and it may well be absent. Most crimes of state are not addressed through law. While this is changing, most crimes committed by the state are not subject to legal redress, particularly when the government committing the crime remains in power. This is particularly the case with harm of indigenous peoples. The use of law generally requires a change of government, and is intimately linked to the formation of the new state, as partner in this creation. Yet we also see that recognition may not be all encompassing – the failure to acknowledge and address the crimes committed against the Romani (Gypsies) in Nazi Germany is a tragic example of this. Further, even when law is used, changing political realities can mean that this recognition is fleeting – as we saw in the Hungarian Peace Treaty.

The history of law addressing state crime is a fairly short one. The genocide perpetrated by the Ottoman state against the Armenians under cover of the First World War was addressed by law only briefly. The Courts-Martial established under the Sultan was abolished with the rise to power of the Kemalist party. The trials promised by the Allies never eventuated. The Second World War saw the first sustained attempt at prosecution, with the main International Military Tribunal at Nuremberg that saw the chief architects of the devastation wrought by Nazi Germany put on trial, as well as a raft of other smaller trials held by the United States and European nations. We then had a hiatus for years in law addressing state crime (despite attempts by non-governmental organizations to bring the Khmer Rouge to justice), until the first political-legal processes in South America to consider systematic human rights violations by the states through the use of government inquiries and truth commissions.

Since the 1980s, we have seen a far higher proportion of state crime being addressed through law. From the approximately one sixth of state crimes perpetrated since the Second World War that were addressed through law prior to the 1980s, this has changed to an estimated one half, and it continues to increase.[3] This increase is across the board – from providing redress for massive crimes committed by the state against its own citizens such as genocide, to addressing long-standing crimes of oppression and subjugation such as apartheid, to playing a role in regime change and institutionalization of the new system of governance such as in post-communist Eastern Europe and in the wake of military rule in South America. Law is increasingly playing a role in the resolution of conflicts, state crime and political change within societies. Its absences, however, are keenly felt by victim communities.

The twentieth century has also seen the increased codification of acts of mass harm committed against civilians. Defined as 'wrongful acts of states', acts committed by state officials, in particular heads of states, formerly did not warrant criminalization, nor were they defined as crimes, but were, if deemed necessary, mediated by diplomacy or force. The move to define such acts as crimes began only in the wake of the Second World War (although the genocide of the Armenians had been termed a 'crime against humanity' by the Allies during the First World War). It was at this time too that the International Law Commission began considering the topic of 'state responsibility', deliberations which ended (for now) in November 2001. We have a *Convention on the Prevention and Punishment of Genocide* that outlines the crime of genocide, we have a permanent International Criminal Court with a mandate to try genocide, crimes against humanity, war crimes and aggression, and we have expanded definitions of these crimes that now include crimes of gender. We do not, however, have a concept of state crime within international law.

The evidence, thus, is that law is increasingly being called upon as a tool to address mass harm and to facilitate societal changes. It is being asked to play an ever increasing role in the redress of acts involving the perpetration of human rights violations by the state. The book addresses these more recent developments and considers how well it does this in light of the nature of state crime, these crimes perpetrated 'in the name of the state'.

Law and the constitution of the state

Law's addressing of state crime can play a powerful role in the constitution of this crime. How, and of course, if law addresses state crime can determine how it is understood, what accountability is possible, and what the prospects for reconstruction and reconciliation may be. Law has power to constitute a society. Law frames a society. At its best, as James Boyd White argued, the law should take as its most central question what kind of a community we should be (White 1985: 42). At its worst, law can do the same. Law establishes boundaries and exclusions as well as inclusions. We see this clearly during the state crime, as well as afterwards. The 'effects of law', to use Sarat and Kearns' phrase (1993), can be broad.

Law can define the limits of perception. In the wake of state crime, legal processes are aimed at reconfiguring the normative framework and reference points of that society. Justice Richard Goldstone said at the time of the South African Truth and Reconciliation Commission that if it were not for the Commission, people who today are saying that they did not know about apartheid would be saying that it did not happen. The Commission, as an authoritative state legal framework, was able to establish a new reality that acknowledged and condemned the truth of the apartheid state. We see the difficulties in this too. When the International Court of Justice in its judgement says that the acts committed against Bosnian Muslims (with the exception of Srebrenica) are not genocide, does this mean they are not? And if a legal process focuses solely on individual perpetrators and not the broader parameters of this crime as state crime, does this then mischaracterize the crime (the focus on individual perpetrators in Rwanda and not the state directed nature of the genocide for example)? When it only includes parti-cular harms, over certain time periods (the Nuremberg Tribunal began its deliberations from 1939, thereby excluding the systematic exclusion and persecution prior to the Second World War), does it also paint a different picture? Or when it omits causes or ongoing consequences, such as the legacy of colonialism or continuing economic injustices?

Law can be a powerful tool in providing a clear verdict on the past, in creating a line between the old and the new. Law draws this line through a variety of mechanisms, from the criminal tribunals established by the United Nations, to national criminal trials, to truth commissions established by national governments, to the constitutional courts of Central Eastern Europe, to policies of lustration and denazification, to compensation and tort claim hearings. This line can be clearly visible. The Truth and Reconci-liation Commission of South Africa in having Archbishop Desmond Tutu at its helm and with a focus on hearing from the victims of apartheid within a discourse of reconciliation was a clear statement that there was a new and inclusive regime. The Allies' denazification programme in the wake of the Second World War made a point about the 'penetration of Nazism through all layers of German society' and the need to separate between Germans and Nazis. One former victim of the Khmer Rouge noted in relation to the joint United Nations and Cambodian criminal tribunal for the crimes of the Khmer Rouge, 'I feel excited about the trial. The trial is for the future of our children' (Mam 2010).

We can observe the norm-making function of law in processes for state crime, in both establishing new realities and repressing old ones. Law marks the telos of the new state. Law can be the basis for acknowledgement and change. As such, its effect can be as a 'foundational moment' for the society.[4] The potential of the legal process at such a time can be as a reference point for the society, one that can provide an important basis, as well as a framework, for wider restoration and reconstruction, both institutional and societal. This was the hope of the Truth and Reconciliation Commission of South Africa with its focus on 'reconciliation through truth', and has been the impact of other mechanisms, from the Australian High Court *Mabo* decision that declared that Australia was not *terra nullius* (empty land) at the time of white colonization, to the establishment of the joint Cambodia – United Nations 'Extraordinary Chambers in the Courts of Cambodia' that marked an end to the integration of the Khmer Rouge in the Cambodian state. It is this norm-making function of law that holds great promise and why it is important that we get it right.

How state crime is constituted, how it is understood through law, can have wider implications for the life of that society. When we understand genocide and other state crime as a crime of state, then this has implications for any later reconciliation. How state crime is prosecuted, as individual perpetrators, as in the case of the national Rwandan criminal trials, or as a more 'state crime' approach, as in the Truth and Reconciliation Commission of South Africa, can have implications for how a society mends in the wake of state crime. The understanding of state crime as state directed can mean a greater chance for bringing a society together. Through considering the broader dimensions of state crime, and not focusing solely on individual responsibilities, there is a chance to create a space for a re-constitution.

Equally, law's constitutive ability is most severely tested in the aftermath of state crime. The tendency, in the wake of state crime, is to use law as another nation-building tool. We see this in Rwanda, with new legislation that has had the effect of silencing opposition. We also see it in the lack of adherence to due process in the 'Red Terror' trials of the Dergue and former Ethiopian president Mengistu Haile-Mariam. All legal processes in the wake of state crime are used to establish the new regime. While law is used to create the new nation through creating boundaries between the old and the new, and establish new understandings of who is included in the new state, these can be constrictive too.

The impact of law in the wake of state crime, however, can be still-born. With the rise of the Kemalist government and the demise of the Sultan, the findings of the Ottoman state's Courts-Martial in the wake of the First World War genocide of the Armenians were placed outside the public sphere and consciously transformed into another message of Turkish martyrdom rather than institutionalized harm against the Armenian people and other Christian minorities by the Ottoman state. The marginalization and transformation of these legal proceedings meant that the constitutive role they ended up playing was that of the reconstruction of the nationalist Turkish party.

We see the constitutive role of law during state crime as well. While law is never used to perpetrate state murder, law does provide a framework, and

LIVERPOOL JOHN MOORES UNIVERSITY
LEARNING SERVICES

makes the crimes allowable. Law is both companion and bystander. So in Germany we see legislation that segregated Jews out from public life creating a space in which their eventual disappearance was less remarked upon. Or in South Africa under apartheid, legislation played a dominant role in the exclusion and oppression of black South Africans, allowing for even further oppressions that were the subject of the Truth Commission hearings. Or law fails to protect, as in the case brought to the International Court of Justice during the war of dissolution whose orders to cease the harms against Bosnians were not heeded.

The laws introduced during state crime – or law-like directives – are fashioned to work with the dominant normative orders of that society. As Sally Falk Moore (1973) showed with her examination of different societal microcosms in the 1970s, similarly to the early legal sociology of Eugen Ehrlich (1913), laws intended to direct change may indeed fail or have unintended consequences due to existing strong social arrangements. Law during state crime sticks close to pre-existing normative orders, utilizing these in the establishment of the new regime, backed up by force. Very rarely do they go outside this, rather staying close to what will be accepted by the majority in power. One example of law straying outside what was accepted was the protest in Nazi Germany of non-Jewish wives of their arrested 'Mischlinge' (Germans of Jewish ancestry) husbands – forcing the state to return the men. But otherwise there was little protest. We see this particularly in the Khmer Rouge regime, who together with a regime of terror in effect supplanted the authority of the former 'wise men' of the Buddhists and appealed to the 'ordinary Khmer'.

Perpetrator regimes have a particular relationship with law. So the first decree of the Khmer Rouge regime was a new Constitution, designed to illustrate their legitimacy – and their new direction – to the world. Even when law is little used, as in Rwanda, the manner of perpetration resonated in part with local practices – killing was sometimes referred to as taking the Tutsi 'to the *bourgmestre*' in an echo of past practices of taking suspected criminals to the local authorities.

Facilitating both accountability and reconstruction through law is a core challenge. We need to be careful in our expectations. When a people has been almost destroyed, the expectation of immediate reconciliation is premature, despite it sometimes being a practical need, as in Rwanda. Reconciliation here we may term something else, a kind of co-existence.

Further, in a focus on reconstruction and reconciliation it is critical that we do not neglect accountability. State crime involves the cooption and transformation of state and non-state institutions, the utilization of a state structure towards these ends. Accountability, thus, should not be solely individual accountability, important as this is, but an institutional reckoning that is key to any full redress for state crime. This is a recognition of the parameters of state crime, that it includes both institutional perpetrators as well as institutional beneficiaries. Organizations whose job it is to protect the population end up harming them or being a companion to or beneficiary of this harm. In the case of Rwanda, this was the state, the army and the police. Or in South Africa, a host of institutions, state and non-state were both perpetrators and beneficiaries. As the Congress of South African Trade Unions submission demonstrated at the institutional hearings for business of the Truth and Reconciliation Commission of South Africa, 'capitalism in South Africa was built and sustained precisely on the basis of the systematic racial oppression of the majority of our people' (Truth and Reconciliation Commission of South Africa 1999b: 22). That is, as they pointed out, 'apartheid's labour laws, pass laws, forced removals and cheap labour system were all to the advantage of the business community' (ibid: 24).

This direct involvement of the state in the victimization of its own civilians, and the deep implication of the institutions of the state (the military and the police, the bureaucracy, the judiciary and the executive) and of civil society, raises particular issues for redress. The crimes are ones committed by individuals, however committed as state policy, harnessing institutions of the state and of civil society. What is being asked here is how to address the institutions of the state that constitute the basis of the state and its legitimacy.

There has been some acknowledgement of this in terms of who is responsible for genocide and other forms of state crime. That is, naming both individuals, as well as states, governments, and state and non-state institutions as responsible for state crime. Truth commissions and inquiries are starting to name a range of actors as responsible. For example, the South African Truth and Reconciliation Commission held institutional hearings that examined the many institutions, both government and non-government, that supported the apartheid system. Hearings were held on the legal profession, the medical profession, the security forces and the churches, among others, in an investigation into how these organizations that we hope may protect, such as religious institutions, were involved. It found damningly that many institutions, in their collaboration with the state and apartheid policy, were responsible for the perpetuation of apartheid. More recently, the East Timor Commission for Reception, Truth and Reconciliation in its findings named the Indonesian state, as well as bystander nations such as Australia and the United States, as responsible for the systematic oppression in East Timor over decades. The location of institutional responsibility can even be seen weakly at the International Tribunal at Nuremberg in terms of grouping individuals on trial into the organizations, such as the 'SS', of which they were members.

It is through addressing the causes and structures that make state crime possible – and these can be different – that we have a chance at creating a stronger basis for the future. When we address both institutional as well as individual responsibility, and we are thus accounting for all actors responsible, we have a greater chance of any future prevention. If reconstruction is to become a goal of law, as it seems it increasingly is, then we will need to be considering justice as multi-faceted, encompassing both strict accountability for state crime as well as taking a more broad reconstructive approach that pays attention to the parameters of crimes committed by states. The concept of civic liability – liability for institutions as well as for individuals – as a form of institutional reconstruction, and one that is a possible link between immediate legal remedy and broader societal and state reconstruction is one concept put forward in the book. In considering law's claim to be a re-constitutive actor it is necessary that we consider what will make it so. *When* law is able to be transformative is a key concern of this book.

Structure of the book

Each chapter in the book addresses an aspect of the relationship between law and state crime. It aims at a broad socio-legal analysis of the interconnections between law and mass harm by the state, and considers what these mean for our understanding and addressing of these state crimes. It considers these acts in their socio-political context, considering the place they occupy in the life of the nation, rather than purely as acts that are 'illegal' and which require a legal response. In this way, it is hoped that we can consider further the role that law plays, both in perpetration and in redress, and, ultimately, in prevention.

Through its examination of law, state crime and genocide, this book also intends to contribute to our consideration more broadly of the role of law in society. It is at these times that we see the schism within law most vividly. Law can include and exclude. It can be a site for justice and for injustice. It is what we appeal to, yet what may not hear us. It can be a basis for change, yet entrench existing prejudices. *Genocide, State Crime and the Law* asks that we consider what this means for law's role and its place.

The book focuses on the genocide of the Armenians by the Ottoman State 1915–18, the Holocaust and Nazi Germany 1933–45, Cambodia under the Khmer Rouge 1975–79, apartheid South Africa 1948–91, Ethiopia under Mengistu and the Dergue 1974–91, the genocide in Rwanda 1994, and the conflict in the former Yugoslavia 1992–94. A broadly comparative approach was chosen in order to highlight the similarities and differences between different forms of state crime and the particular issues this throws up for legal redress. The selection of case studies was guided by wanting to consider how law addresses mass harm perpetrated in the course of nation-building, in the 'name of the state'. These are all instances of state crime. Further, they are all situations in which (state-initiated) law has played some role in redress.

The cases selected illustrate a spectrum of the use of law during the mass harm, from weak legal redress such as the trial in absentia of Pol Pot and Ieng Sary by Vietnam in the wake of the defeat of the Khmer Rouge, to a strong response such as the series of trials in the wake of the Second World

War. They also illustrate a spectrum of the use of law during the mass harm. It is clearly not an exhaustive list. While some were not included due to the lack of any state legal redress, such as Biafra 1967–70, the crimes of Stalin, or of China under Chairman Mao, other examples of legal proceedings for state crime have been brought into the discussion. These include post-independence East Timor, Bangladesh 1971, truth commission processes in Liberia, Sierra Leone and in South America, and post-communist legal processes, as well as, in Chapter 5, in the context of reconstruction and reconciliation, victim-initiated legal proceedings for indigenous genocide in Australia. There will be gaps in this book, but it is intended, rather than as a comprehensive guide to all case studies of state crime and their relationship to law, to be an indicative one.

Chapter 1 begins with a consideration of the nature of state crime. It locates genocide and other forms of mass harm perpetrated by the state as *state* crime, crimes committed in the pursuit of nation-building. It shows how these are systematic actions taken by the state or the emerging state against particular groups for their destruction or subjugation. It puts forward a schema of state crime that defines and differentiates acts of gross human rights violations perpetrated by the state, yet locates them all as 'crimes against humanity', violations of human rights on a *sufficiently savage or systematic scale*. It argues for a recognition of the particular parameters of this type of crime, and their differences, that will assist both in legal redress and in prevention.

The book continues its consideration of the relationship between genocide, state crime and law with an examination of the use of law during the perpetration of genocide and other state crime. This is the first step in contextualizing the use of law in redressing state crime. Chapter 2 examines the use of law in the perpetration of state crime in the seven core cases: the genocide of the Armenians by the Ottoman State 1915–18, the Holocaust and Nazi Germany 1933–45, Cambodia under the Khmer Rouge 1975–79, apartheid South Africa 1948–91, Ethiopia under Mengistu and the Dergue 1974–91, the genocide in Rwanda 1994, and the conflict in the former Yugoslavia 1992–94. It outlines a spectrum of the use of law, from companion to bystander. It shows that while law is not used as a central tool in murder, perpetrator regimes define themselves peculiarly in relation to the law, and in fact law makes 'allowable' the perpetration of state crime. This, I suggest, has important implications for the perpetration, and later the redress, of atrocities.

Chapter 3 shows how law is used as a further tool of nation-building and governance in the wake of state crime. Law is used to constitute the new society, to provide a clear break between the old and the new. Legal processes are designed to create new realities. These narratives of law, however, in partnering the new state, may be overtaken by political change. The second part of the chapter provides a systematic overview of the seven core cases of state crime and the legal redress used, illustrating a dominant focus on perpetrator and victim redress rather than a more future oriented broader societal redress through law.

Carried out 'in the name of the state', state crimes involve the use and transformation of a state structure and its institutions, both civil and state. Chapter 4 examines the attempts in legal redress for state crime to address these institutional parameters. It shows that while we may see individuals placed according to institutional affiliation, the institution itself, and the state, is rarely specifically addressed. While there may be an account of the harm that includes institutions and the state, there is little accountability. The chapter suggests the concept of civic liability to bring institutions, both state and non-state, into an overarching framework of liability for state crime, drawing on the duty of care owed by our core state and non-state institutions to its society.

Chapter 5 investigates the relationship between reconciliation, reconstruction, and law. It considers the ever-increasing call for reconciliation in the wake of genocide and state crime, examining its place and function as a component of law and of the post-conflict landscape. The chapter examines what can make law a constitutive actor, and how law may provide a basis for reconstruction and reconciliation. It shows the necessary interdependence between institutional and societal reconstruction, and the conditions for law being transformative. It illustrates that the institutional design of legal processes and the path taken by a government in the wake of such crime do impact on societal reconstruction. However, this does not mean that legal proceedings *create* societal reconstruction or reconciliation. At best they establish spaces that open up these possibilities.

The book concludes in Chapter 6 with a consideration of the connections between law in perpetration, law in redress and law in prevention. It illustrates the critical power of acknowledgement of law, both in perpetration and in redress. Law is companion in determining who is citizen and who is protected. Yet in its still providing a space for injustice, in providing a record, and in stopping short of partnering extermination and killing, it may provide a space for future justice. Law is thus able to occupy a space between the past and the present. Law is companion, collaborator and bystander. Law can also be preventer. In this we see the fundamental dichotomy within law itself, simply that between law as facilitator of harm, and law as facilitator of redress. Law can both enfranchise and disenfranchise, be a tool of empowerment as well as of exclusion. This is fundamental to understanding both genocide and state crime, but also the institution of law.

Law's addressing of state crime can play a powerful role in the constitution of this crime. How it is constituted through law, however, can have wider implications for the life of that society. Equally, law's constitutive ability is most severely tested in the aftermath of state crime, and it is in observing the addressing of the 'crisis' situation of state crime and genocide through law that we may observe both the potentials and limitations of law to re-constitute in the wake of harm.

It is a complex process, well articulated by Chief Justice DP Mahomed in judgement on the case brought before the Constitutional Court of South Africa that challenged the constitutionality of the amnesty provision of the Truth and Reconciliation Commission of South Africa:

> It is an exercise of immense difficulty interacting in a vast network of political, emotional, ethical and logistical considerations.
> (*Azanian Peoples Organisation* (*AZAPO*) *and Others* 1996: para 21)

It is this interface that the book grapples with; the limits and potentials of law in addressing state crime conceived of as state perpetration of crimes against humanity.

Notes

1 Hannah Arendt wrote:

> The great danger arising from the existence of people forced to live outside the common world is that they are thrown back, in the midst of civilization, on their natural givenness, on their mere differentiation. They lack that tremendous equalizing of differences which comes from being citizens of some commonwealth and yet, since they are no longer allowed to partake in the human artifice, they begin to belong to the human race in much the same way as animals belong to a specific animal species. The paradox involved in the loss of human rights is that such loss coincides with the instant when a person becomes a human being in general – without a profession, without a citizenship, without an opinion, without a deed by which to identify and specify himself – *and* different in general, representing nothing but his own absolutely unique individuality which, deprived of expression within and action upon a common world, loses all significance.
> (Arendt 1959: 302)

2 The Commission of Fifteen Members, created by the Preliminary Peace Conference in January 1919, found by majority in its report that the First World War 'was carried on by the Central Empires together with their allies, Turkey and Bulgaria, by barbarous or illegitimate methods in violation of the established laws and customs of war and the elementary *laws of humanity*'. *Violation of the Laws and Customs of War*. Report of Majority and Dissenting Reports of American and Japanese Members of the Commission on Responsibilities, Conference of Paris, 1919 (in Schwelb 1946: 180).
3 This is a reanalysis of data, primary sources of which are documented in Balint 1996: 231–47.
4 My use of the term 'foundational moment' has been inspired by Elizabeth Jelin's earlier use of the term, although I have applied it in different ways throughout the book. In the context of the transition in Argentina, Jelin saw the trial of the military commanders as the institutional authentification of 'truth', through the authority of the judiciary, and the foundational moment of 'justice' (Jelin 1994: 51).

Chapter 1

Conceptualizing genocide and state crime

At the end of the First World War, in his opening speech to the Ottoman Senate on 19 October 1918, the president, Senator Ahmed Riza, invoked the memory of 'the Armenians who were savagely murdered'. Two days later, when challenged on this, he described the mass murder of the Armenians as an 'officially' (*resmen*) sanctioned 'state' crime (*devlet eliyle*) requiring 'some kind of intervention' by the authorities (Dadrian 1994a: 110). The subsequent Courts-Martial into the genocide of the Armenians heard one witness speak of doing 'government business' (Höss 1992: 220).

Genocide and other forms of mass harm directed against civilian populations are a particular kind of crime. These are systematic actions taken by the state or the emerging state against particular groups for their destruction or subjugation. What makes these crimes particular is both their enormity, but also their position in relation to the state. These are acts done 'in the name of the state'. These are not individuals committing crimes, but programmes of mass destruction initiated and carried out by governments or governments in waiting. They are perpetrated over longer (apartheid in South Africa) or shorter (the genocide in Rwanda) periods, with the aim of creating the state in a particular image. They can include crimes of settler-colonialism, that as Patrick Wolfe has suggested, can be understood, unfolding as they do over longer time periods, as 'a structure rather than an event', yet with the same logic of destruction and nation-building (Wolfe 1994: 96). They are state orchestrated, harnessing institutions and expressing state policy. The recognition of this mass harm and destruction as state crime is critical for our understanding of these crimes and for their legal redress.

This opening chapter considers different approaches to conceptualizing state crime. State crime, as will be shown, has been defined ranging from unlawful acts committed by state officials, to the denial of sufficient housing, to the commission of systematic human rights violations. The state crimes that I discuss in this book are acts of mass harm perpetrated by states, or states to be. My focus on state crime includes what is core to the international legal conception of 'crimes against humanity', in particular its original usage as being violations of human rights on a *sufficiently savage or systematic scale*, yet being attentive to the state orchestrated nature of such crime. While this kind of orchestrated mass harm is mostly perpetrated by states, it can also, as seen in the case of the Republika Srpska in the conflict in the former Yugoslavia, be perpetrated by organizations with links to existing states or who themselves are attempting to be the state, what I term 'states to be'.[1] As M. Cherif Bassiouni has noted, non-state actors can 'parall[el] the organizational power structure of the state' and thus can be 'the functional equivalent of state actors' (Bassiouni 2003: 69).

While 'crime against humanity', 'crime against peace', and 'war crime', as considered within international law, possess a necessary individual dimension, they also importantly possess an institutional state dimension. This chapter argues for a conceptualization of genocide and other forms of state crime that cuts through the disciplinary borders of the social sciences and international law. It considers how we may understand these crimes of the state as a nation-building, and state-directed set of acts – and what this means for our defining mass harm by the state. This becomes important both in terms of how we may address state crime through law, as well as in how it may be prevented. Considering our internationally defined harms of 'crimes against humanity' and genocide through a 'state crime' lens allows us to address the particular nature of state crime, its institutional and nation-building character. Yet we can also distinguish between these crimes, and what I suggest in the chapter is a conceptualization of mass harm that allows us both to allow for their difference and focus on the institutional and state nature of these crimes. Further, it allows us to consider what appropriate legal redress may look like.

'In the name of the state'

The use of the state and its resources marks genocide and other forms of mass harm as a different kind of crime, requiring a particular kind of legal response. The destruction wrought is in the name of the state and part of state policy. It demarcates who is citizen in this state and who is not. It uses the institutions of the state, or state to be, and others to perpetrate crimes of destruction and oppression against civilians under its control.

The vision of a greater Germany, a Third Reich that would be eternal, meant the extermination of an estimated six million Jews throughout occupied Europe (as well as the killing of Romani and other 'undesirables'). Christian anti-semitism and scientific racism, together with the will and organization of the Nazi state, conspired in the destruction of European Jewry. The Nazi party implemented a raft of legislation for the exclusion of Jews, and then began a system of further segregation, ghettoization, and concentration and death camps. What began with legislation, ended in extermination. At the end of the war, the National Socialist vision, its 'Weltanschauung', had resulted in death never before seen, with Auschwitz becoming a symbol of evil. With knowledge of what was happening, as Martin Gilbert (1981) has outlined, came no action from the Allies. In an introduction to the transcripts of the British war crimes trial of the camp commandant Josef Kramer and other officials of the concentration camp Bergen-Belsen, Raymond Phillips writes that when on 15 April 1945 the first British officer arrived at the camp, and Belsen became a symbol of 'all that had been told (and scarcely credited) of the vileness and rottenness of the Nazi system',

> with public horror at the stories that came from Belsen went a public demand that those responsible should be punished for their deeds ... and to many it seemed superfluous that there should be a trial at all, and the popular cry was for a summary identification and execution of the offenders.
>
> (Phillips 1949: xxiii–xxiv)

The Hutu Power of the government and political elites in Rwanda after the Arusha Accords that had sought a power sharing arrangement meant the murder of an estimated 800,000 Rwandan Tutsis (together with some moderate Hutus). Over 100 days, Tutsis were hunted down, rounded up and killed.

Organized months before, the genocide in Rwanda was facilitated by militia armed by the state, communication between the government and the communes, and hate propaganda through radio. As Rene Lemarchand was to write, 'Planned annihilation, not the sudden eruption of long-simmering hatreds, is the key to the tragedy in Rwanda' (Lemarchand 1995: 8). Alison des Forges observed:

> Extremists used its administrative apparatus, its military and its party organizations to carry out a 'cottage-industry' genocide that reached out to all levels of the population ... Those with state power used their authority to force action from those reluctant to kill.
>
> (des Forges 1995: 44)

International observers refused to call it genocide. Nesam McMillan (2008) has charted the international failure to stop the genocide, noting, 'There was a wholesale turning away from the suffering of the Rwandan Tutsis as they were methodically exterminated because they were Tutsi' (ibid: 1).

From April 1975 to January 1979, an estimated 1.8 million Khmer people were killed by Pol Pot and the Khmer Rouge. Buddhist monks, the Cham Muslim, and Vietnamese, Thai and Chinese in Cambodia, as well as those defined as 'non-Khmer', were targeted by the Khmer Rouge. The 'Democratic Kampuchea' established by the Khmer Rouge after their taking power in Cambodia was a violent regime. Survivors were to call it *kuk et chonhcheang*, 'the prison without walls' (Hinton 1998: 93). Hundreds of thousands of

Khmer were forcibly moved from the cities to the countryside and worked to death. This was to be 'an era more remarkable than the age of the Angkors', a slogan they would repeat. The vision of a Cambodia that would be ' … a State of the people, workers, peasants, and all other Cambodian working people' (*Constitution of Democratic Kampuchea* 1976, Art. 1) was implemented violently by the Khmer Rouge and their cadre, and ended only with the invasion by Vietnam.

On a platform of 'black peril swamping the cities', as David Dyzenhaus (1991: 40) notes, the Afrikaner Nationalists in South Africa swept to power in 1948, implementing a system of segregation and disenfranchisement of South Africans that was institutionalized through law. The vision of apartheid resulted in the systematic segregation and subjugation of black South Africans. This gross disenfranchisement that lasted until 1991 with the negotiated settlement between the National Party government and the African National Congress was realized through practices of forced removal, 'pass' laws that meant limited movement and access, banning from services, imprisonment and torture and a system of a state within a state. Over 14,500 civilians were killed and many more affected as a result of the apartheid policy, this vision of separateness that was violently implemented by the South African state.

In Ethiopia, what started as a popular uprising against the government of Emperor Haile-Selassie ended as a military coup installing Lieutenant-Colonel Mengistu Haile-Mariam as President, together with a governing body, the Dergue Military Council. Over their 17-year reign, from September 1974, an estimated 200,000 civilians were killed, with many more detained and tortured. Legislation marked out the new regime, orchestrated by Mengistu and the Dergue, and the army and police were used as state executioners. The regime of Mengistu was intent on a 'new page' of Ethiopian history, a socialist regime committed to protecting the 'Revolutionary Motherland'. The new Special Penal Code referred in its preamble to the 'historic revolution now in progress', a revolution which had at its core terror, torture and killings, encircling the Ethiopian people. It only ended in May 1991 with the overthrow of the regime by the EPRDF (Ethiopian People's Revolutionary Democratic Front) and the EPLF (Ethiopian People's Liberation Front).

The conflict in the former Yugoslavia was a deliberate, orchestrated attempt by the Bosnian Serb and Serbian state leadership, with support from Croatian Serbs, to establish a 'Greater Serbia'. In reality, this meant a future with, in a particular geographical area of the former Yugoslavia, no non-Serbs, in particular no Bosnian Muslims. Gow puts it succinctly when he writes 'the war in Yugoslavia was a war for borders, statehood, identity and ideology' (Gow 1997: 12). What may be termed both a 'conventional' war and a 'war of extermination' was waged. The objective of Serbian political and military forces was to carve out new borders; as Gow notes, the creation of a new mini-Yugoslavia, to be detached from Bosnia in the east to Serbia, in the south to Montenegro, and in the west to Serb-populated and occupied regions in Croatia (ibid: 35).

The breakdown of Yugoslavia was orchestrated by the former Serbian republic under Slobodan Milošević, who, as Gow notes, rose to power in 1987 promising to make Serbia 'whole' again (ibid: 17). The creation of a Greater Serbia meant the destruction of Bosnian Muslims, orchestrated by the Serbian state in conjunction with the newly formed 'Republika Srpska' in Bosnia – through concentration camps, rape camps and mass killings. The International Criminal Tribunal for the former Yugoslavia found in the *Tadić* case that the Bosnian Serb army was largely established, equipped, staffed, and financed by the Yugoslav Peoples' Army, the JNA (*The Prosecutor v Duško Tadić* 1997). This was a case of both the state and the 'state to be' following a plan of destruction in the name of the new 'nation to be', a 'Greater Serbia'. Their actions resulted in the deaths of an estimated 300,000 former Yugoslavs, mainly Bosnian Muslims, killed in Bosnia-Herzegovina, the dissolution of what was formerly known as Yugoslavia, and the traumatization and dislocation of many thousands more.

The genocide of the Armenians was perpetrated by the Ottoman state under cover of the First World War. With the entry of Turkey into the war, an opportunity arose for the destruction of what was seen as an alien nation, preventing the establishment of a 'Pan-Turkic empire'. This Greater Turkey had no room for Christian Armenians, mostly tolerated, albeit as second-class citizens, over centuries. With political incursions into the Ottoman Empire and internal instability in the years leading up to the First World War, this was to change. The 'Committee of Union and Progress' (known as the 'Young Turks'), which had on its establishment been a force for change, moved away from what Richard Hovannisian has described as egalitarian Ottomanism to the new ideology of Turkism, which would 'give justification to violent means for transforming a heterogeneous empire into a homogeneous state based on the concept of one nation, one people' (Hovannisian 1986: 28). Under the leadership of Talat Paşa, Enver Paşa and Cemal Paşa, the leaders of the 'Young Turks', the Ottoman state began a programme to annihilate the Armenians. This began with the arrest, deportation and killing of leaders of the Armenian community in April 1915, followed by the mass deportation of Armenians designed to result in their death, and the killing of Armenians in the Ottoman armies. An estimated 1.2 million Armenians were killed from 1915 to 1918. The American Ambassador at the time wrote: 'I am confident that the whole history of the human race contains no such horrible episode as this. The great massacres and persecutions of the past seem almost insignificant when compared to the sufferings of the Armenian race in 1915' (in ibid: 30). Telegrams sent by the Minister of the Interior Talat Paşa to the Governor of Aleppo show the intent of the genocide by the ruling Young Turk Ittihadist Party. The account of Arnold Toynbee shows the systematic and thorough nature of the destruction – as he observed: 'It was a deliberate, systematic attempt to eradicate the Armenian population throughout the Ottoman Empire, and it has certainly met with a large measure of success' (in Melson 1986: 64).

These are all state crimes and systematic, directed, purposeful acts that are state policy, intended to result in mass harm and destruction. These are searches for the perfect society, a search, which as Isaiah Berlin noted, is a recipe for bloodshed (Berlin 1991). It is a search harnessed to the institutions of the state, and as such has far wider implications and results than any mere fantasy of any group. The destruction and systematic oppression is integrally connected to the definition and the future of a state, and is a violent exercise of consolidation, targeting groups who are seen to conflict with the interests and vision of the state as defined by the ruling political elite. It defines who is citizen and who is not, and ultimately, who is perceived as human and who is not.

Understanding state crime

The concept of state crime for mass harm by states has been largely missing in the social science literature. This is beginning to change. In criminology, for example, we see a dominant focus on domestic crime, 'ordinary' individual acts of murder, rape, gang violence and so on. This has been expanded to a consideration of state violence, as we see in the work of Kauzlarich (1995), Barak (1991) and Ross (1995) for example, and Cunneen's (2008) work on the role of the state in colonial violence. Smeulers and Roelofs (2008) have developed a framework of 'supranational criminology' designed to encompass international crimes, to which we can add earlier work such as George Yacoubian's (1997) on including genocide within a criminological framework, Green and Ward's (2004) work on state crime, and most recently Alex Alvarez's (2009) work on genocide.

Political scientists and sociologists have worked closely on the concept of genocide and crimes of the state. R.J. Rummel proposed the term *democide* to denote killing by governments, demonstrating that there are different types of killing by the state (Rummel 1994). Alex Schmid examined the connections between repression, state terrorism and genocide (Schmid 1991). Barbara Harff and Ted Gurr have examined the nature of state harm against civilians, proposing the term 'politicide' (Harff & Gurr 1989). Zygmunt Bauman (1989) showed how the Holocaust must be considered as part of modernity rather than outside it. Irving Horowitz and Pieter Drost recognized the link between genocide and the state (Drost 1959a, 1959b; Horowitz 1976). Colin Tatz (2003) examined genocide as an example of race politics. Leo Kuper (1981) examined genocide as a political crime.

In international law we in fact have no concept of state crime. What we do have are references to state responsibility and state policy. The Rome Statute of the International Criminal Court in its definition of 'Crimes against humanity' notes the existence of a 'State or organizational policy to commit such [an] attack' [a widespread or systematic attack directed against any civilian population]. The Genocide Convention notes in relation to the use of the International Court of Justice as the organ for the settlement of disputes in interpretation, application or fulfilment of the Convention the 'responsibility of the state for genocide' (Article IX). The main international legal drafting body, the International Law Commission, has written of state responsibility, but fallen short of confirming the term 'state crime'. In earlier discussions, the Commission discussed a 'special regime of responsibility' for 'international crimes of the state' (see Spinedi 1989), yet this debate has been shelved for now. Rather, international law considers genocide, crimes against humanity and war crimes as separate acts, with little explicit conceptualization of their state nature. This has led, as William Schabas has suggested, to a misplaced focus on lesser leaders in international criminal prosecutions (Schabas 2008) and, overall, I would suggest, a misunderstanding of the nature of these kinds of crimes.

In the social sciences, state crime has been defined variously as the act of governmental officials breaking laws, to the commission of systematic human rights violations including crimes of omission such as the denial of housing to the homeless, to the coercive or covert behavior of states against other states. It has also been termed 'state terror' or 'state terrorism'. Michael Stohl and George Lopez define state terror generally as one aspect of governmental violence, suggesting that it is necessary to discern the different forms of state-directed violence, in particular oppression, repression and terrorism. State terrorism, in their definition, involves the act or threat of violence to create fear and/or compliant behaviour in a victim or audience of the act or threat. It occurs, they suggest, where oppression defines the political arena within which repression and terrorism transpire (Stohl & Lopez 1984: 3–10). This is along the lines of the focus of Ted Gurr, in his discussion of coercive states (Gurr 1988). Stohl moves beyond the perpetration of domestic human rights violations as state terror to examine state terrorism in international relations, for example what he terms the coercive diplomacy of the Nixon–Kissinger bombings of Hanoi in December 1972 (Stohl 1984: 43–45). Alex Schmid defines state terrorism as acts which go 'beyond the legitimate use of violence by those holding the reins of power, just as war crimes go beyond what is considered permissible in warfare' (Schmid 1991: 29). In his discussion of state-organized crime, William Chambliss emphasizes the 'institutionalized policy of the state' as a core aspect, including the policies of torture and violence by the police in apartheid South Africa as these practices were both state policy and in violation of South African law, yet excluding the excessive use of violence by the police in urban ghettoes for lacking the 'necessary institutionalized policy of the state' (Chambliss 1989: 184).

David Kauzlarich, Ronald Kramer and Brian Smith discuss state violence in the context of law and crime, arguing that organized violence committed by governmental agencies needs to be discussed in the context of crime, in particular international law (Kauzlarich et al. 1992). Their focus is primarily an outward one, in their examination of United States policy of threatening to use nuclear weapons in ensuring 'peace', and United States intervention in Nicaragua. Gregg Barak argues the necessity of focusing on the structural and organizational nature of governmental abuse, drawing a spectrum from proactive state criminality such as the repression of the Chinese demonstrators in Tiananmen Square in 1989, to crimes of omission in the domestic context of the United States such as the denial of sufficient and adequate housing to the homeless, the informal economy and the traditional forms of criminal activity it produces, and the denial of the fundamental right to work for an adequate income (Barak 1991: 6, 12; Barak 1994: 260). He connects a concern with state criminality to class and social justice worldwide (Barak 1991: 12). Jeffrey Ross's scope of state crime includes 'cover-ups, corruption, disinformation, unaccountability, and violations of domestic and/or international laws. It also includes those practices that, although they fall short of being officially declared illegal, are perceived by the majority of the population as illegal or socially harmful (e.g. worker exploitation)' (Ross 1995: 5–6). Peter Grabosky focuses on governmental illegality and public corruption (Grabosky 1989). Penny Green and Tony Ward define state crime as 'state organisational deviance involving the violation of human rights' (Green & Ward 2004: 2). They draw a link from organizational deviance to natural disasters, corporate crimes, corruption, police crime, state terror, war crimes and genocide.

We can thus identify a range of state crimes, from corruption, to omission of services to purposeful harm against civilians. What is common to all is the involvement of the state, and the perpetration of harm against individuals and communities within the reach of the state. It is this 'institutionalized policy of the state', as emphasized by Chambliss, that is core to our understanding of state crime. That we consider systematic and gross violations of human rights, the genesis of 'crimes against humanity', to be state crimes, part of this 'family' of state crime, is core to our understanding of both what they are and how we might address them.

That genocide and other forms of systematic harm perpetrated by states be recognized as state crime appears to me to be a critical conceptual acknowledgement. I use the term state crime to describe the systematic and state-orchestrated actions targeted at particular groups for their destruction or subjugation. These include genocide, apartheid and other forms of 'crimes against humanity'. The core component then of state crime as I discuss it is the action taken against specific groups, as defined by the state, to destroy and oppress.

'Crimes against humanity' as state crime

The acts currently defined in international law as 'crimes against humanity' can be understood as state crime. These include (in summary from the list in the Statute of the International Criminal Court): murder, extermination, deportation or forcible transfer of populations, imprisonment, torture, rape, sexual slavery, enforced prostitution, forced pregnancy, enforced sterilization, persecution against any identifiable group on political, racial, national, ethnic, cultural, religious or gender grounds, enforced disappearance of persons, apartheid, and other inhuman acts of a similar character intentionally causing great suffering, or serious injury to body or to mental or physical health.

According to international legal definitions of crimes against humanity, these are acts perpetrated as part of widespread or systematic attacks directed against civilian populations. The definition in the Statute of the International Criminal Court notes,

> 'Attack directed against any civilian population' means a course of conduct involving the multiple commission of acts referred to in paragraph 1 against any civilian population, pursuant to or in furtherance of a State or organizational policy to commit such attack.
> (Rome Statute of the International Criminal Court 2002, Art. 7.2.a)

This idea that the acts are 'pursuant to or in furtherance of a State or organizational policy' points to the link to the state. The argument can be made as to whether a 'crime against humanity' or 'war crime' can be committed by an individual or individuals without the consent of the state apparatus. While we may find cases (for example, the massacre of Vietnamese civilians during the Vietnam War at My Lai – and even here it can be argued the subsequent cover-up demonstrated the link to state policy), the majority of such crimes have been committed within the context of a state policy or state to be. This is recognized or at least alluded to in international law (yet not sufficiently taken up in case law at international tribunals and at the international criminal court, as noted by Schabas 2008) and is a key element of these crimes.

State crime as I conceptualize it draws on the genesis of the international legal concept of crimes against humanity. One conceptualization of the developing notion of 'crimes against humanity' post-Second World War, as noted by Sydney Goldenberg, was that crimes against humanity are *co-extensive in scope* with human rights, being violations of the converse duties on a *sufficiently savage or systematic scale* (Goldenberg 1972: 13).[2] It is this idea that my understanding of state crime tries to capture. It is a focus on the systematic human rights violations perpetrated by states against their civilians, geared to their destruction or oppression.

This form of state crime is an attempt to carve a society in a particular image, to disallow diversity and a common citizenship. It is put well by Otto Kirchheimer, who wrote of the matter of the human condition, that the lasting contribution of the Nuremberg trial [the International Military Tribunal] was that 'it defined where the realm of politics ends, or rather, is transformed into the concerns of the human condition, the survival of mankind in both its universality and diversity' (Kirchheimer 1961: 341). Genocide, in its decree, as Karl Jaspers put it, that 'a people should not exist', can be understood as the ultimate crime against humanity (Jaspers & Augstein 1966: 35).

State crime, then, to describe mass harm by states, includes what in international law are defined as 'crimes against humanity', and genocide. These are all systematic acts taken by states or states to be against civilians in their control. It is the institutional and state-directed character of state crime, as an expression of state policy, that is critical to its conceptualization. This concurs with previous, although wider, definitions of state crime put forward by Stohl and Lopez, Schmid, Kauzlarich, Kramer, Smith, Ross, Chambliss, Barak, and Green and Ward. State crime to include systematic mass harm can be thus seen as a subset of a broader understanding of state crime.

Genocide as state crime

Genocide is a form of state crime. What separates it out from other forms of mass harm perpetrated by states is its purpose of the intended destruction of a group. As the United Nations noted in its General Assembly resolution passed on 11 December 1946 introducing the proposal for a Convention on genocide and affirming that genocide is a crime under international law, 'Genocide is a denial of the right of existence of entire human groups, as homicide is the denial of the right to live of individual human beings'. Genocide as state crime and as crime against humanity is in line with the original usage and conception of crimes against humanity that included genocide as a component offence: Sydney Goldenberg noted that with the opening for ratification of the Convention for the Prevention and Punishment of the Crime of Genocide on 9 December 1948, 'the criminality of genocide, a component offense of crimes against humanity, was now incontestably clear in international law' (Goldenberg 1972: 17).

State crime as I define it includes genocide. In this I follow Alex Schmid's conceptualization of genocide as 'sui generis' yet still placed within a continuum of repression-state terrorism-genocide (Schmid 1991: 33). This is not an unbroken continuum. John Thompson and Gail Quets suggest that rather than thinking in terms of one boundary between genocide and not-genocide, we should think in terms of a continuum from no group destruction to complete destruction (Thompson & Quets 1990: 248). It is a useful starting point; however, it is too broad a conceptualization for sharp analysis. Genocide is conceptually and structurally different to racism, to torture, to mass discrimination. Many levels of destruction can be found in societies; however, not all are on a continuum towards genocide, nor do all contribute to the act of genocide. The spectrum within which genocide can be situated is a truncated spectrum, one in which there are both specific linkages as well as significant departures.

It is crucial to place genocide, the destruction of a people, within global and state processes, to conceptualize genocide as connected to war, statehood and nationhood. The act of genocide can be viewed within the frame of national state-building: in weak states, in states in the process of formation or collapse, in states which are on the periphery of the global system, and in states asserting internal control. In a similar vein, Charles Tilly drew a connection between state-making and war (Tilly 1985). Genocide can be viewed as a form of war, a war that is fought against the state's own citizens, resulting in their ultimate disenfranchisement. It is often portrayed this way by the state. In her analysis of the Holocaust, Lucy Dawidowicz argued that Hitler was fighting two wars simultaneously: the conventional war of conquest for *Lebensraum* to establish the Thousand Year Reich, and the ideological war of murder against the Jews (Dawidowicz 1975). In this sense, both genocide and war can be seen as integrally connected to nation-building.

Mahmood Mamdani wrote, linking the Nazi Holocaust and the Rwandan genocide, of *race branding* whereby it becomes possible not only to set a group apart as an enemy, an 'alien presence', but also to exterminate it with an easy conscience (Mamdani 2001: 13–14). It is reminiscent of Etty Hillesum waiting at the transit camp of Westerbork in Holland in July 1943, when she wrote in a letter, 'For us, I think, it is no longer a question of living, but of how one is equipped for one's extinction' (Hillesum 1986: 100). Genocide is a political decision: as Irving Horowitz notes, always a conscious choice and decision (Horowitz 1976: 39). There may be a gap in which we ask 'how is it humanly possible?' (see Charny 1982); however, it is never inevitable.

The concept of genocide as a crime of state has been used by authors such as Irving Horowitz (1976) and Pieter Drost (1959a, 1959b), and more recently Alex Alvarez (2009) and Penny Green and Tony Ward (2004). Placing genocide within a state crime framework allows us to focus on the state nature of the harm perpetrated, that these are actions taken by states or states to be, for the purposes of nation-building. As genocide scholar Helen Fein has noted, 'The victims of twentieth-century premeditated genocide – the Jews, the Gypsies, the Armenians – were murdered in order to fulfil the state's design for a new order' (Fein 1979: 29–30). This becomes important in considering the ways in which law may adequately address genocide.

The term genocide was first proposed by Raphael Lemkin in 1944 in his book, *Axis Rule in Occupied Europe* (Lemkin 1944). Lemkin devised the word in two parts: the Greek word *genos* (race, tribe) and the Latin *cide* (killing). Interestingly, he also proposed that another term – ethnocide (derived from the Greek *ethnos* for nation) – could be used to express the same idea. Genocide, wrote Lemkin, does not necessarily mean the immediate destruction of a nation, except when accomplished by mass killings of all members of a nation:

> It is intended rather to signify a coordinated plan of different actions aiming at the destruction of essential foundations of the life of national groups, with the aim of annihilating the groups themselves.[3]
>
> (Lemkin 1944: 79)

The term genocide was thus designed, at least by Lemkin, to describe the intended destruction of *enduring* groups. Lemkin's definition took into account the different means of destruction of groups, including biological intervention. In his conceptualization of genocide, Lemkin distinguished it from the forced assimilation of 'denationalization', suggesting that genocide includes the element of physical destruction that denationalization does not. It is the destruction of peoples and nations that genocide is intended to describe.

Lemkin's definition was partially codified in the 1948 *United Nations Convention on the Prevention and Punishment of the Crime of Genocide*. We see this in particular in the acts that are included in the Convention, that lead to the destruction of groups, from killing members of the group, to causing serious bodily or mental harm to members of the group, to deliberately inflicting on the group conditions of life calculated to bring about its physical destruction in whole or in part, to imposing measures intended to prevent births within the group, to forcibly transferring children of the group to another group (Article II). This has, however, generated concern that there exists a lack of distinction or gradation between genocides: killing members of the group is on the same level as causing mental harm to members of the group.

What has to be noted in a discussion of genocide and definition is the gap between legal codification and social scientific reality. One core compromise, for example, was the exclusion of political and cultural groups from protection under the Convention. The Soviet and Eastern bloc delegates argued against the inclusion of political groups, while the Western powers argued against the inclusion of cultural groups (on this see Robinson 1960). This has generated much discussion about the nature of genocide and demonstrates how legal codification can shape how we view state crime.

The non-inclusion of political, social and gender groups, and the omission of cultural genocide (which existed in the first draft of the Convention), has been said to make the definition of genocide too narrow, excluding situations which have otherwise been defined as genocide (for example, the 500,000 alleged Indonesian 'communists' killed by the Indonesian government in 1965–66 and the over one million Bangladeshis killed during the secession of Bangladesh from Pakistan in 1970–71). David Hawk has noted that the absence of political groups from the coverage of the Genocide Convention has unfortunately had the effect of diverting discussion from what to do to deter or remedy a concrete situation of mass killings into a debilitating, confusing debate over the question of whether a situation is 'legally' genocide (Hawk 1987: 6). Helen Fein has noted that 'genus' means 'basic kinds, classes, subfamilies of humanity' and, that this can include political groups who can be as enduring as other groups noted in the Convention (Fein 1990: 23). Israel Charny has argued for a far broader conceptualization of genocide, that includes all mass harm (Charny 1994).

By making the signatories of the Convention responsible for punishing genocide, it relies on the state, the organization that perpetrates genocide, to sanction its own crime. It relies on state officials to combat crimes by state officials, and until the establishment of the International Criminal Court there existed no provision for individuals or non-governmental groups to bring charges of genocide. Further, the intent requirement is too high and too difficult to prove – as Kuper noted, the government of Paraguay can reply to accusations of genocide that as there was no intention to kill the Guayaki (Aché Indians), it being an unfortunate result of the clearing of land and building of new roads for settlers, there can be no genocide (Kuper 1981: 33–34).

Proposed at a United Nations General Assembly meeting in 1946, the Convention was codified in December 1948. Its comparatively rapid passage, if we compare it with the only recently defined crime of aggression after years of discussion, can be attributed to the context within which it arose, namely the horrors and human destruction of the Holocaust. In essence, it filled Lemkin's vision, as seen in Article II's recognition of different acts and thus different means of destruction of a group. The text of the Genocide Convention was adopted unanimously and without abstentions by the United Nations General Assembly on 9 December 1948, and came into force on 12 January 1951.

The examination of genocide as an act of state, and of state-making, is an approach which focuses on *how* it is that genocide is committed. It views genocide as committed as part of state policy, whereby political elites of the executive of the state harness institutions of the state in order to perpetrate these acts. The institutions of the state are utilized in order to fulfil a vision of a 'better state' by those who seize control or hold control. What this means is a recognition of the state as the chief instigator, the institutions of the state as co-opted, and complicated and complex relationships between perpetrator, victims and bystanders, including a particular historical relationship. Genocide can be understood as a crime of state, and with other state crime shares particular characteristics as well as significant differences. A key similarity, as discussed, is the institutional and state nature of the harm perpetrated, that the action taken is state policy and the institutions of the state are utilized for this purpose. A key difference is what is intended for a group. In the case of genocide, destruction, and in the case of other state crimes of mass harm, subjugation.

A schema of mass harm as state crimes against humanity

What characterizes mass harm by states is that it is both state policy, and that the institutions of the state are utilized for this purpose. This includes the police, the army and the legal system. It also includes non-state institutions such as the church or business that may participate or collaborate. State crime includes both acts perpetrated by the state that result in the destruction of groups, and acts perpetrated by the state that result in the oppression and subjugation of groups. Who is the 'group' is defined by the state. So the 'non-Khmers' of Pol Pot's Democratic Kampuchea as defined by the Khmer Rouge are a group, as are the Jews of Europe as defined by the Nazi state (bearing in mind that many Jews, particularly in Germany, may have identified as Germans first and Jews second, and many secular and converted Jews not as Jews at all).

These systematic acts of human rights violations that result in destruction and subjugation include those acts defined within international law as 'crimes against humanity' (persecution of a group, apartheid, forcible transfer and so on). State crime also includes genocide, currently listed outside the definition of 'crimes against humanity' in international law, yet which was originally considered within the concept of 'crimes against humanity'. Here, the crime of extermination, as included within the list of 'crimes against humanity' may be considered as genocide.

I suggest a differentiated spectrum of state crime that includes genocide and other forms of mass harm perpetrated by states. Within state crime as mass harm, we can identify three forms of state crimes against humanity:

- State destruction of a group
- State systematic killing
- State systematic subjugation

This conceptual classification allows for a differentiation of state crime within a framework that highlights the institutional and state-directed nature of this type of crime. These are all acts which are found within current international law as crime, and which can be found within the list of acts of 'crimes against humanity' defined in international law. They are all systematic and state-orchestrated actions targeted at particular groups to result in their destruction or subjugation. What this classification does is both highlight the state-directed nature of the harm, and distinguish between the different forms of mass harm perpetrated by states (bearing in mind of course that the boundaries are not always that sharp).

Within the state crime of destruction of a group we can place the Armenians in Turkey under cover of the First World War, the Jews in Greater Germany during the Second World War, and the Tutsis in Rwanda 1994. These are all examples of genocide, of destruction of a group. Here we can also place the attempted destruction of the Cham Muslim by the Khmer Rouge, and the attempted destruction of the Bosnian Muslims by the Serbian state of the former Yugoslavia (Serbian sponsored Republika Srpska).

Within the state crime of systematic killing we can place the killings in Ethiopia under Mengistu and the Dergue, the killings of the 'non-Khmers' of Pol Pot and the Khmer Rouge's Democratic Kampuchea, and the broader killings in the former Yugoslavia. These are examples of systematic killing.

Within the state crime of systematic subjugation we can place the apartheid regime in South Africa.

All the above are state crime, all are state directed, either by the current state or state to be, and all can be considered state crimes against humanity. But why distinguish between destruction, systematic killing and systematic subjugation or oppression? Why not just use the current definitions of international law of genocide, crimes against humanity and war crimes? The point of this differentiated spectrum of state crime is twofold: to distinguish between different forms of mass harm against civilian populations that are state directed, and to consider the different characters of state crime and thus to capture something from a socio-legal and social science perspective that politicized legal definitions do not.

As the discussion has shown, state crimes are state orchestrated, harnessing institutions and expressing state policy. They also require a particular legal response. Yet it must also be a differentiated response. There exist significant points of meeting and departure between genocide and other state-directed mass harm. The institutional nature of such crime is an important meeting point. So too is the perpetration of such acts for the broader purposes of state consolidation and state power. A point of dissimilarity, however, is what is intended for the targeted groups – subjugation in the case of apartheid for example, or destruction as in the case of genocide.

These distinctions throw up different issues again for legal redress and, in particular, reconstruction and reconciliation in the wake of such crime. This is not to establish a hierarchy of suffering, these different forms of state crime are not of different 'worth', but to define as closely as possible the different kinds of mass harm perpetrated by states against civilians. This schema defines and differentiates acts of gross human rights violations perpetrated by the state. This becomes important in considering the ways in which law addresses these crimes.

This conceptual framework for state crime and genocide includes genocide within a spectrum of differentiated state crime, as state destruction. Genocide is an act committed by states to create the state in a particular image, a tool of state-building. Zygmunt Bauman described it as 'a means to an end', with 'the end itself a grand vision of a better, and radically different, society' (Bauman 1989: 91). There are other violent tools of state-building, acts committed in the name of the state which are not genocide yet which share some similarities – hence, it is necessary to discuss genocide in the context of other forms of state crime. In particular, for the purposes of a discussion of the role law may play in redress, comparing acts of genocide with other acts of state crime is necessary and fruitful in that it allows us to compare state-initiated mass harm together.

Yet their differences too must be identified. Genocide, as the intended destruction of a group, is placed in its own category in the spectrum of state crime. Genocide is the attempt to end a lineage. There is to be no return and no retrieval. That is why it is different to many listed 'crimes against humanity' for example. It is the destruction of a people, the fulfilment of a decree, as Karl Jaspers noted, that 'a people should not exist', a judgement as to 'which groups of people are permitted or not to live on earth' (Jaspers & Augstein 1966: 35). Genocide can encompass more than murder, as indigenous genocide with its many destructions in addition to killing demonstrates – forced assimilation and child removal for example. With indigenous genocide, we see the intent from the state that this group *as it is* no longer exists, which may be achieved with little killing.

As the United Nations General Assembly declared in 1946, 'Genocide is a denial of the right of existence of entire human groups'. It is not only, as Irving Horowitz states, the irreversibility of state murder that gives the subject of genocide its unique and awesome dimension – it is the *meaning* of this irreversibility (Horowitz 1989: 12). Is the intent to irrevocably remove, to *destroy* a particular group, as in the case of the Armenians, the Jews, the Bosnian Muslims or the Tutsi. This makes it genocide, state destruction of a group.

There are other intents – the 'pragmatic' one in apartheid South Africa of subjugation of black and non-white South Africans, or the intent to promote terror through the killings and torture of Mengistu's Ethiopia, or the use of mass killing for radical restructuring and control as in Khmer Rouge Cambodia. These are situations in which groups of people were killed – however, the intent of the killing was not primarily the inalienable destruction of these groups, but control and subjugation of the population as a whole. The group, then, can include both enduring or specified groups, as well as the citizenry as a whole.

In Pol Pot's Cambodia we can see the destruction of groups such as the Cham Muslim and the Vietnamese, yet the main project of the Khmer Rouge was not destruction of the Khmer people as such, but control and subjugation. The killing of Buddhist monks was part of this plan, in order to destroy the old normative order. The Khmer Rouge wanted to shape a society in their image, one that was 'fully Khmer' as defined by the new state. The mass killing was a tool of this. There was no plan to kill all Khmers, only Khmers not in their image. The ever-shifting definition of 'intellectuals' (anti-Khmer) is an illustration of this. Yet we also see the intent to destroy particular groups – the Cham Muslim for example. Cambodia under Pol Pot can thus be seen as both systematic state killing and genocide. This illustrates the difficulty of absolute boundaries, the necessity of grey areas in definition and the importance of using typologies as conceptual tools rather than statements of fact. When we are discussing mass harm on the scale of genocide and other state crime, this becomes important.

The acts committed inside Bosnia-Herzegovina present us with another hybrid. They were not, as unfortunately argued in the Memorial of the Government of the Republic of Bosnia and Herzegovina to the International Court of Justice, 'random mayhem' (*Memorial of the Government of the Republic of Bosnia and Herzegovina* 1994: 197). As cases at the International

Tribunal for the former Yugoslavia have shown us, they were systematic, planned and ordered. The acts committed against Muslims in Bosnia-Herzegovina were an attempt to destroy the group – at least in that part of Yugoslavia (Bosnia-Herzegovina) – and in the use of rape camps, an attempt to transform the biological reproduction of that group. Not all Bosnian Muslims were sought out to be killed, yet a substantial part were – thus, there was intent to destroy *in part* (using the Convention definition of genocide) – and the practices carried out against them indicate more than a regime of terror calculated to compel them to flee the territory. The acts perpetrated constituted a systematic attempt to destroy this group, in substantial part (the Genocide Convention refers to the destruction of groups 'in whole or in part'). Although the term 'ethnic cleansing' was popularly used to describe what was done in the former Yugoslavia, genocide is the more appropriate term, together with, in this schema, state destruction of a group and state systematic killing.

In the concept of systematic killing, and its overlap with genocide, we may see the term introduced by Leo Kuper of 'genocidal massacre'. The intent in genocide is to remove a particular group, perceived as a threat. The intent of mass killing by a state is generally to induce terror among a population and to institute a system of control – it may include the destruction of particular groups within that population, but unless this is for the purposes of their intended destruction as such, the acts are not genocide. Yet such acts can also have elements of genocide, as Kuper showed. Kuper wrote of the 'incidence of genocidal massacres in the establishment and maintenance of colonial domination', introducing this term to describe 'the annihilation of a section of a group … as for example in the wiping out of whole villages', 'in part because the genocidal massacre has some of the elements of genocide' (Kuper 1981: 10, 60). He then continued, 'But I hope too that the inclusion of genocidal massacre will reduce controversy over the selection of cases, so that the human concern for the prevention of genocide may prevail over the almost insuperable problem of precision in classification' (ibid: 10). We see important connections, then, between systematic killing and destruction of a group.

We can draw further distinctions for the purposes of legal addressing, between crimes 'in the life of a nation' (genocide, apartheid, totalitarianism, some crimes against humanity) and crimes committed in pursuit of conventional war (war crimes). Where war crimes may be served by a trial (and civic liability processes, to be discussed in Chapter 4), other crimes perpetrated against a state's own civilians may be better served by a raft of legal processes that address both the crimes as such, their institutional parameters, and their underlying causes. We saw this happening, for example, in the case of the truth commission process in South Africa that included institutional hearings aimed at transformation of institutions central to the apartheid policy such as the education, health and legal sectors. In Guatemala, this manifested in the drafting of a socio-economic accord which focused on addressing the poverty, discrimination and social and political marginalization in that country, which the accord recognized as key contributing factors to the conflict.

Conclusion

State crime, as considered in this book, includes a range of systematic actions undertaken by the state against groups within the state. It harnesses state institutions, invites and coerces collaboration from non-state ones, and follows these actions as state policy. We can differentiate between these state crimes, as discussed above, from genocide, to state killing, to state subjugation and oppression. All are state crimes against humanity. In their actions against civilians within their control, they deny a common humanity and forge a path that envisions the state, and its citizenry, in a particular image. As such, they use state crime in the pursuit of nation-building.

Yet our current approach to the use of law in addressing state crime lacks specificity. By this I mean that in our thinking about how law may best address these kinds of crimes we fail to distinguish between different kinds of state crime (for example, between genocide, apartheid, systematic oppression, mass killing) and what they may require in adequately tackling them. We have no typology of state crime to which we can connect our various legal responses and this is why a conceptual framework of state crime is important. What we have is a list of state crimes, and various approaches to legal redress, but little guidance as to which may fit best and when, what kinds of accountability are needed, what it may mean to repair and to provide redress – as well as to prevent. While we have important typologies of genocide and some of state crime (as I have discussed earlier, see Balint 2008), the link to law has not been made.

The recognition of the role of the state and the link to nation-building is an important starting point as well as the classification discussed earlier of state destruction of a group, state systematic killing, and state systematic subjugation within a schema of state crime. Yet we also need a causal schema that considers the differences and similarities in the perpetration of state crime. While we can identify certain similarities between crimes perpetrated by the state, what are often called the gravest international crimes (genocide, crimes against humanity, war crimes), we can also find certain differences, which then require different forms of legal redress. Considering the different types of state crime that require redress will mean thinking differently about the types of accountability and restoration needed to achieve justice. It will mean thinking about how and when law can be an active player in reconciliation, reconstruction and prevention.

Matching the types and causes of crimes to redress is important not only in establishing true accountability, but also in establishing a preventative foundation for the future. This book attempts to begin this conversation, of considering the legal redress for different forms of harm perpetrated by states. In considering a range of state crimes, from the genocide of the Armenians and other Christian minorities by the Ottoman state in the First World War, to the systematic oppression of black South Africans under the apartheid regime, it asks how we might best approach these crimes of the state and how, as well, these crimes of the state have been mediated through law.

Notes

1 These can also include what Penny Green and Tony Ward have termed 'proto-states', those 'political entities (for example, the FARC – Revolutionary Armed Forces of Columbia) which deploy organized force, control substantial territories and levy formal or informal taxes but are not accepted members of the international society of states' (Green & Ward 2004: 3).
2 Goldenberg was interpreting two immediate post-Second World War documents defining crimes against humanity, the general report on the nature of crimes against humanity presented to the Eighth Conference for the Unification of Penal Law in July 1947 and the May 1946 committee of the United Nations War Crimes Commission that agreed upon general propositions to define the term crimes against humanity under the Nuremberg Charter and Control Council Law No. 10. He noted, referring to Egon Schwelb's work on the development of crimes against humanity that this is 'not a novel or strained interpretation of the category' (Schwelb 1946: 178–226).
3 He had previously proposed two other classifications: *barbarity*, consisting of the extermination of racial, religious or social collectives, and *vandalism*, consisting of the destruction of cultural and artistic works of these groups. These had been submitted to the International Conference for Unification of Criminal Law in Madrid, Spain, in 1933. The Conference did not accept the proposal (Rosenthal 1985: 120).

Chapter 2

The toleration of harm

Law and perpetration

Perpetrator regimes define themselves peculiarly in relation to the law. Buddhist monks were among the first to be killed by the new regime of Pol Pot and the Khmer Rouge in Cambodia 1975. As bearers of the 'old order', they were a clear threat to the new state. In killing the monks, the Khmer Rouge destroyed a central plank of the normative order of the Khmer people. One moral code was replaced with another. The new order of *Khchatkhchay os roling* – scatter them out of sight – for those who were not 'real' Khmer replaced the old. However, as David Hawk reminds us, in real life entire groups of people cannot be simply legislated or defined out of existence, and legal prohibition and sociological dissolution were accompanied by substantial physical liquidation (Hawk 1988: 137). At the same time, after destroying the old normative order, the Khmer Rouge drafted a new Constitution, a legal document for the world to see.

Nazi Germany took a different approach initially. Hitler began with the direct utilization of the law, using it to facilitate his rise to power. The Enabling Act gave the government the power to enact legislation on its own, resulting in Hitler declaring the unity of the Nazi Party and the German state. Hitler then embraced law as an effective tool in the implementation of his policies, beginning with the removal of Jewish judges and other civil servants from office in 1933, and moving on to the Nuremberg Laws that separated Jew from non-Jew in Nazi Germany, removing their rights and citizenship. In his speech to the Reichstag in September 1935, Hitler declared the Nuremberg laws an 'attempt to regulate by law [the Jewish] problem'. He then went on to say 'which, should this attempt fail, must then be handed over by law to the National-Socialist Party for a final solution'.[1] Later, at the 1942 meeting in Berlin known as the Wannsee Conference, where the 'final solution' was discussed, it was stated (in relation to the policy of increased emigration), 'The aim of this task was to cleanse the German living space of Jews in a legal manner'.

Despite the takeover of the Weimar legal system, the appearance of a *Rechtstaat*, a state based upon the rule of law, was maintained, and through this an appearance of normalcy. The Nazis then proceeded to use law in its barest and most abusive form – as a direct extension of political will. Increasingly more repressive and segregationist laws were introduced, new courts established, and the powers of existing courts curtailed. In using law so prominently, the Nazi Party managed to establish an initial, and essentially enduring legitimacy, one necessary for their acceptance, both externally at first, and internally.

In the Germany of the National Socialists and in Khmer Rouge Cambodia, law was used to establish a new reality. In both, law played a legitimating role, specifically tailored to the position of law in that society. In neither system, however, was law used in the perpetration of state murder. What it did do was allow for its toleration. It acted both as a shield, allowing the perpetration of the state harm, and a framework, providing a context for it. We see this elsewhere too. The national truth commission inquiry into the role of the legal profession in apartheid South Africa found that, in fact, 'Part of the reason for the longevity of apartheid was the superficial adherence to the "rule of law" by the governing National Party, whose leaders craved the aura of legitimacy that "the law" bestowed on their harsh injustice' (Truth and Reconciliation Commission of South Africa 1999b: 101).

Political elites involved in the perpetration of state crime are at pains to locate this 'new reality' at least superficially within the 'old reality' of that state. Often this means a central use of law. However, this is generally only in the initial stages of the persecution, and even when law continues to play a role in the latter stages (for example, the use by Nazi Germany of the Nuremberg Laws as a 'precondition for the total clearing up of the problem' as specified at the 1942 Wannsee Conference), law is never used to authorize murder. The closest we come to law authorizing murder is the Ottoman State's Deportation Law ordering the removal of the Armenians, a removal which was understood would result in their death – yet this legislation was in fact enacted after the deportations had begun. What we do see is a use of law that both contributes to the legitimacy of the harm perpetrated as well as providing a framework for the state crime. Further, we can observe a similarity in the use of law prior to and during the state crime. The law that is used is the law that was used before – in the case of Nazi Germany, court-based and legislative law, in the case of Khmer Rouge Cambodia, the dominant use of informal legal orders.

As this chapter will show, we can say four things about the use of law in genocide and state crime: law never authorizes murder in the perpetration of state crime; law can be used as a central tool in state oppression but not genocide; law assists in making state crime 'allowable' and is an important tool in attaining quiescence from the wider population and establishing state legitimacy; the type of law used during such periods is similar to the type of law used prior to the state crime. This chapter considers the examples of the perpetration of the genocide of the Armenians by the Ottoman State 1915–18, the Holocaust in the Second World War 1933–45, Cambodia under the

Khmer Rouge 1975–79, apartheid South Africa 1948–91, Ethiopia under Mengistu and the Dergue 1974–91, the genocide in Rwanda 1994, and the conflict in the former Yugoslavia 1992–94 in light of the role played by law and how law is used.

The Holocaust is shown as an example of the legal system being changed and law used to create a deep legal framework for legitimation. The apartheid era in South Africa is shown as an example of the legal system not being changed, but particular criminal legislation introduced to create a deep framework of legitimation. The Armenian genocide, Cambodia under the Khmer Rouge, and Ethiopia under Mengistu are shown as examples of law having a less obvious presence, but still being used for legitimation, within a change of the legal system for Cambodia and no change for the Ottoman state nor Ethiopia. Rwanda 1994, and the war in the former Yugoslavia are shown as examples of no change of the legal system nor introduction of specific legislation.

The chapter concludes with a consideration of how the harm committed is made 'allowable' by law, and that although in none of the cases discussed does law authorize the full scope of the crime committed, even when law appears to play no role, the rhetoric of law and justice is used alongside the act of perpetration.

Law's involvement in state crime

We can identify a spectrum of the use of law in regimes that commit state crime. This ranges from a strong use of law to a weak or non-existent use of law. Within the spectrum are examples of legal systems being destroyed, and new ones implemented, legal systems that have been radically changed, legal systems that change over time, and legal systems that are not changed. A number of differentiations can be made within such a spectrum. One central differentiation, I suggest, can be made between 'criminal legislation' and 'criminal state'.

The German philosopher Karl Jaspers defined a criminal state as one that in principle neither establishes nor acknowledges the rule of law (Jaspers & Augstein 1966: 34). He defined the Nazi German state as such. As he noted in 1965 in a conversation with *Der Spiegel* editor Rudolf Augstein, 'the decisive point is whether one acknowledges that the Nazi state was a criminal state, and not merely a state that committed crimes' (ibid). At the time, the West German Parliament was debating the question of whether to extend the statute of limitations on Nazi murders, and Jaspers and Augstein were considering, among other things, the matter of responsibility.

When the legal system of a state is changed to destroy the rule of law and separation of powers, and to impose directly the rule of the executive, we can, following Jaspers, term this a 'criminal state'. When the system complies with the doctrine of separation of powers, and still maintains a semblance of the rule of law, legislation introduced to frame the harm can be termed 'criminal legislation'. We can differentiate between Nazi Germany and apartheid South Africa in this way, although with the changing relationship of the National Party government to the courts in South Africa from the mid 1980s we can see that this distinction is not always an absolute one.

Nazi Germany effectively abolished the doctrine of separation of powers – Hitler spoke of the judiciary belonging to the state. The law was an extension of the will of the Führer. On the other hand, in apartheid South Africa, the separation of powers effectively still existed – court decisions could still run counter to the will of the executive. The acquittal of Nelson Mandela in 1961, after his trial for treason from 1956 to 1961, is an example of this. The courts did not always maintain independence, and numerous examples of abuses of law were given to the Truth and Reconciliation Commission. Yet, certainly at the beginning of apartheid the courts could maintain their independence, and there are examples of this, despite their sometimes choosing not to.

In South Africa, unlike Nazi Germany, the rule of law did continue to exist, at least in a formalistic rather than any substantive sense, with apartheid legislation introduced 'on top' of the existing legal system. Although the extent to which such criminal legislation corrupted the rule of law can be debated, and the independence of the judges has been questioned (the Truth and Reconciliation Commission of South Africa final report argued in its findings that in their silence, the courts and the legal profession, 'connived in the legislative and executive pursuit of injustice': 1999b: 101), even if we accept that South Africa maintained a 'weak' rule of law, this is still different to Nazi Germany where the rule of law was destroyed. Such a difference, I suggest, contributed to the difference in attitude towards the legal system by Germans and South Africans. Susanne Karstedt suggests that the German people were accepting of what was meted out in the wake of defeat due to their profound mistrust of the internal German judiciary (Karstedt 1998). Yet in relation to South Africa, Hugh Corder notes:

> it is a matter of some astonishment to many lawyers who lived through the desecration of the rule of law under segregation and apartheid that the law .... and the courts ... should have been chosen as the single most important and least distrusted medium for the transfer of power from a minority to a majority.
>
> (Corder 1998: 1)

Such a difference, I suggest, can be attributed to the level of transformation of the legal system by each regime, and the level of independence of the judiciary. In South Africa judges could still maintain some independence (Corder 1984 has argued that judges could decide differently), and the courts could still be used as an avenue of appeal, whereas in Nazi Germany they could not. That said, in South Africa under the apartheid regime the courts have been viewed as participants and co-conspirators in the systematic oppression of South African apartheid.

When the legal system is not changed, two further possibilities are presented. Either specific legislation is introduced in relation to the particular crimes perpetrated (this we see in South Africa and in the Ottoman state), or no specific legislation is introduced. The Ottoman state passed the Deportation Law (albeit once the deportations of the Armenians that would lead to their death had begun) as well as special legislation to release prisoners and to confiscate property. The South African state passed a raft of legislation aimed at systematic repression of black South Africans and denying them their citizenship.

The 1994 genocide in Rwanda and the war in the former Yugoslavia are examples of the second possibility, in which no legislation relating to the harm was introduced. The killings in both continued without any recourse to law, although in Rwanda the rhetoric of customary practice was used in the process of killing in some instances, perpetrators saying they were taking Tutsis 'to the *bourgmestre*' (a reference to the local practice of taking suspected criminals to the local mayor) when they were taking them to be killed.

Four central possibilities then for law during the perpetration of genocide and other forms of state crime can be identified.

Law authorizes state murder

No such cases can be found in the case studies. Legislation in relation to the crime may exist (most notably in Nazi Germany and in apartheid South Africa), however the legislation provides a framework, or basis for, rather than being the sum of, the harm perpetrated. While legislation of separation and repression existed within Nazi Germany and apartheid South Africa, this still did not encompass the breadth of what was perpetrated. Law did not authorize state murder.

In apartheid South Africa, the extrajudicial killings and torture were not authorized by the formal laws of the state. Such activities may have been accepted, and encouraged, by particular institutional cultures (the police and the security organizations) who had their own form of living law, what we may see as a parallel and hidden structure of the state. They may also have been supported by laws that allowed indefinite detention and interrogation and that provided a space for torture and death. Yet in apartheid South Africa extrajudicial murder by the state was still 'outside' the law. Similarly, the murders in the death camps of Nazi Germany were not 'allowable' under the enacted formal law of the Nazi German state. In fact, any legislation that did relate to the Jews was enacted at a time when the plan was emigration, not extermination. Murder, however, was allowable within the parallel and hidden structure of the state and the death and concentration camps. In apartheid

South Africa and Nazi Germany, the legislation of separation was not legislation for murder. This was kept outside of the law.

The decision to implement a policy of genocide in particular (and the more horrific aspects of the policy of apartheid, for example) is generally not public, nor officially legal. This means it is not articulated within legislation. The decision to commit such crime is always secret or coded. This is clear in the genocide of the Armenians, the Holocaust and the genocide in Rwanda, and is illustrated by there being no or little public documentation regarding the actual plan of destruction, compared to other plans of exclusion, segregation and oppression.[2]

The Armenian genocide is the only case in which legislation (the Deportation Laws) directly framed the perpetration of murder – however, even here, the wording was deliberately non-specific ('deportees' not Armenians), the actual meaning was known only to those at the top, and it was passed once the murder was almost complete. Legislation that allowed the release of prisoners to serve in the Special Organization Unit that was primarily responsible for the killing of the Armenians was rushed through, yet once most of the killings had taken place. Here, law provides a framework of legitimation for the implementation of murderous policy, yet does not play a role in its practical implementation.

Law is used to create a deep legal framework for facilitation of state crime

We have seen that this can happen either through a total change of the legal system ('criminal state'), or legislation introduced to frame the harm ('criminal legislation'). In both, I suggest, law *facilitates* the crime, yet does not formally circumscribe it. Both Nazi Germany as a 'criminal state' and the apartheid regime in South Africa through 'criminal legislation' (although arguably moving towards a criminal state in the later years of apartheid) used law to create a deep framework for facilitation of state crime.

When law is used to create a deep framework for state crime, the use of law in achieving the aims of the new regime is overt. The legal system is changed to reflect the goals of the new regime, or particular legislation is introduced, geared towards achieving these goals. The legal system makes it clear who is included and who is excluded in the structure of the state. We saw this with the Nuremberg Laws of Nazi Germany, as well as with the raft of apartheid legislation in South Africa. It is law that overtly defines the boundaries of the state and functions as a central tool in implementation and regulation of these boundaries.

Law may be used in the first stages of the state crime, but not always in the final stages of actual perpetration of the crime. In National Socialist Germany, law was used as a framework for the removal of Jews from German society. This was in the first stages of the Nazi regime, when the plan was exclusion not extermination. At the point of full exclusion, of murder, law played no part – although, as Koch notes, the Reich Minister of Justice was represented at the 1942 Wannsee Conference where the plan for destruction was laid out (Koch 1989: 117). The role played by law was in establishing the groundwork for the perpetration of state crime. Formal law was irrelevant during the actual perpetration. Those directives that were given were not law, rather they were decrees and communications from and within the inner elite. What law did do, however, was provide a layer of legitimation for the subsequent killing.

Some law is used, although it cannot be characterized as a deep framework

In this category, the use of law is somewhat covert. The previous law may still exist, yet be subsumed under the new state of affairs. The new system (military law, rules or state of terror) will take precedence over the old, without necessarily changing the old system – often through use of a legal technique (for example, the declaration of a state of emergency). Mengistu used this during his reign in Ethiopia, introducing particular laws, in particular the new Penal Code, on top of existing legislation, with the existing Ethiopian legal system remaining much the same. Or law may be a charade, existing on paper but never given any life (the Cambodian Constitution for example), or existing on paper in contradiction to actual practice (the Armenian Deportation Laws for example).

Examples of where some law is used in perpetration are the Armenian genocide and Mengistu's 'Red Terror' in Ethiopia ('criminal legislation') and Cambodia under the Khmer Rouge ('criminal state'). At the beginning of the regime of Pol Pot, law was used as a tool to signal the new regime's goals. Yet enacted legislation was essentially stillborn, developed as a signature of the new regime (common for communist regimes) and not designed to be operational. Law in relation to the killings of the Armenians by the Ottoman state was used as a tool of post-facto legitimation, although unlike Khmer Rouge Cambodia, at the end rather than at the beginning of the harm perpetrated. In this manner it too used law as a weak framework of legitimation.

Law is neither instrument nor obstacle to the state crime

Here, law is not explicitly utilized in legitimation or perpetration of harm; however, the victims are not given the protection they are entitled to within the existing national (or international) legal system. The legal system has not been changed, and nor has any specific legislation been introduced (with the potential exception of state of emergency legislation). Law is thus neither instrument of, nor obstacle to, the offences committed. We may identify law as bystander. However, even here, some minimal involvement of law can be found – either in the declaration of a state of emergency, or in the way in which criminal actions may be framed by the rhetoric of law. In Rwanda 1994, customary law was referenced in Tutsi victims being taken to the *bourgmestre* as 'suspected criminals'. Slobodan Milošević used the 1974 Constitution and its 'deficiencies' as a rallying call for his rise to power, forcing through amendments that set the stage for dissolution in the 1992–94 conflict. Orders to stop made by the International Court of Justice in response to Bosnia and Herzegovina's call to the Court in 1993 while the atrocities were being perpetrated went unheeded by Serbia and Montenegro. Both nationally and internationally, law fails to protect.

The use of law in state crime is not always one or the other. For example, Cambodia under Pol Pot can be considered both a case of law being used to create a deep framework yet also as neither instrument nor obstacle to the state crime. The existing legal system was destroyed and then radically restructured to reflect the goals of the new regime, yet the new system was then abandoned in favour of a system of rule by force. In the case of the genocide of the Armenians, law was used to legitimate the actions taken (the Deportation Laws and the release of prisoners), yet in its being pushed through after the state crime had been perpetrated, it cannot be considered a deep framework.

Each of these categories will now be discussed in relation to the case studies.

Law used to create a deep legal framework for facilitation of state crime

Here we can place the Holocaust in the Second World War, and apartheid South Africa.

Nazi Germany and the Holocaust

> Guarantees of justice are no longer located in the statute, but in the extent to which the individual decision accords with National Socialist thinking.
>
> (Kirchheimer 1935: 144)

In Nazi Germany the movement from racial separation to exclusion to extermination was facilitated within the framework of law. This was deliberate National Socialist strategy. Not only were laws enacted to legitimate and to frame this exclusion, the entire legal system was oriented towards the creation of the particular National Socialist vision of the German state, a vision that excluded Jews, and that restricted the entry of Roma, Slavs and other 'undesirables'. In addition, the form and operation of the legal system reflected National Socialist logic. As Peter Caldwell, suggests, Nazi anti-constitutionalism – meaning the dominance of radical, crisis-oriented policies over attempts to find stability – was an essential part of the National Socialist worldview (Caldwell 1994: 400). Constitutional theory under Nazism, writes

Caldwell, operated under the same radical social-Darwinist logic as Nazi institutions themselves (ibid).

Law was the key first tool for the crimes perpetrated by the Nazi state. The Protocol of the Wannsee Conference, held on 20 January 1942, and widely held to be the 'blueprint' for the extermination of European Jewry, notes in a review of 'the struggle conducted up to now against this foe [European Jewry]' with regard to the initial National Socialist approach of increased Jewish emigration, that 'The aim of this task was to cleanse the German living space [*Lebensraum*] of Jews in a legal manner'. In addition, it notes:

> In the implementation of the plan for the final solution, the Nuremberg Laws are to form the basis, as it were; a precondition for the total clearing up of the problem will also require solutions for the question of mixed marriages and *Mischlinge*.
>
> (Protocol of the Wannsee Conference 1942)

In both Nazi Germany and the Ottoman state, law was used for the facilitation of separation, of the Jews and the Armenians. What distinguishes the use of law in Nazi Germany from the use of law in the Armenian genocide, however, is that whereas in the Ottoman State these laws were introduced in addition to already existing legislation, with no change to the existing legal system, in Nazi Germany the legal system, and in particular, the relationship between the legal system and the political system, was radically changed.

Hitler and the Nazi party were able to gain power initially through channels located within the German system. Hitler was appointed Chancellor legally (under Article 48 of the Weimar Constitution), and legally invoked various measures including the dissolution of Parliament, the calling of new elections, and a ban on public meetings, all in the name of national security. In the wake of the *Reichstag* fire in 1933, Hitler was able to build on these measures, issuing a series of emergency decrees, described as measures to ward off 'Communist acts of violence endangering the state'. These decrees included the suspension, through the *Decree for the Protection of Volk and State*, of basic freedoms and imposed the death penalty for treason, arson and such acts. A subsequent set of decrees addressed high treason, which essentially covered all forms of dissidence. It was the *Reichstag* fire, and the judicial response to it, that was a defining moment in the relation between the Nazi state and the judiciary. In the wake of the fire, the *Reichsgericht* (the highest appellate court in the Weimar Republic) acquitted several members of the Communist Party of involvement for lack of evidence. As Stolleis notes, the Nazi party responded by establishing the *Volksgerichtshof* (People's Court) in early 1934 to adjudicate political cases (Stolleis 1998: 2). This would be a common scenario. When, for example, administrative courts tried to protect Jewish synagogues or Jewish tradesmen, the Nazis would issue police decrees to counter this.

A combination of intimidation and direct violence preceded the new election, in which the NSDAP (the National Socialist German Workers Party) gained almost 44 per cent of the vote, yet still without a majority. In the wake of the election the SA (Sturmabteilung) 'brownshirts' accelerated its campaign of terror against Communists, Socialists, trade unionists and Jews. The next act by Hitler was to obtain passage of an Enabling Act, *The Law to Remove the Distress of Volk and State* (1933), that would give the government, without recourse to the Reichstag, the power to promulgate emergency legislation. On 21 March 1933, the Reichstag opened, and on 23 March in its first working session, the Enabling Act was passed. The Enabling Act (Article 2) gave the government the power for four years to enact any legislation, even if it deviated from the Constitution. On 8 July 1933 Hitler declared 'the party has now become the state', with the NSDAP, through a campaign of terror and forced dissolution, being the only remaining party. Consequently, on 1 December 1933, a law was enacted declaring the unity of the Nazi Party and the German state. With this fact legally decreed, as Lucy Dawidowicz writes, Hitler held full control (Dawidowicz 1975).

German legal scholar Ulrich Scheuner was to write in 1934 in the legal journal *Archiv für Rechts-und Sozialphilosophie*, 'numerous concepts and principles of the earlier period, the right of parliaments and the parties, the principle of separation of powers, the idea of basic rights, and so forth, have been stripped of their meaning by the new organization' (cited in Stolleis 1998: 96). Yet, as Ernst Fraenkel also noted at the time, 'the National Socialist *coup d'état* of 1933 was, at least technically, facilitated by the executive and judicial practice of the Weimar Republic' and they were able to 'pay lip service to the laws' (Fraenkel 1941: 5, 6). As he argues, long before Hitler's dictatorship, the courts [unlike English courts] had held that questions as to the necessity and expediency of martial law were not subject to review by the courts (ibid: 5).

In assuming control of the German state, Hitler set out to change the basis and the functioning of the German legal system. This was done both through a re-conceptualization of the role of law, as well as through changing the components of the legal system. Minister of Justice Franz Gürtner explained the role and place of law in the following manner in 1937:

> National Socialism substitutes for the conception of formal wrong the idea of factual wrong: it considers every attack against the welfare of the people's community, every violation of the requirements of the life of a nation as wrong ... As a result, the law gives up all claim to be an exclusive source for the determination of right and wrong ... The legislator is aware of the fact that he cannot give exhaustive regulations for all the situations in life; therefore he entrusts the judge with filling the remaining gaps ... [The judge] interprets the existing regulations not literally but according to their spirit and basic thoughts.
>
> (Miller 1995: 49)

Law thus became an overt tool in nation-building and in creating the new National Socialist state according to the principles outlined by Hitler as Führer, the 'requirements of the life of a nation'. Otto Kirchheimer wrote of the 'metajuristic concept of the Führer' (Kirchheimer 1935: 156). It was the Führer's concept of justice that was embodied in the legal system. The nature of the totalitarian state meant that there could be no independent competing authority. As Kirchheimer accurately predicted in 1935, changes in the criminal law functioned primarily to produce a system of total state repression (ibid: 166). It was a legal system based primarily on belonging to the greater *Volksgemeinschaft*, as defined by the National Socialists, the boundaries of which were carefully and brutally maintained.

We can learn from Adam Podgórecki's analysis of the character of law in totalitarian societies. He showed that totalitarian law contains two opposite tendencies. Firstly, a tendency to pretend that it respects the requirements of normative consistency, legal hierarchy, and internal coherence; and secondly, a tendency to conform blindly to the political requirements of the actual power (Podgórecki 1996: 6–7). In Nazi Germany, as will also be seen in the case studies of Pol Pot's Cambodia and Mengistu's Ethiopia, these tendencies were evident. Ernst Fraenkel termed this 'the dual state' – a state in which there was 'constant friction between the traditional judicial bodies which represent the Normative State and the instruments of dictatorship, the agents of the Prerogative State' (Fraenkel 1941: xiii). There were exceptions to this – in the areas that did not impact on the vision of the National Socialist state, law still maintained some independence. Private property and taxes, as Fraenkel (ibid: 78–79) discusses, were an example of this. Yet elsewhere law was an extension of the power in control. The Nazi Party was clear on this – in a speech to prosecutors and judges, Goering was to say, 'The judges are bound by the law which is the promulgation of the Leader's will' (cited in ibid: 74).

Although for 'ordinary' Germans, parts of life and legal regulation may have appeared to remain virtually unchanged, the arbitrary nature of National Socialist power meant that a certain order could not be guaranteed. Radical changes were made to the system. The principle against retroactive law was abolished immediately. As Kirchheimer notes, persons who committed crimes between 1930 and 1932 were prosecuted under laws enacted between 1933 and 1935 (Kirchheimer 1935: 147). This meant in reality that persons who earlier may have faced a period of imprisonment could now face the death penalty. In June 1935 the principle *nulla poena sine lege* (no crime without a law) was abolished. The criminal code was amended, and Article 2 of the 1935 new criminal code read as follows:

> Whoever commits an act which the law declares as punishable or which deserves punishment according to the fundamental idea of a penal law or the sound sentiment of a people, shall be punished. If no specific

penal law can be directly applied to the act, it shall be punished according to the law whose underlying principle can be most readily applied to the act.

(Miller 1995: 49)

Thousands of individual decrees were enacted, with titles such as 'Decree for the Repulsion of Malicious Attacks Against the Government of National Renewal' (enacted 21 March 1933). Special courts (*Sondergerichte*) were established. The old internal military courts were re-established. A 'people's court' (National Socialist People's Court: *Volksgerichthof*) was created on 24 April 1934 to prosecute political opponents, made up, as Kirchheimer notes, of administrative functionaries from the civil service, military and NSDAP, and judges who had proven their trustworthiness to the regime (Kirchheimer 1935: 154).

It was law that provided the framework for the gradual exclusion of Jews and Romani from German public life, and it was law that was harnessed for the formulation of the greater telos, the 'new reality' of the Third Reich. Law as maintainer of order and definer of borders distinguished between citizen and non-citizen, between crime and non-crime. The two became synonymous. As Ingo Müller has remarked, the general criminal law of the Third Reich saw its role as an attempt to judge whether a 'member of the *Volk* could still be tolerated by society, or whether she or he should be removed from society, either temporarily or permanently' (Müller 1991: 77). Law thus defined who was citizen:

The purpose of a trial now became not so much to determine whether the wrongdoer had broken a law, but rather, whether the wrongdoer still belongs to the community.

(Müller 1991: 79)

This is exemplified in Paragraph Two of the German Criminal Code that was reworded to read:

Punishment is to be inflicted on anyone who commits an act which has been declared punishable under the law or who deserves to be punished according to the fundamental principles of a criminal statute and healthy public sentiment.

(Kirchheimer 1935: 146)

The separation of German Jew from German non-Jew was carried out through a number of formal legal steps, enforced by violence – in particular, that from 9 to 10 November 1938 initiated by the SA 'brownshirts' that became known as 'Kristallnacht', the Night of Broken Glass, a period of destruction and intimidation against German and Austrian Jews.

A raft of legislation was enacted during the 1930s that formally and brutally excluded Jews from public life. The first law that specifically excluded Jews was the 'Law for the Restoration of the Professional Civil Service' on 7 April 1933, removing Jews from the civil service: 'Civil servants who are not of Aryan descent are to be retired' (Section 3.1). At the same time, as Dawidowicz notes, a law cancelled the admission to the bar of lawyers of 'non-Aryan' descent and denied permission to those already admitted to practice law (Dawidowicz 1975: 58). To appease President Hindenberg, an exception to both of these new laws was made for those who had been 'employed on or before August 1, 1914, or who, during the World War, fought at the front for Germany or her Allies, or whose fathers or sons were killed in action in the World War' (ibid). Further laws included those that severely limited Jewish attendance at schools, that 'retired' Jewish university professors and lecturers, that excluded Jews from the arts and from film, that only allowed farmers with 'no Jewish blood' to inherit land, that revoked citizenship of Jews from Eastern Europe, and that excluded Jews from the German army (ibid: 58–61). As Dawidowicz remarked, 'what had begun as popular anti-Semitism … now received complete legal sanction' (ibid: 61).

The key legal instrument was the 1935 Nuremberg Laws. These were specifically the *Nuremberg Law for the Protection of German Blood and German Honor* and the *Nuremberg Laws on Reich Citizenship*, both promulgated on 15 September 1935. The Reich Citizenship law clearly demarcated who would have protection from the state. A 'Reich citizen' was to be of 'German or related blood', and as such is a 'person who enjoys the protection of the German Reich'. Critically, 'The Reich citizen is the sole bearer of full political rights in accordance with the Law'. The Protection of German Blood and German Honor law forbade marriage 'between Jews and subjects of the state', employment by Jews of 'female subjects of the state … who are under 45 years old', and further stated that 'Jews are forbidden to fly the Reich or National flag or to display the Reich colors'.

German Jews, as classified by the state, were thus abruptly disenfranchised. Clear borders for the Third Reich were to be drawn, and law was the instrument through which to achieve this. Law was thus the central instrument in the separation of Jew from non-Jew in Nazi Germany, and in laying the foundations for the new order. The enactment of these laws brought together what had been in some ways an *ad hoc*, albeit violent, policy towards the German Jews. In 1935 Kirchheimer wrote:

> Especially in the case of the 'Jewish Question', the development of so much of the German legal system remains in a state of flux. Indeed, the dynamic nature of National Socialism conflicts with any attempt to establish a set of determinate legal guarantees.
>
> (Kirchheimer 1935: 160)

With the introduction of the Nuremberg Laws, a level of 'stability' was established. Indeed, their enactment was welcomed by sections of the Jewish community who saw them as a potential firm grounding, a respite from the indeterminacy that had existed until then. With the articulation of their place in the Third Reich, it was believed that some level of normalcy may return to their lives. The *Reichsvertretung der Juden in Deutschland* (National Representation of the Jews in Germany) stated in part in response to the Nuremberg Laws:

> The Laws decided upon by the Reichstag in Nuremberg have come as the heaviest of blows for the Jews in Germany. But they must create a basis on which a tolerable relationship becomes possible between the German and the Jewish people.
>
> (*Jüdische Rundschau*, No 77, 24 September 1935)

In introducing the Nuremberg Laws in the *Reichstag*, Hitler stated the following:

> The only way to deal with the problem which remains open is that of legislative action. The German government is in this controlled by the thought that through a single secular solution it may be possible still to create a level ground [*eine Ebene*] on which the German people may find a tolerable relation towards the Jewish people. Should this hope not be fulfilled and the Jewish agitation both within Germany and in the international sphere should continue, then the position must be examined afresh.
>
> (Hitler's Speech in the Reichstag on the Nuremberg Laws, September 1935)

Legislative action, backed up by violence, was the first stage of Nazi exclusion of Jewish Germans from the wider German society – 'Forcing the Jews out of the various areas of life (*Lebensgebiete*) of the German people', as stated in the 1942 Protocol of the Wannsee Conference. The next stage, as outlined at Wannsee, was emigration – 'Forcing the Jews out of the living space (*Lebensraum*) of the German people'. A 'Reich Central Office for Jewish Emigration' was established in January 1939. As the minutes of Wannsee indicate, 'The aim of this task was to cleanse the German living space of Jews in a legal manner'. Law thus was an important initial framework for the policy of separation and for the fulfilment of the National Socialist vision.

There is debate as to why legislative action was replaced by a policy of murder. Why indeed was there legislative action at all? Was legislation always supposed to be sufficient, or was this some kind of initial stage, to mask later intentions? Hitler seems to have left this open in his *Reichstag* speech on the Nuremberg Laws, stating 'Should this hope not be fulfilled and the Jewish agitation both within Germany and in the international sphere should continue, then the position must be examined afresh'. As the minutes of Wannsee indicate, emigration was a first primary goal: 'Forcing the Jews out of the living space (*Lebensraum*) of the German people'. It was only with the 'opening up of the East' and the grim 'possibilities' this introduced, as the Protocol of the Wannsee Conference notes, that other measures were contemplated, and that extermination, not emigration, became official National Socialist policy.

With the commencement of the Second World War, punishment became harsher, laws were even more encroaching, and there was greater interference by Hitler into the workings of the judiciary. In February 1942, for example, Hitler expressed the opinion that the German judiciary were not 'sufficiently elastic' (Koch 1989: 110). In Hitler's last speech before the *Reichstag* he stated:

> I expect the German judiciary to understand that the nation does not exist for the judiciary but the judiciary for the nation, that is to say that the whole world, including Germany, is not to be blown to smithereens just in order that a formal law can exist, but that Germany must live on, however much the formalities of the judiciary may be in contradiction with this. I cannot – to quote one example – understand a judgment in which a criminal, who had married in 1937 and ill-treated his wife until she was taken to a mental hospital where she died from the last maltreatment, is sentenced to five years' hard labour when tens of thousands of brave Germans must die to protect their homeland from destruction by Bolshevism. This means that, in order to protect their women and children, from now on I shall intervene in these cases and remove judges who are obviously not aware of the necessity of the hour.
>
> (Koch 1989: 113–14)

Already in 1941 in occupied Europe Jews were no longer subject to German law (Stolleis 1998: 19).[3] In Germany, however, many jurists were still struggling with their position, and still attempting to find their place in Hitler's Germany, to rationalize the developments in Nazi Germany. A 1942 memo from State Secretary of the Reich Ministry of Justice, Curt Rothenberger to Hitler, titled 'Reflections on a National Socialist Judicial Reform' and presented at the United States Nuremberg Military Tribunal in the 'Justice Case', includes statements such as 'What can I do to put at the disposal of the Führer a justice and judges in which he may have confidence?', and argues for complete judicial reform 'in readiness for after the war' (*Trials of War Criminals before the Nuremberg Military Tribunals* 1949–53, Vol 3: 469–83). At the same time, the tension between order and arbitrariness continued. The case of Johann Meisslein, a military trial held in March 1943 in which Messlein, a road engineer from Nuremberg in charge of a group of Jewish slave labourers in the Ukraine, was found guilty for the 'unauthorized' killing of two Jewish women, illustrates this (Kwiet 2000: 125–35).[4]

Johann Meisslein, a road engineer from Nuremberg, had been drafted into the German army, as had other professionals, to work on projects of military importance in German occupied Eastern Europe. He was in charge, assisted by a Polish foreman, of a group of Jewish slave labourers from the Ozitna camp, in the Ukraine, who were building a road. The practice was that if it was seen that a Jew was too ill to work, they would be sent back to the camp. The policemen in charge of the camp would then ascertain whether they were ill and if so, would instruct the Lithuanian guards they should be killed. The Court found that on 5 June 1942 Meisslein noticed that two Jewish women were unable to walk and were being carried along by the group. He instructed the foreman that the two should be taken away. The foreman interpreted this as meaning they should be killed, so instructed one Lithuanian guard to kill the two women. The Court found that the foreman could not have interpreted it any other way. When Meisslein found out what had happened, he reported it to the police. Despite this, Meisslein was found guilty, according to para. 132 of the Penal Code, of *Amtsanmaßung*, that is, assuming powers one didn't have. When considering the sentence, the court took into consideration that the accused assumed the power over life and death. That is, he did something which must not be done except through the authorization of public office. Importantly, the Court stated that the execution of the Jews was a matter for the police and the SS (Schutzstaffel), and not members of the OT (Organisation Todt; the labour battalion Meisslein was a member of). It was the state, and the state only, who was to assume powers over life and death.

1943 was the year in which the 'Jewish solution' (extermination, not deportation) was finalized. Jewish emigration from the 'Government-General' (German occupied Eastern Europe) had already been banned in a Decree of 25 October 1940. Jewish emigration from Germany was banned one year later, through the *Order Banning the Emigration of Jews from the Reich, October 1941*. As the 1942 Protocol of Wannsee noted, 'Emigration has now been replaced by evacuation of the Jews to the East, as a further possible solution, with the appropriate prior authorization by the Führer'. This was to fulfil the task 'charged' to Heydrich, as contained in Göring's Memorandum of 31 July 1941, to make 'all necessary preparations with regard to organizational, practical and financial aspects for an overall solution (*Gesamtlösung*) of the Jewish question in the German sphere of influence in Europe'. The order banning emigration was critical to the genocide to be perpetrated. The world of the Jew in German territory was now confined to death and concentration camps, ghettos and hiding. Law had facilitated this, yet law was to be quite absent, there was to be no recourse to law for the victims.

Law presented a rational face of the Nazi state. When law was used as the key tool, when the actions of the new (Nazi) state took a similar form to the old (Weimar Republic) state, this familiarity of form was on one level reassuring. The separation by degree, and by law, lulled many into a false sense of security. The catchphrase for the Jewish community in Germany in this early stage of the mid-1930s was *überleben*: if we can only 'live through' this time. The use of law meant that the Nazis were able to maintain a balance of normalcy and terror. The terror was to be on the periphery of German life. From the beginning, this seemed clear, with the demotion in status of the SA (Sturmabteilung) 'brownshirts' who were responsible for most of the *Kristallnacht* violence. After 10 November 1938 they were moved out of the central sphere of Nazi power.

Law was the symbol of the rational and the modern society. The use of law by the Nazi state meant that on some level they followed in this modern tradition. And the Jewish community, particularly the German Jewish community who were fairly assimilated, who embraced and celebrated modernity for giving them enfranchisement, were reassured in this. What was not known at this stage, was the grim reality of the underside of modernity. Modernity without any checks, any sustaining ethics, a modernity filled with the emptiness of rationality as Zygmunt Bauman was to later illustrate (Bauman 1989). That, as modernity could enfranchise, so too could it disenfranchise. And that reason was no guarantee of life.

By the end of the Second World War, six million Jews had been killed – almost three-quarters of European Jews – as well as three million Poles, 500,000 Romani, and thousands more political opponents and 'undesirables'. They had been segregated, dehumanized and killed. In the occupied East, some had been killed first through the 'mobile killing units', the *Einsatzgruppen*. The Jews in occupied Europe had been forced into ghettos, and then deported to concentration and death camps. Law had failed to protect, in fact law had facilitated this ultimate removal orchestrated by the Nazi state.

Apartheid South Africa

South Africa gives us another example of the deep use of state law in the orchestration of state crime. Law played a key role in the establishment of a segregated state in South Africa. From the beginning of the formation of the Union of South Africa in 1909, as Dyzenhaus discusses, the political-legal-social system was a segregated one (see Dyzenhaus 1991: 32–40). This followed the earlier practice of discrimination and exploitation (with some exception in the Cape) in the united four provinces of the Transvaal, the Orange Free State, Natal and the Cape. An underlying principle of segregation existed, which was further consolidated with the disenfranchisement of previously enfranchised Africans from the common electoral roll in 1936. Africans, according to Lord Alfred Milner, High Commissioner of South Africa, were 'not fit to be equal partners in civilization' (ibid: 34). Dullah Omar has noted that with the Union of South Africa, 'an apartheid state ... was thus imposed on the indigenous inhabitants of this land and the dual political system of a parliamentary democracy for whites and a dictatorship for blacks was born' (Omar 1990: 19).

Segregation, however, was not deeply institutionalized nor uniform until 1948, with the election win of the Afrikaner Nationalists over the ruling United Party, on a platform of 'the "black peril" "swamping" the cities' (Dyzenhaus 1991: 40). It was in 1948 under the Afrikaner Nationalist government that the apartheid policy was established. The National Party came to power on a platform of apartheid, an Afrikaans word meaning 'apartness' or 'segregation'. While segregation was no new condition for the South African states, the apartheid policy signalled an increase of discriminatory laws relating to black South Africans, and a harsher regime.

Dyzenhaus notes that three statutes formed the basis of apartheid: the Population Registration Act 30 of 1950 (classifying the entire South African population as a 'white person, a coloured person or a Bantu, as the case may be ... '), the Abolition of Passes and Coordination of Documents Act 67 of 1952 (requiring all African men to carry passes, which extended in 1956 to all African women) and Section 10 of the Natives Laws Amendment Act 54 of 1952 (which limited Africans with the right to live permanently in the white urban areas to those who were born there, those who had lived there continuously for fifteen years, and those who had worked continuously for the same employer for ten years) (Dyzenhaus 1991: 40). These were enacted alongside existing laws such as the Prohibition of Mixed Marriages Act 55 of 1949 which banned marriages between 'whites' and 'non-whites', and the Group Areas Act 41 of 1950 that segregated urban areas, creating zones for exclusive white use. The Group Areas Act was seen as a 'keystone of the system' – as the International Commission of Jurists 1988 report on South Africa noted, this was highlighted when P.W. Botha announced prior to the constitutional referendum of 1983 that apartheid was to be extinguished, yet vowed that the Group Areas Act was to remain, demonstrating the falsity of this claim (International Commission of Jurists 1988: 15).

A further law that was to be highly used later was the Suppression of Communism Act No 44 of 1950 that allowed for the 'listing' of members or supporters of any banned organization resulting in a severe curtailing of their movements, employment and education. 'Banishment' grew out of this, using the Native Administration Act of 1927 which gave the State President the power to 'order any tribe, portion of a tribe, or individual African to move from one place to another and to remain in the area stated until permission to leave is granted' (Fullard 2004: 354). Madeleine Fullard notes that banishment was especially directed at Africans in rural areas and was generally abrupt and severe, exiling them to a remote rural area often thousands of kilometres from their home and family (ibid). This was later to become the practice of 'banning orders' of the Internal Security Act of 1982.

Campaigns by black Africans against the implementation of these laws, orchestrated by the African National Congress together with the South African Indian Congress and other political organizations, resulted in further oppressive legislation. As David Philips notes, in 1952, together with the South African Indian Congress, the African National Congress staged the Defiance Campaign, targeting six laws of the new apartheid government to defy non-violently (Philips 2008). For example, African men refused to carry passes, as required by law, or deliberately entered areas marked 'Whites Only', allowing themselves to be arrested (ibid). The Public Safety Act 8, which gave wide-ranging powers to the Governor-General if he were satisfied that a state of emergency existed, and the Criminal Law Amendment Act 8 which made it an offence to violate any law by way of protest against any law, were both enacted in 1953.

Black South Africans were to have their recourse to courts taken away. As noted by the International Commission of Jurists in their 1960 report, The Natives (Prohibition of Interdicts) Act, 22 June 1956 meant that,

> Any African threatened by an official with forcible removal from any land, building or area, whether unlawful or not is by that Act precluded from access to the courts to obtain a restraint upon such illegal action. His sole remedy is to obtain compensation after the wrong has been committed.
> (International Commission of Jurists 1960: 63)

Later protests led to more draconian laws and measures. The state of emergency legislation was first employed in 1960, after the massacre at Sharpeville by government troops (Ellmann 1992: 19). As Dyzenhaus notes, 5,000 people had gathered peacefully at Sharpville, an African township not far from Johannesburg, as part of a nation-wide campaign aimed at the planned burning of passes, when 'the police panicked and opened fire, leaving 69 dead and 180 wounded' (Dyzenhaus 1991: 45).

New political crimes were created. The Unlawful Organizations Act No. 34 of 1960 allowed the African National Congress and Pan Africanist Congress to be declared illegal organizations. As Fullard notes, they were to remain banned for thirty years, and throughout the 1960s membership of an illegal organization was to be the most common charge faced by thousands of ordinary members and supporters of the African National Congress and Pan Africanist Congress (Fullard 2004: 344). In 1961, the Indemnity Act was passed. Made retrospective to 21 March 1960, its purpose, as Fullard notes, was to protect the government and its officials against claims regarding security forces actions taken during demonstrations – its retrospectivity meant it covered the demonstrations and their violent repression in Sharpeville, Mpondoland and elsewhere (ibid: 345).

Following the call for a National Convention and 'stay-away' (a general strike) in May 1961 by the African National Congress (ANC), further oppressive laws were brought in. A law that allowed detention without bail for twelve days, and criminalized the organization of prohibited gatherings, the General Law Amendment Act No 39 of 1961, was rushed through Parliament. The defendants in subsequent trials, 'challenged the right of the state to charge Africans in terms of laws and institutions from which they were excluded' (ibid: 345). The ANC decided to change tack, and focus on establishing a government in exile and engaging in sabotage in South Africa. With the beginning of armed attacks by the new military wing of the ANC, came new repressive legislation and new political crimes. The General Law Amendment Act No 76 of 1962, known as the Sabotage Act, created the political offence of sabotage. A wide definition was adopted, and it included the death penalty. As Fullard notes, it widened the powers to declare organizations unlawful, and included house arrest in banning orders (ibid). Nelson Mandela and most of the leadership of the opposition organizations were subsequently arrested and found guilty under the Sabotage Act.

Numerous pieces of legislation detailing the order of life for black Africans and giving the government tools for their oppression followed. The General Law Amendment Act 37 of 1963, also known as the 90-day law, allowed for arrest and detainment of up to ninety days (in practice, many would be held for a further ninety days). Together with the Sabotage Act, this resulted in thousands of arrests in the early 1960s and an increase in torture in detention. The 90-day law was increased to 180 days in 1965 with the Criminal Procedure Amendment Act No 96. The Terrorism Act 83 of 1967 enhanced the powers of the police, allowing for arbitrary arrests and detention without trial for an indefinite period. As Fullard notes, this built upon the provisions of the Sabotage Act and the detention laws, and created the new offence of participation in terrorist activities (ibid: 347). The Terrorism Act authorized the actions of the security police, who were accountable only to the Minister. The courts could not order the release of a detainee or arbitrate on the validity of action taken under the detention provisions (ibid: 348). With prolonged detention came prolonged torture, much of which has been documented by survivors such as Albie Sachs and others (Sachs 1970), as well as through the Truth Commission process.

Millions of black South Africans were progressively stripped of their South African citizenship (Dyzenhaus 1991: 41). This was through the Black Homelands Citizenship Act 26 of 1970 that provided that every black person in the Republic was to be a citizen of one or other designated black area. Through subsequent statutes, ten million South African blacks had their South African citizenship taken away and allocated another, 'designated … as citizens of places with which many had no ties' (ibid).

The 1970s saw the formation of the Black Consciousness Movement through growing unrest among black South Africans (ibid: 46). It also saw the 1976 'Soweto uprising' – begun as a protest about 'Bantu Education'. As Dyzenhaus notes, 'the police, by firing on a peaceful demonstration of school pupils in Soweto, sparked off a country-wide protest against apartheid and a period of repression which dwarfed Sharpville in brutality, destruction, and death-toll' (ibid). This repression was to include the crushing of the Black Consciousness Movement and the death of Steve Biko in police detention (ibid).

Later, the Internal Security Act of 1982 authorized arrest, detention and interrogation without trial and the banning of individuals, organizations and gatherings. 'Banning' was to be an effective and draconian means of oppression. Its implementation ranged from house arrest to confining individuals to certain geographical areas, suburb, district or farm, and included bans on communication with other banned individuals. Anthony Mathews wrote that 'The combination of all these restraints amounts to a civil death, and to a large extent a personal and social death, for the victim of the banning order' (Mathews 1986: 125). Fullard describes its effects as follows:

> The consequences of banning orders were severe. Whites lost the right to vote and many banned people became unemployed. Zollie Malindi lost his job at a laundry in Cape Town after being confined to a particular magisterial district. The onus of containment was placed upon the shoulders of the banned and they became their own jailers. Cut off from most social interaction, they entered an isolated twilight zone with little stimulation, a severe loss of income and were under perpetual surveillance.
> (Fullard 2004: 352–53)

Apartheid law can be understood in a number of stages. Firstly, the initial legislation of separation that set out the boundaries of the apartheid state (building on boundaries already in place) and further repression. In the very early stages, recourse through the courts in some instances may be found. The first two attempts to remove the 'Coloureds' from the electoral roll was invalidated by the Appellate Court (Dyzenhaus 1991: 50). However, there are also examples of the courts anticipating government intent. Dyzenhaus discusses one case, *Minister of the Interior v. Lockhat* 1961, in which, he suggests, the judge looked to the public record revealed by the general design and implementation of apartheid policy (ibid: 18). By 1960, it was clear what apartheid was meant to represent.

Law was used as a key tool in oppression, both in its demarcation, and through the use of the trial. Fullard notes that from the late 1960s, the courts were used to serve the regime's political goals, that they were a bare 'legitimising device' (Fullard 2004: 341). By 1970 'the rules and safeguards ... have been eroded to such an extent ... that the mere skeleton of the ordinary criminal trial remains' (Norton in ibid).

This had not always been the case. Activist Joe Slovo commented:

> In a sense, up to about 1960/1, the underground struggle was fought on a gentlemanly terrain. There was still a rule of law. You had a fair trial in their courts. Nobody could be held in isolation.
> (Fullard 2004: 356)

The courts until this time had been a place of often fair adjudication. It was in reaction to many of these decisions that numerous acts of separateness were legislated by the government. As the International Commission of Jurists in its 1960 report noted, 'The evolution of separate, but not necessarily equal, facilities and amenities can be traced in recent years as a legislative reaction to judicial decisions' (International Commission of Jurists 1960: 59). These decisions included, for example, a decision by the Appellate Court in 1950 'which ruled that a regulation reserving a portion of all trains to whites, but not restricting them to those sections, led to "partiality and inequality in treatment"', and that this was 'not authorised by the Railways Act of 1916' (ibid). But before the judgement had even been handed down, the Railways and Harbours Acts Amendment Act 1949 was introduced by the government, allowing the reservation of railway premises and trains 'for the exclusive use of particular races provided that equal facilities were available for all races' (ibid: 60). This was later tested as false with a further case that acquitted a black South African for entering the waiting room at Cape Town railway station, yet the intentions of the government were clear. As the Commission of Jurists noted,

> That the Government had no intention of providing parallel facilities for the different races in any of the social or public services was made explicit by Mr. Swart when he said [in Parliament], 'we will always find that reasonable amenities are provided for all classes according to their standard of civilisation and according to their need'.
> (International Commission of Jurists 1960: 60)

The government was intent on implementing their apartheid vision without interference from the courts. As the Commission recounts, Mr Swart (former Minister of Justice and then Acting Prime Minister) went on to say, 'to leave the interpretation in the hands of the courts … is an impossible task for which we are not prepared' (ibid).

David Philips notes that the Treason Trial that ended in 1961 'proved to be the last time that the South African Government used conventional legal means, through the courts and under the normal restraints imposed by the Rule of Law, to deal with its opposition' (Philips 2008). Thereafter, 'the Government moved to the use of arbitrary repression, and largely by-passed the courts and the restraints of the Rule of Law' (ibid). In the wake of the Defiance campaign of 1952 that had sought non-violent opposition to apartheid law, in 1955, what was known as the 'Freedom Charter' was drawn up by a congress of various groups calling itself the Congress Alliance. As Philips notes, the 'government responded to the aspirations of the Freedom Charter with repression. A year and a half after the Congress of the People, in December 1956, the authorities arrested all 156 leaders of the Congress Alliance and charged them all with High Treason' (ibid). This was to be known as the Treason Trial, lasting four years. None of the defendants were found guilty, yet this trial was to mark the end of the rule of law.

What was seen as fair, however, was not necessarily on the basis of equality. Nelson Mandela made this point powerfully. In his trial in Pretoria in 1962, conducting his own defence, Mandela argued that the system could not provide any equality before the law. As he stated:

> a judiciary controlled entirely by whites and enforcing laws enacted by a white parliament in which we have no representation, laws which in most cases are passed in the face of unanimous opposition from Africans, cannot be regarded as an impartial tribunal in a political trial where an African stands as an accused.
>
> (Mandela 1986: 135)

Any semblance of the rule of law was to be removed. As the apartheid regime harshened, the rule of law was pushed to the side. The Final Report of the Truth and Reconciliation Commission argued that, with the use of emergency executive decrees as the 'chosen medium of government', from the mid 1980s 'a climate of "state lawlessness" prevailed and the pretence of adherence to the rule of law was abandoned by the Botha regime' (Truth and Reconciliation Commission of South Africa 1999b: 101). While the 1980s saw the repeal of some laws forbidding contact between black and white South Africans (for example, the Marriage Act was repealed), it also saw a period of a greater abuse of law. Detention without trial and the banning of individuals was core to this, part of the 'statutory armoury' of the South African security system (Dyzenhaus 1991: 46). The state of emergency was proclaimed again in June of 1986, 1987, and again in 1988 and 1989 (Dyzenhaus 1991: 40–49). A new Constitution was enacted in 1983, which, as the International Commission of Jurists noted in their 1988 report, 'provides for the first time parliamentary representation for non-whites, that is so-called coloureds and Indians [and] was claimed by the government to be a major breakthrough' (International Commission of Jurists 1988: 11). Yet, as the Commission report noted, 'No genuine shift in political or economic power has taken place, however, and the Constitution excludes from parliamentary representation the huge disenfranchised African majority', further it 'reinforces the apartheid structure' (ibid).

In the late 1980s the Restoration of Citizenship Act 1986 was introduced, also a major change, to reinstate the citizenship taken away from black South Africans assigned to 'homelands'. Yet as the International Commission of Jurists noted, 'citizens of the independent homelands who now see the possibility of reclaiming South African citizenship are likely to be disappointed. Only those already permanently resident with home and job outside the homeland will qualify, and they are at the mercy of bureaucratic discretion' (ibid: 13). They concluded that 'The structure of apartheid remains untouched by the cosmetic changes which the government has so far made', noting that no changes were proposed to the segregated public school system, the Group Areas Act, or the Population Registration Act which racially classified each South African (ibid).

At the same time, in the 1980s, the 'people's courts' became prevalent. Abel describes them as follows:

> Although their reliance on mediation followed the traditional makgotla, brought to the city by elders, they differed dramatically in three ways. The personnel were youths. They attacked traditional values like patriarchy. And they used, often abused, corporal punishment.
>
> (Abel 1995: 374)

The corporal punishment used was often the grotesque practice of 'necklacing', killing alleged informants or collaborators. These 'courts' held in black townships were seen as an alternate space to the apartheid law, and, as T.W. Bennett notes, filled a 'vacuum in law enforcement' in townships in the wake of the state of emergencies called (Bennett 2004: 155).

An informal court system had existed in South Africa since colonization. The 'people's courts' were an incarnation of what had been prevalent parallel to the official state system. Sandra Burman and Wilfried Schärf note that 'A dual system of colonial state (or formal) and noncolonial state (or informal) courts existed in the rural areas from the arrival of the first magistrates in African territories' (Burman and Schärf 1990: 693). There was recognition of this informal court structure at the Truth and Reconciliation Commission as well, that many civil legal matters in South Africa are decided by bodies outside the formal court structure, namely tribunals administered by chiefs in the former homeland areas, under laws dating from the colonial period (Truth and Reconciliation Commission of South Africa 1999c). The dual system of law provided both an alternate space for mediation, but a repressive one as well, reflecting the repressive policies of the state.

It was law that framed and institutionalized the policy of apartheid. It was through legal means that the policy of segregation, present from the beginning of South African statehood, was institutionalized and harshened. Colin Tatz has noted that the 'South African way of life', one of exploitation and oppression, was a system kept in place by custom and convention, and later buttressed and 'invigorated' by law (Tatz 2003: 118). Fullard notes that 'The legal system was the key mechanism through which the state could simultaneously crush opposition and depict banned organisations as violent, communist and a dangerous threat to white security' (Fullard 2004: 342). Law played an important role both in implementing apartheid as well as providing a forum for government policy. Law was both collaborator and companion. Within this context it is difficult to reconcile the rule of law and apartheid law. The argument can be made that it is impossible for discriminatory or segregationist laws to be 'separate' to the main legal system – for any legal system is a comprehensive one. There may be separations and distinctions within a legal system – for example, affirmative action legislation, different status legislation – yet these exist for the addition, not the removal, of rights and privileges.

What is being discussed here is legislation that corrupts the total legal system. It defines those living within the borders of the nation state, between citizens and non-citizens, between those with full rights and those without such rights. It may be the case that a substantial proportion of the population is not affected by such legislation, that it does not affect their day to day living, yet this does not mean that such legislation is separate to the society. Judges may act independently, yet they are working within a legal system that is a discriminatory one. They may not make decisions which are arbitrary. The rule of law tradition as such may be followed. Yet even though the state does not interfere generally in the system of law, does this mean that a rule of law system substantively exists, and that the judges cannot be seen to be complicit with the discriminatory and oppressive policies of the state?

The role of judges in South Africa during apartheid has been fiercely debated. The Truth and Reconciliation Commission was disappointed that no judges attended the Legal Institutions hearing (despite putting in submissions). Arguments have been made that judges protected the legal order, that judges could do nothing else, and that judges protected the apartheid state. Hugh Corder has described the relationship as 'while formally independent from political influence, manifestly incorrupt, and consciously impartial, [judges] were integral parts of the very structure which had created and now maintained injustice, from which they made little effort to extricate themselves' (Corder 1984: 240). In his study of judicial decision making in the Appellate Division in South Africa, he shows that 'In most of the cases … either of two decisions could have been defended as legally proper' (ibid: 237).

South Africa has been understood as a bifurcated state – one democratic and one authoritarian, one for whites and one for blacks. Michael Mann found 'an impeccably liberal society and democratic state for whites' that 'coexisted with authoritarian and militaristic rule over blacks' (Meierhenrich 2008: 171). Meierhenrich suggests that South Africa be seen as an example of Fraenkel's dual state, that there existed both 'rational' and 'irrational' law within the apartheid state and that a culture of 'legality' was maintained (ibid: 170–74). As Chanock notes, 'a culture of "constitutionalism" was successfully maintained among and for whites' and thus 'Power was limited to protect white democracy, but not limited where Africans (and Asians) were concerned' (Chanock 2001: 41). In his analysis of administrative law under apartheid, Chanock concluded that the reason why the courts failed to protect constitutional freedoms during apartheid, despite arguments as to South Africa following the rule of law, was because 'they made choices as to which part of the bifurcated state each case belonged to' (ibid). In this way law played a partnership role in the implementation of apartheid.

Law, however, was also used in the fight against apartheid. These include, as Richard Abel has documented, challenges to the pass laws, unfair labour practices, the practice of banning and eviction, and of torture by the security forces, among others (Abel 1995). Yet despite appeals to law, which in some cases were successful, these did not succeed in any immediate wider change (although Abel argues they laid the groundwork for later change). It is of note, too, that under apartheid, most of the framework of rights remained intact – who had access to those rights was determined by the government, and to an extent, the courts. Interestingly, Fullard notes that 'with all possibility of legal protest excluded, the courtroom became the last remaining space in which banned organizations could articulate their views' (Fullard 2004: 342). That is, that despite the trials being used by the government as a form of showcase, they were also used, as she notes, 'by the liberation movements as a platform for expressing their policies and perspectives', and that 'the Rivonia Trial provided an important legacy of imagery, speeches, iconic figures and other symbolic representations that were used to mobilise international support and domestic resistance for decades to come' (ibid).

The formal apartheid legislation, however, did not encompass the full and harsh reality of apartheid. There was no law authorizing torture, or extra-judicial killings, for example. These 'excesses', which were the reality of the apartheid era, fell outside law. Yet while they may have fallen outside law, they were framed by law. Apartheid legislation may not have fully encompassed the crimes perpetrated, but it did make them allowable, and even expected. It certainly made them possible.

Some law is used in state crime, although it cannot be characterized as a deep framework

Here we can place the genocide of the Armenians by the Ottoman state in the First World War, Cambodia under the Khmer Rouge in the 1970s, and Ethiopia under Mengistu and the Dergue.

The Ottoman State and the genocide of the Armenians

The role played by law in the Armenian genocide was primarily that of legitimation. The enactment of law served as a mask for killing. The law was also used in an attempt to implicate others in the crime, to widen the web of responsibility. The Temporary Law of Deportation of 1915, allowing for the deportation and consequently the death of the Armenians as the 'deportees' (ostensibly for their safety in wartime), not only failed to be passed through the correct channels but was drafted after the deportations had begun. The 1915 law relating to the release of prisoners to serve in the Special

Organization Unit (the unit primarily responsible for the killing of the Armenians) was pressured through Parliament as well as being drafted after the commencement of the deportations, after most of the Armenians had been killed, and after most of these criminals had already been drafted into the unit. The 1915 Temporary Law of Expropriation and Confiscation, the appropriation of property bill, was the only piece of legislation that appears to have been passed in accordance with usual procedure and not after the fact.

It is true that law did frame the massacres. Yet the decision to carry out the policy of murder against the Armenians was formulated before any laws were passed. The facilitation of the genocide of the Armenians was independent to the enactment of law. While the laws passed during this time relate specifically to the genocide, it cannot be said that law was a primary tool in the implementation of the killings. However, that laws authorizing actions taken against the Armenians were passed, albeit after the fact, showed the place of law and the importance placed on the legitimacy of these actions.

The Christian Armenian population within the Ottoman Empire had always held the status of 'subject peoples'. As Dadrian notes, Ottoman law was a combination of Islamic doctrine and common law. Non-Muslim subjects were required to enter into a quasi-legal contract, the *Akdi Zimmet*, whereby the ruler (the Sultan-Khalif), guaranteed the 'safeguard' of their persons, their civil and religious liberties, and, conditionally, their properties, in exchange for the payment of poll and land taxes, and acquiescence to a set of social and legal disabilities (Dadrian 1997b: 4). Further, these contracts marked the initiation of a customary law in the Ottoman system that regulated the unequal relations between Muslims and non-Muslims (ibid). The status of the Armenian population was thus inferior to those of their fellow Muslim subjects, with the Armenians being 'tolerated infidels' (ibid). While the Ottoman Constitution of 1876 stated (Article 17), 'All the Ottomans are equal before the law. They have the same rights and same duties toward the country, without prejudice to religion', as Stephan Astourian notes, such protection was largely fictional (Astourian 1992: 63). Although the Constitution was reinstated after having been suspended in 1878 by Sultan Abdul Hamid II, and reinstated under the pressure of the Young Turk revolution on 23 July 1908, this did not change the situation of the Armenian minority. The large-scale massacres in Cilicia supported by the Turkish army in April 1909, in which 20,000 Armenians were killed, only confirmed this. Any hopes of Armenian Christian equality came to an end, as Astourian notes, with the military coup engineered by Enver, ousting the relatively liberal government that had ruled the Ottoman Empire since July 1912, and installing a dictatorial regime led by the triumvirate of Talat, Cemal and Enver (ibid).

In the lead-up to the massacres of the Armenians, earlier agreements, such as the Armenian Reforms, which had sought to provide a level of international protection to the Armenian minority, were annulled by the Young Turk leadership.[5] The following explanation was given by then Interior Minister Talat Paşa to an Armenian Deputy of the Ottoman Parliament:

> Don't Armenians realize that the implementation of the reforms depends on us … They don't seem to have learned their lessons; all undertakings opposed by us are bound to fail. Let the Armenians wait, opportunities will certainly come our way too. Turkey belongs only to the Turks.
>
> (Dadrian 1997b: 214)

This expression, 'Turkey belongs only to the Turks', was to be heard again and again, and provided the ideological rationale for the actions taken against the Armenian population. In his memoirs, Cemal Paşa states that 'our sole objective was to free ourselves from all the measures [imposed upon us] in this war and which constituted a blow to our internal independence' (Paşa, cited in ibid: 208). Further, in a conversation with Hans Humann (German naval attaché and Enver Paşa's childhood friend), Enver is reported to have said that the main rationale of the anti-Armenian measures was 'the total elimination of any basis for future interventions by the Powers on behalf of the Armenians' (Lepsius, cited in ibid).

There was a clear build-up of such a plan prior to the actual genocide. It can be seen as combination of internal belief (Young Turk ideology) and reaction to external pressure to improve the situation of the Armenians. Already in December 1913, British leaders had warned the British government that Turkey was intent on destroying the Ottoman Armenian population in the event the Powers imposed upon Turkey the Reform Act; that there was the 'great fear of a massacre' in Turkey (Nassibian, cited in ibid: 216). Moreover, there is evidence that the actual plan for destruction was decided prior to the entry of Turkey into the First World War. Indeed, there is evidence that Turkey entered the war in order to facilitate this destruction, to provide a mask for the killings. A document dubbed 'the Ten Commandments' was discovered by the British in 1919. Titled by the British, 'Documents relating to Comite Union and Progres Organization in the Armenian Massacres', and subtitled 'The 10 Commandments of the Comite Union and Progres' (The Committee of Union and Progress was the Ittihadists' name, for both their association and their party), it has been identified as the record of one of a series of meetings of top-level Ittihad leaders during the early part of the First World War (Dadrian 1994b). It lists from one through ten the actions to be perpetrated against the Armenian population, simultaneously, in order to ensure their destruction.

This plan was put into action just prior to the entry of the Ottoman state into the First World War. The first stage was the conscription of male Armenians into the army, as part of a general mobilization on 2–3 August 1914. Many were worked to death, and many Armenian soldiers killed by the Turkish army. The second stage was the targeting of Armenian political and community leaders: on 6 September 1914, an instruction was sent by the Interior Ministry to the provincial authorities to keep these leaders under surveillance. With the entry of Turkey into the First World War in November 1914, military 'emergency measures' served as a cover for the appropriation of Armenian property in the provinces, and widespread harassment of the Armenian population (to which there was isolated Armenian resistance). Historian Taner Akçam comments:

> Under the pretext of searching for arms, of collecting war levies, of tracking down deserters, there had already been established a practice of systematically carried-out plunders, raids and murders [against the Armenians] which had become daily occurrences.
>
> (Akçam, cited in Dadrian 1997b: 221)

On 24 April 1915 an Interior Ministry order authorized the arrest of all Armenian political and community leaders ostensibly suspected of anti-Ittihad or nationalistic sentiments. Thousands of Armenians were arrested, most were executed, all without any specific charges being laid or trials held (ibid).

It was the act of deportation by the Ottoman authorities that claimed the most lives in the genocide against the Armenians. Deportation was intended death: deportation meant the mobilization of women, children and the elderly, rounded up to walk across Turkey, without adequate food or water, with no shelter, subject to the harsh terrain and thus to die. It meant to be subject to multiple abuses along the road: rape, removal of children (particularly girls for 'Islamicization'), and arbitrary killing by those who were their 'guides'. The American Ambassador Henry Morgenthau observed:

> The real purpose of the deportation was robbery and destruction; it really represented a new method of massacre. When the Turkish authorities gave the orders for these deportations, they were merely giving the death warrant to a whole race; they understood this well, and in their conversations with me, they made no particular attempt to conceal the fact.
>
> (Morgenthau 1918: 309)

The deportation was formalized through the Temporary Law of Deportation. In a Memorandum dated 26 May 1915, the Interior Minister requested from the Grand Vizier the enactment through the Cabinet of a special law authorizing deportations (Dadrian 1997b: 221). The law did not specifically refer to the Armenians, rather to 'deportees'. As Dadrian notes, it authorized the Commanders of Armies, Army Corps, Divisions and Commandants of local garrisons to order the deportation of population clusters on suspicion of espionage, treason, and on military necessity (ibid).

The law was endorsed by the Grand Vizier and taken to Cabinet on 30 May 1915, which approved it. It was, however, already announced by the press on 27 May. Yet the draft bill was in fact never approved by the Parliament, which was required under Article 36 of the Ottoman Constitution, as the Parliament had been temporarily suspended. It is suspected that this suspension (on 1 March 1915, one and a half months earlier than stipulated by law) was directly connected to the anti-Armenian measures (ibid: 236). It is known, however, that the deportations commenced prior to the draft bill being presented. And although it was never formally approved by Parliament, it was accepted as a legitimate law, due to its announcement in the press and the fact that it was already under way.

Law thus provided a public framework for the deportations, a level of legitimacy for the actions taken against the Armenians. Despite being rushed through and not in fact endorsed by Parliament, it provided a veneer of legality. While law did not provide a deep framework for the actions against the Armenians, it did provide retrospective legitimacy.

A supplementary law was enacted on 10 June 1915 regarding the registration of property of the deportees. The Temporary Law of Expropriation and Confiscation followed. It allowed the state to appropriate and sell the Armenians' belongings and properties. This law was publicly debated as required in the Ottoman Senate, from 4 October to 13 December 1915. The one voice of opposition was Senator Ahmed Riza, who put forward an alternate bill proposing that the application of the law be delayed until the end of the war, on both constitutional and humanitarian grounds, arguing that the law was 'inimical to the principles of law and justice' (ibid: 223). This did not happen, and the law, with pressure applied from the Ittihadist leadership, was approved.

The other law intimately connected to the acts perpetrated against the Armenians was the draft bill to enlist convicted murderers in the Special Organization. The Special Organization was the group formed in secret by the Ittihadist leaders to facilitate the murder of the Armenians. As Dadrian notes, their mission was to deploy in remote areas of Turkey's interior and to ambush and destroy convoys of Armenian deportees (ibid: 236). A draft bill was enacted in 1916 to enlist convicted murderers in the Special Organization. Its passage was requested and secured by the under secretary of the Justice Ministry as an 'emergency bill' (*müstaceliyet*), on 12 December 1916. Yet by the end of 1916 the actions against the Armenians had almost been completed, and in fact the release of prisoners had already been authorized by the Justice Minister Ibrahim. It appears that the purpose of the law was to ensure the appearance of legality, as well as to possibly implicate those beyond the Ittihadist leadership in the killing of the Armenians. Evidence presented at one of the later Courts-Martial trials established the role played by the 'escorts' of the deportee convoys. As Höss notes, in the Yozgat trial the cipher telegrams presented (with their handwritten signatures) confirmed, according to the judgement of the Court, 'the nature of the real purpose of these guards – the massacre of the people of these convoys. There can be no hesitation or doubt about this' (Höss 1992: 218). One telegram contained the phrase 'deported, namely, annihilated' (ibid: 216).

By the end of the First World War, 1.8 million Armenians had been killed, in a systematic plan conceived and initiated by the Young Turk triumvirate. The constitutional provisions designed to protect non-Muslim minorities had proven a hollow shield. Hollower still were the Armenian Reforms, internationally executed yet not followed through, due to the onset of the war, Turkey's alliance with Germany (one of the international signatories) and Turkey's annulment of this international contract. There was a gesture to law in the form of bills presented after action had commenced (the deportation law) and bills passed once actions had commenced (the release of the prisoners bill), as well as debate on the confiscation of the property bill. Yet the Young Turks' vision of a 'Turkey for the Turks' meant that the rule of law was secondary to their aims, and that law would in fact be used as a tool of legitimacy for genocide. Any appearance of legislative independence was a sham, subsumed under the genocidal policy of the state.

Khmer Rouge Cambodia

In Cambodia under Pol Pot and the Khmer Rouge, we see law being put even more to the periphery. At the very beginning, law played a minor role – the enactment of a new Constitution – but then law ceased to play any role. The judiciary of Cambodia was destroyed, and the 'law' of the Khmer Rouge was communicated via rules and directives, rather than through any legislation. Many of these directives were not disseminated to the Khmer people, the rationale being that what was right and wrong was expected to be 'known' by the ordinary Khmer. This absence of formal law was due in part to the small role played previously by formal law in Cambodian society; however, it was also due to the Khmer Rouge will for absolute control. Their destruction of what can be seen as the alternative to formal law – Buddhism – demonstrates this. What law did very clearly (in the enactment of the new Constitution) was establish the 'telos' of the new regime. In a similar but far more superficial manner to that of Nazi Germany, law (the Constitution) demonstrated the ideological goals of the Khmer Rouge and their own *Weltanschauung*, that Cambodia was ' … a State of the people, workers, peasants, and all other Cambodian working people' (*Constitution of Democratic Kampuchea* 1976, Art. 1).

However, law in the sense of courts and judges and centralized rules has not played a central role in the history of Cambodia, nor did it in the assumption of power by the Khmer Rouge. Law in the form of norms, religion and common culture has been absorbed integrally in a way that centralized law never was. There exists a culture of conciliation and mediation framed within a tradition of external yet penetrating and framing power relations. Writing in the 1990s, Dolores Donovan noted the preference for dispute resolution outside the state legal system, particularly in the countryside, and the Khmer preference for turning to monks or persons higher in the social hierarchy for resolution of disputes (Donovan 1993: 453).

The emphasis on community conciliation rather than on formal decisions by courts of law, was framed and ordered by the moral tenets of Buddhism and infused with the spiritual tenets of the gods, within a greater regional hierarchy of traditions. That which was meted out was considered justice, in the sense of satisfying the principles of order and authority. There were a number of different types of ordering, culture and law which framed Cambodian life: a hierarchical tradition, the monarchy, the 'spirit' culture, a rich oral tradition, a culture of conciliation, the Buddhist order, the family unit and a state legal system. Different forms of law played different roles, non-formal law played a large part in the establishment and maintenance of law in Cambodia. The Khmer Rouge used this to their advantage, particularly the interplay between informal normative ordering and power.

The first formal Cambodian legal system was the promulgation of a new Law Code presided over by King Duang on his anointment in 1848 (Chandler 1992: 135). With the establishment of the French Protectorate in 1863, the French brought in a French-style formal legislative and judicial system, including a Constitution. In 1884, as a condition for France's 'invited protection' of Cambodia, the French forced the king to sign a treaty, Article 2 reading: 'His Majesty the King of Cambodia accepts all the administrative, judicial, financial and commercial reforms which the French government shall judge, in future, useful to make their protectorate successful' (ibid: 144). The French system was retained after Cambodia's declaration of independence, and destroyed by the Khmer Rouge.

The Buddhist order provided an alternative value system to the colonial one. Buddhism was woven into the very fabric of Khmer life. Before the Khmer Rouge took power, Cambodia was considered to be the most Buddhist country in Southeast Asia: to be Khmer was to be Buddhist. Most Khmer men spent an average of two years as a monk (Jackson 1989: 68). A transplant from India, following Hinduism, Buddhism meshed with local culture and religion. Many Cambodians speak of Buddhism as the 'soul' or 'core' of Khmer culture and civilization (Sam, cited in Hannum 1989: 87). In order to secure full control of the Khmer people, the Khmer Rouge needed to destroy Buddhism, which, after a gradual process beginning in Khmer Rouge controlled areas as early as 1973, they did after 1975 in less than twelve months.

It could be argued that the Buddhist orders embodied formal law, at least for those outside the main cities (or even just outside of Phnom Penh), and that Buddhism provided an ordering structure, as well as a mode of conduct. Buddhist leaders (monks) were also community leaders, they were seen as learned men, they embodied order. The spirits possibly embodied will. When the formal judicial system did not even touch those in the country, the combination of Buddhism and spirit culture played an important formative role. Demonstrative of this combination, Chandler and Mabbett relay an incident from the 1960s:

> A witness at court was strongly suspected of telling lies. He persisted with his version of the case, even after swearing on a pile of volumes of Buddhist texts. In order to test whether a more plausible version could be extracted by other means, the magistrate asked him to swear by the spirit of a nearby sacred tree, which should kill him if he did not tell the truth. He promptly changed his tune.
>
> (Jacques, cited in Mabbett & Chandler 1995: 111)

These levels of informal ordering, framed within the hierarchy of relations – the relationship between the majority of Khmer and the spheres to which they related (local religion, local culture and local authority) – may provide some indication as to how the Khmer Rouge was able to get so close to the majority of the population. Namely, that one authority was swapped for the other. As long as the central tenets of life were not affected, the Khmer Rouge could be welcomed (this was in the early stages, before 1975).

The spirits – the *Neak Ta* – were still believed in. Khmer peasantry held an inherent belief in the rhythm of power and authority. The power of the spirits was that, if transgressed, they would react. As the spirits on the whole did not react, the actions of the Khmer Rouge fitted in with Khmer folklore: tales of spirits being overpowered by courageous men unafraid to face them. The spirits still existed, but it was now the Khmer Rouge who held the power. As one 32-year-old peasant who lived under Khmer Rouge rule said:

> But since the Khmer Rouges rule the country, the *Neak Ta* don't dare do anything, they're afraid of the Khmer Rouges' meanness. When we spoke about the *Neak Ta* to them, they would say: 'Where is he, I'm going to shoot him.' Even the *Neak Ta* were afraid of them, they didn't dare act up against them.
>
> (Ponchaud, cited in Jackson 1989: 168)

The Khmer Rouge were seen to replace the 'powerful men' in the Cambodian belief system of those in the countryside. They were able, to an extent, to be included in the normative ordering of the Khmer. Further, Eisenbruch has shown how the Khmer Rouge used the language of traditional healing, in particular its explanatory framework of 'threats coming from outside and those from within' in their fundamentalist message to the population (Eisenbruch 2007: 76–77). The Khmer Rouge drew on the 'living law' of the Cambodian people in their brutal practices.

Formal law was used in the first instance in Cambodia to declare the beginning of the new regime and the cessation of the old. The Khmer Rouge marched into Phnom Penh on 17 April 1975, four days after the traditional

Khmer New Year. The Khmer Rouge proclaimed their entering Phnom Penh as the beginning of a new age, and the implementation of a new reality. 'The 17th of April 1975, a glorious date in the history of Kampuchea, has ushered in an era more remarkable than the age of the Angkors' was a slogan often repeated over the Radio Phnom Penh domestic service (Ponchaud 1978: 9).

This new era was violently implemented. One of the first acts of the new regime was the elimination of all Khmer who had been involved in the civil and military administration of Cambodia. 'What is infected must be cut out', 'it isn't enough to cut down a bad plant, it must be uprooted': these were slogans heard frequently on the radio and at Khmer Rouge meetings (ibid: 70). As François Ponchaud writes, the belief of the Khmer Rouge was that the authorities of the former regime were not fellow-creatures who had been misled, rather they were enemies and as such had no place in the national community (ibid). Thus were the judges and the lawyers killed, and the old colonial law destroyed. For one of the doctrines of the new regime was an independent path, that all must be fully Khmer: as such, international food and medicine aid was refused by the new government.

In May 1975 the Khmer Rouge enacted the new Constitution of the renamed Democratic Kampuchea. Law then ceased to function in the usual manner. The old law was destroyed, and the new became a tool in the hands of the Khmer Rouge, for brutal implementation of their specific ideology. As in other totalitarian regimes such as National Socialist Germany and Mengistu's Ethiopia, and as Adam Podgórecki (1996: 19) points out, the preconceived function of the law was more important than the law itself.

Article One of the *Constitution of Democratic Kampuchea* 1976 declared Cambodia to be 'a State of the people, workers, peasants, and all other Cambodian working people. The official name of the State of Cambodia is "Democratic Cambodia [Kampuchea]"'. Article Five declared that 'Legislative power is invested in the Representative Assembly of the People, workers, peasants and all other Cambodian working people'. The Assembly was to be known as the Cambodian People's Representative Assembly, composed of 250 members, of whom 150 represented the peasants and fifty each the workers and the Revolutionary Army. Article Seven stipulated that the People's Representative Assembly was responsible for legislation and for defining the various domestic and foreign policies of Democratic Cambodia. The Assembly, as Article Eight noted, was to be responsible for selecting a State Presidium of three members to function as head of state, as well as electing a government to 'give effect to laws and political lines laid down by the Cambodian People's Representative Assembly'.

Articles Nine and Ten of the Constitution dealt with 'Justice'. Article Nine read as follows:

> Justice is administered by People's Courts which represent and defend the people's justice, defend the democratic rights of the people and

punish any act directed against the people's state or violating the laws of the people's state.

The judges at all levels shall be chosen and appointed by the People's Representative Assembly.

Article Ten read:

Actions violating the laws of the people's state are as follows:
hostile and destructive activities which threaten the popular state shall be subject to the severest form of punishment;
other cases shall be handled by means of constructive reeducation in the framework of the state or people's organisations.
(*Constitution of Democratic Kampuchea* 1976)

The first and only plenary session of the People's Representative Assembly was held from 11 to 13 April 1976. No laws and decrees were enacted: rather, a press release was issued (Carney 1989: 90). Timothy Carney comments that the government of Democratic Kampuchea appeared to relate more to the outside world than to the administration of the nation itself. The Standing Committee of the People's Representative Assembly would regularly send congratulatory messages abroad, yet never discussed any laws (Carney 1989). The tone of Democratic Kampuchea seemed to be that a 'good Khmer' would 'know' what was right and what was wrong. And that following orders would be enough – for although government was said to be in the hands of the people, real authority clearly resided in the central body of the Khmer Rouge, and particularly in its elite. Formal law thus played a peripheral role in the new Cambodian state.

According to David Chandler there is no evidence that any judges held office in Democratic Kampuchea or that a legal system existed in Cambodia between 1975 and 1979 (Chandler 1991). Rather, the evidence is that 'justice' was meted out on the spot for any infractions against the new regime and thereby against Democratic Kampuchea. Justice was harsh, violent, and usually meant death. Upon entering Phnom Penh in 1979, the Vietnamese forces were surprised to find no political or other prisoners. It appears that during the time of 1975–79 there was no jail system, no organized system of courts or hearings, and no penalties other than death. There were to be 'people's courts' which were not defined and the Constitution contained a blunt warning that anyone 'threatening the popular state' could look forward to the 'severest form of punishment'. In their plan to start anew, there could be no half measures – if you were not suitable for the new nation, then you had to be 'removed'.

The Khmer Rouge instituted a '12-point Moral Code', engaging in a process of moral inversion (ibid: 242–43). Violence and terror became virtues, pacifism became a vice. Family loyalty became state disloyalty. 'Old people' (peasants) were initially better off than 'new people' (those who fled or were forced out of the cities in April 1975 into the countryside, including both peasants who had been sheltering from the civil war, and urbanites who were permanent residents). 'New people' were only tolerated. But for both groups, the slightest infraction or aggravation meant death, and the differences in treatment steadily narrowed for the worse during the Khmer Rouge years. 'Guilt' extended to family members, perhaps encouraged, as Lek Hor Tan suggests, by a tragic aspect of the traditional Cambodian penal system that political criminals or 'traitors' and their whole families were executed together (Tan 1979: 9).

Anthony Barnett writes that the power of arbitrary life or death was placed in the hands of the cadre on the spot. Although the central and zonal security forces had sweeping powers of intervention, there existed no guidelines for such intervention or for the local cadres. Importantly, there existed no public law or Party regulation to safeguard, even by process let alone appeal, the lives of ordinary Cambodians from the authority of their local rulers (Barnett 1983: 216). With the traditional institutions destroyed – the monarchy, family ties, village and land organization, Buddhist and other religions – and their place taken by the Khmer Rouge, there no longer existed the traditional normative sources of ordering. Order (which in reality was raw power) was in the hands of individual cadres in the Khmer Rouge constructed districts. Yet in the Khmer Rouge world view, power and authority, that is, freedom, were in the hands of all peasantry, all 'true' Khmers, so this dispersal of power was in theory, 'natural'. The individual had no place in the 'old Cambodia', nor did he or she have a place in the 'new Kampuchea'.

Control of the population was termed 'management measures'. The Khmer Rouge pamphlet *Revolutionary Flags* published a piece titled 'Sharpen the Consciousness of the Proletarian Class to Be as Keen and Strong as Possible'. Under the heading 'How do we solve them' (the manifestations of the class struggle) it stated:

> At the same time [as an awareness of common contradictions which are common and continual and must be resolved through continuous education], we must have *careful management measures, all kinds of careful measures* [emphasis added]. Of all these measures, one is basic, implement the dictatorship of the proletarian class over these groups of people. We must make the proletarian class dictatorial meaning that regarding these groups of people, we are not confused. Give freedom to the worker-peasant people. As for the capitalists, feudalists, there must be a tight framework. Freedom must be given to some and withheld from some. We must be clear. Be careful so that the feudalists, landlords cannot wander about. Whether on the way to seek salt, to seek roots for medicine or going to tend cattle. If these people wander at will, they will get together. We must educate our cooperatives to be wary of these people.
>
> (*Revolutionary Flags* 1976, in Jackson 1989: 279)

Law in Democratic Kampuchea thus consisted of rules and directives. Party directives were the nation's laws, and party committees supervised their implementation (Carney 1989: 97). The rule of law did not exist. There was no separation between formal law and government.

The Constitution was the only law enacted by the Khmer Rouge – that is, the only law which took the form of formal law. Despite the provision in the Constitution (Article Seven) for the enactment of law by the People's Representative Assembly, law in the form of legislation could not be found in Democratic Kampuchea. It appears that rules, ordinances and proclamations substituted for legislation as such. One document titled 'Decisions of the Central Committee on a Variety of Questions' (30 March 1976) has as its first subtitle 'The Authority to Smash (People) Inside and Outside the Ranks' (Chandler et al. 1988: 1, 3).

By the time of the Vietnamese invasion in 1979, an estimated 1.8 million Khmer had been killed. This included Buddhist monks, ethnic groups such as the Vietnamese, Thai, Cham Muslim and Chinese, as well as persons defined only as 'dissidents', and 'non-Khmer' by the Khmer Rouge. After the initial killings of soldiers and officials of the former government, most of those killed were ordinary Cambodians, either forcibly resettled from the cities, or living on the land. They were killed through inhumane working conditions, or outright murdered. There was no protection from being targeted in the New Kampuchea. Dissidence and 'treachery' were determined by the Khmer Rouge cadre. There were no rules to be relied upon. The people were at the mercy of the Khmer Rouge, and ultimately, at the mercy of the inner elite, for their very lives. Formal law played little role in the perpetration of state crime. It provided, like the Armenian genocide, a framework of legitimacy for the new regime, yet all killings and repression occurred outside of law. What we can observe, however, is that informal legal orders played some role, both in the initial acceptance of the Khmer Rouge, as well as in the way the Khmer Rouge may have been perceived.

Ethiopia under Mengistu and the Dergue

There were a number of significant laws introduced by the regime of Lieutenant-Colonel Mengistu Haile-Mariam and the Dergue military council on their seizing power in 1974. Although the legal system was left largely as it was during the period of Emperor Haile Selassie, it was used instrumentally by Mengistu, and laws declared, and repealed, according to his policies. Paul Brietzke notes a similarity in legal style between the regime of Haile Selassie and the Dergue, characterizing it as the rough and ready formulation of perfunctory rules conferring a broad discretion, these rules adding up to a chaotic body of laws, formal legal authorization being subsumed by the political, embodying the demands of a small elite (Brietzke 1982: 179).

The main Ethiopian legal codes were maintained, with a few articles amended, including those relating to the protection of the rights of the Royal Family and the King (there being no more Royal Family) and land ownership (as the new Socialist doctrine was state land ownership). The courts too remained intact. Previously there had been four levels of courts. However, although courts had always constitutionally been independent, they had never been independent in practice, and this certainly did not change under Mengistu. A new level of court was added by Mengistu, the Special Courts-Martial.

The first key law introduced was *The Special Penal Code Proclamation* No. 8 of 1974. It was designed especially for the new court, the Special Courts-Martial, and in fact was not to be applied in other courts. It was meant both to herald and to frame the new order, to be a 'supplement' to the Penal Code of 1957. Yet it was also designed to demonstrate the appearance of continuity in the new laws. As the Special Penal Code stated:

> most of the offences provided for herein have previously been defined in the criminal laws and the rest have long been recognized by natural law, custom and the practice of the professions and as such have solid basis in the law.
>
> (*The Special Penal Code Proclamation* No. 8 of 1974: 19)

In its preamble, after first stating that the 'historic revolution now in progress in our country is being steered under the motto "Ethiopia Tikdem" (Ethiopia First)', *The Special Penal Code Proclamation* continued, 'one way of facilitating the implementation of the said motto is by adapting the criminal laws relating to grave offences to the changed situation which the new order demands', adding, 'as a result of the change new acts hitherto not dealt with by the criminal law have come to light'. The Special Penal Code dealt with 'offences' ranging from Offences against the Ethiopian Government and the Head of State to Offences against National Progress and Public Safety and Security. Significantly, Article 3 dealt with armed uprising and civil war, making punishable armed revolt, mutiny or rebellion against the Government, and civil war, with imprisonment or death. It was the Dergue's tool to deal with the EPLF (Ethiopian People's Liberation Front) and EPRDF (Ethiopian People's Revolutionary Democratic Front), and those 'suspected' of being members. However, as with all other regimes of state terror, the vast majority of deaths occurred far beyond the reach of the law, as extrajudicial killings, and severe torture. While the Penal Code was a signifier of the path of the state, it did not circumscribe all the state's actions.

Further Proclamations dealt with the composition and functions of the Provisional Military Administration Council. Another significant Proclamation provided for the Establishment of a National Revolutionary Operations Command. Imbued with socialist rhetoric of protection of the 'Revolutionary Motherland', this established a National Revolutionary Operations Command vested with the 'necessary powers and duties to coordinate the set-up and working procedures of government offices and mass organizations and the participation of the broad masses and patriots which is essential to achieve the[se] goals'. It established a strict, hierarchical, and controlled command structure, from the National Operations Council right down to sector commands in each of fifteen regions, with punishments of imprisonment and death for failing to comply with the Operations Command. Such a system was designed to encircle the population, and to strictly control them. It was a significant tool in the reign of terror.

Law was certainly a tool of the Mengistu regime. Law was used as a political tool, as further demonstrated by a clause in *The Special Penal Code Proclamation*: 'Whereas, the retroactive application of this Special Penal Code is not repugnant to natural law and basic legal philosophy'. Although the system of killings and torture happened outside of law, the structures in which they occurred (established by the National Revolutionary Operations Command Proclamation) and the crimes for which they were 'guilty' (established in the Special Penal Code) provided a framework for the crimes committed by Mengistu and the Dergue. Law thus provided a level of legitimacy. Yet it was not a deep framework. The crimes committed were perpetrated outside of law, yet legitimized by it. By 1991, with the overthrow of the regime by the Ethiopian People's Liberation Front and the Ethiopian People's Revolutionary Democratic Front, an estimated 200,000 civilians had been killed, their bodies often thrown out onto the streets of Addis Ababa and other smaller cities, relatives having to pay to take the body away to be buried, to 'pay for the bullet'.

Law is neither instrument nor obstacle to the state crime

Here we can place the genocide in Rwanda 1994, and the conflict in the former Yugoslavia.

The genocide in Rwanda in 1994

Rwanda 1994 is an example of the apparent absence of law. The killing of the Tutsi and moderate Hutu by the predominantly Hutu government was implemented quite separately to any legal means. In the hours after the shooting down of President Habyarimana's plane in the evening of 6 April 1994 (the cause of which is still not conclusively known), hardline members of the government wrangled for control, and soldiers and the Presidential Guard 'implemented a preestablished plan that was known to a hidden network' (des Forges 1999). Killings started immediately, and contrary to a press release issued by the hardline Colonel Bagosora in the name of the Rwandan army with regard to 'efforts … to stabilize the situation in the country rapidly …' and to 'restore order in the country', quite the opposite was deliberately carried out (ibid). In fact, Bagosora was reportedly overheard directing the commanders of the elite military units on the morning of 7 April, 'Begin on one side … ', ordering a systematic sweep of Tutsi and opponents of Hutu Power from one side of the city through to the other (Reyntjens, cited in ibid).

Already in these first hours people were killed according to prepared lists. Road blocks were set up, moderate Hutu politicians, including the Prime Minister Agathe Uwilingiyimana, and Tutsi civilians in the main city Kigali were all killed. A civilian government, claiming to be a legitimate continuation of the previous government, was formed on 8 April, chosen by Colonel Bagosora. The killing intensified, with radio broadcasts demonizing the Tutsi population, and demonstrating that the killing was aimed at them, that Hutus should not fear for their lives, but should rather help in the campaign. Radio RTLM (Radio Télévision Libre des Mille Collines), which was to be an accomplice in the genocide, gave out lists of names of 'traitors', inviting its listeners to 'rise up' against these 'spies'. One radio announcer invited listeners who would like to look for these persons to call her for more information.

There were initially attempts to stop the slaughter, by other politicians and military leaders, and later, by the *préfets* (regional governors) of Butare and Gitarama, and the *bourgmestres* (the local councillor or mayor) of Giti in Byumba, and of Musebeya in Gikongoro, among other local administrators. They were subsequently killed. Control was tightened by national leaders, who actively recruited civilians in the killings – 'civilian self-defense' – together with their armed youth wing, the *Interahamwe*. This 'civilian self-defense', as Michelle Wagner points out, was in fact developed prior to the genocide, in late 1990, and became a local ordering mechanism. As she notes, it 'developed the shared vocabulary, as well as the techniques, for identifying and seeking out "enemies of the people" and their "accomplices"' (Wagner 1998: 30). This form of local ordering was to become important in the genocide.

The worst massacres, in schools, in churches, mosques, and in communes, occurred between 12 April and 1 May. Tutsi were prevented from leaving the country: on 13 April, an officer of the army general staff telephoned the official in charge of immigration at the Butare prefecture and ordered him to grant no more authorizations for travel to adjacent countries. Tutsi attempting to cross the river to Burundi that night were slaughtered at Nyakizu (des Forges 1999). With the international community voicing disapproval, particularly after the killing of orphans in Butare, the government ordered 'pacification', interpreted to mean both more secret means of killings, and a stop to the overt killing. The main motivation, it appeared, was the threat by France that they would stop sending arms to fight the Tutsi exile army, the Rwandan Patriotic Front, as well as the recognition by some sections of the government of the importance of international aid and development money. Essentially, however, it was a deception. The killing continued until the Rwandan Patriotic Front took control, and the interim government and key leaders fled the country.

Law played no role during the genocide. There was no specific legislation introduced, nor even the declaration of a state of emergency. There was, however, an attempt at the beginning of the killing to use law as a means of protection. Human Rights Watch notes that in the first days of the genocide, officials in communes opposed to the slaughter had tried to use the judicial system to protect Tutsi. They arrested assailants and pillagers, and began preparing cases against them (des Forges 1999). However, the Report notes that as soon as the leaders at the national level exerted their influence in the communes, the *bourgmestres* released the detainees (ibid). They also note that interim Prime Minister Jean Kambanda's message of 27 April spoke of reopening courts and using the judicial system to punish killings and deter future violence (ibid). Yet the judicial work that was done during the genocide did not concern the killings of Tutsi, rather harm done to Hutus.

The rhetoric of justice was used as a shield and a tool for genocide. Law in Rwanda was a mix of the formal and informal. Although informal systems such as the 'agacaca' system had not been in popular use really since independence, the graduated system of Rwandan law in which most non-criminal disputes were mediated at the level of the commune (an estimated 143 courts existed) or through the services of the local councillors, meant that the system of law was fairly locally based for most people. There was a great deal of interaction between the population and the local authorities. The highly centralized system of control in Rwanda meant a tightly organized local system. Dispute handling mechanisms included the *bourgmestre*, the local judge of the lowest court (located in each commune), Party members, local notables and the 'agacaca' system. There were thus many dispute handling mechanisms: state courts were just one of these.

The translation of this local role for law was that during the genocide, as Human Rights Watch reported, Tutsi would be brought to the *bourgmestre* in a continuation of the earlier practice of handing over any suspected criminal to the local authorities (ibid). They would be 'tried' with being the 'enemy'. In a grotesque extension of this practice, assailants would announce that they were taking the Tutsi 'to the *bourgmestre*' when they led them into a banana grove or off into the bush to be killed (ibid).

By mid July 1994, an estimated 800,000 Tutsis had been killed in Rwanda. They had not been protected by law (international law had been spectacularly absent, as had local and national law), nor did law play a role in their destruction. Yet in the charging of Tutsis as 'enemy', and the role of the *bourgmestres* in the genocide, we see a nod to the forms of local law and local ordering.

The conflict in the former Yugoslavia

Law played an initial role in terms of setting the stage for what James Gow has termed the Yugoslav War of Dissolution (Gow 1997). Slobodan Milošević used the 1974 Yugoslav Constitution, which codified the system established by President Tito of limited decentralization, to rail against in his rise to power. As Gow notes, he came to power in 1987 promising to make Serbia 'whole' again by repairing the damage done by the 1974 Constitution and ending autonomy for the provinces (ibid: 17). William Maley writes that Milošević manipulated Serbian cultural symbols relentlessly in order to mobilize the Serbian masses in support of his policies (Maley 1997: 561). Milošević forced through a series of amendments to the Serbian and Kosovan constitutions between autumn 1988 and March 1990 (when Kosovo lost its autonomy completely), and curtailed Vojvodina's autonomy during 1989. Slovenia responded in kind. In September 1989, Slovenia adopted a series of controversial constitutional amendments, asserting republican sovereignty (Gow 1997: 17). The other republics also made constitutional amendments, and the republics became engaged in a deadlocked discussion of which route to take – a new federation was proposed by Serbia, while Slovenia and Croatia argued for a loose association of sovereign states, modelled on the European Union (ibid: 18). Montenegro supported the Serbian plan, while Bosnia and Macedonia favoured the confederal alternative proposed by Slovenia and Croatia, Bosnia favouring closer links and Macedonia weaker ones (ibid). Croatia declared its sovereignty in 1990, and talks continued until early 1991.

Eleven per cent of Croatia's population were Serbian. After Croatia's declaration of sovereignty, ethnic Serbs, backed by Belgrade, began to act, forming paramilitary units, and violence was orchestrated in Croatia. Gow argues that this was a tactic of intimidation by Belgrade, to coerce the other republics into staying in the federation (ibid: 19). The point at which the federation stopped functioning was on 15 May 1991, when Serbia and its satellites blocked what should have been the automatic rotation of the office of the Presidency of the SFRJ (The Socialist Federal Republic of Yugoslavia – Socijalistička Federativna Republika Jugoslavija) to the Croatian representative. Gow writes that this was done in order to create conditions for a 'state of emergency' in which the army would declare martial law. Yet, interestingly, army chief General Veljko Kadijević elected not to take this route, and, in his own terms, to act constitutionally (ibid: 20).

On 2 June 1991, Slovenia and Croatia declared their independence. The Yugoslav People's Army, the JNA, attacked Slovenia, yet withdrew after less than a month. At the same time, the conflict in Croatia between the government and rebel Serbs escalated into war, backed by the JNA. On 29 February 1992, Bosnia-Herzegovina declared its independence, and Bosnian Serbs declared a separate state (30 per cent of Bosnians were Serb). However, prior to Bosnia-Herzegovina declaring independence, the JNA had begun manoeuvres in Bosnia, in mid-August 1991. Gow writes that although there were many voices attributing the war in Bosnia to the decision by the European Community member states and the United States to grant recognition of full independent international personality to the republic on 7 April, the war seems to have been conceived, planned and prepared, and implementation begun, some months before by the JNA and the Serbian Security Service (ibid: 34). In the Serbian areas of Bosnia-Herzegovina, preparations were made for future administration and statehood probably from mid-August 1991 (ibid). There was close cooperation between the Bosnian Serb leader Radovan Karadžić and the local military commander at Banja Luka, General Nikola Uzelac, with the President of Serbia, Slobodan Milošević.

In April 1992 the Bosnian Serbs began their siege of Sarajevo, and in May the JNA relinquished command of an estimated 100,000 troops in Bosnia, effectively creating a Bosnian Serb army. Meanwhile, the arms embargo imposed on all of the former Yugoslavia by the United Nations on 25 September 1991 was not lifted, creating a great discrepancy of fighting power between the rebel Bosnian Serbs and the Bosnian government.

This was a systematic set of acts by the Serbian leadership in Belgrade. War was not a necessary nor inevitable outcome of the dissolution of the former Yugoslavia. Rather, the war that took place was a decision by Belgrade to draw new borders, and not to allow those they termed Serbs or who saw themselves as Serbs to be under non-Serb rule. The shape the war took was one of organized terror. The JNA and Serbian militias encouraged flight, and at the same time set up a system of concentration camps, mass killings and torture that sought to ensure the absolute removal of non-Serbs, mainly Bosnian Muslims, from Serb areas of control.

The attempted extermination of the Bosnian Muslims was carried out under cover of what was, at least initially to the outside word, a conventional territorial war. Importantly, for the purposes of this discussion, it meant that law played no part in the violations carried out against the Bosnian Muslims – these were carried out as, and under cover of, 'war'. The harm perpetrated was largely done in secret. These included rape camps, massacres, expulsions. The genocidal acts perpetrated were both in support of a greater goal – the attainment of a 'Greater Serbia' as well as for their own sake.

It could be argued that the use of the cover of war allowed the Geneva Conventions, that set out the laws of war, to became the relevant law, thus legitimizing the violence and masking the real goals of the war. As noted by Judge Gabrielle Kirk McDonald, former President of the International Criminal Tribunal for the former Yugoslavia, discussions of whether the war in Yugoslavia was conducted by 'international' or 'internal' forces, and thus whether the Geneva Conventions or the Additional Protocols apply, risked the danger of masking the true nature of this war (McDonald 1998: 34–35, 44–45). Law, in treating all sides equally as combatants in war, can become a shield for atrocities.

While the atrocities were being perpetrated, Bosnia and Herzegovina made an appeal to international law. An application was made to the International Court of Justice in March 1993, asking the Court to intervene in the killing of Bosnian Muslims. The Court in fact ordered that the Federal

Republic of Yugoslavia (Serbia and Montenegro) take measures to 'deter and stop acts of genocide', yet they continued.

The attempt by the United Nations to establish 'safe areas', notably in Srebrenica, where in July 1995 over 7,000 Bosnian Muslim men and boys were executed, despite being under the protection of the United Nations, was a horrific failure (the International Court of Justice was later to term this genocide). In addition, the cover of war meant that the international community could argue that all regulations (in particular the arms embargo) should be applied equally – thus directly contributing to the harm suffered by Bosnian Muslims. All that can be said in the end in terms of the role of law in the conflict in the former Yugoslavia is that it failed.

By the end of 1995, an estimated 300,000 civilians (mainly Bosnian Muslims) had been killed, and Yugoslavia as a federation had ceased to exist. Those who still called themselves Yugoslavs had no place to call home. While law played no direct role in the state crime perpetrated, it can be argued that the international community, by terming it war (and using applicable law), provided a shield for the atrocities, in particular genocide, to be perpetrated. International law proved to be no protection.

Law and the *allowability* of state criminality

Law is both strongly absent and strongly present in these situations of mass harm. Its presence as a framework of legitimacy provides a veneer of allowability. Its absence as protector means that it fails those seeking its protection.

In the state crimes discussed, law was never used in the actual implementation of the policy of murder. Law may facilitate such policy, it may pave a path, it may even offer a method of resistance (instances in Rwanda and South Africa) but it never authorized it. The murder of civilians always occurred outside law. Systematic harm and state crime can occur within law, as we saw in the case of apartheid South Africa. In systems of state oppression, of overt discrimination, law may fully frame and authorize such a system. This could have been the case with apartheid, had it stopped with the segregation and the discrimination, with what was valid and authorized in the statute book. But the reality of apartheid was something more than this; it was a brutal system that operated in its full power at the edge of the law. For the white minority this was at the edge of their lives, yet for many of the black majority it was at the centre of their lives.

Yet while state crime is committed outside formal law, it is arguably law that contributes to its perpetration. It is law that makes such crime allowable. The introduction of legislation which authorized the separation of Jews from the rest of the German population, and which created special rules for certain groups of German citizens, created an official and legitimate space for exclusion. It can be argued that it was this initial legal separateness, accompanied with some public terror in the early years, that made the later disappearance of these groups from the German public space acceptable, and less remarked upon.

Law, in this way, plays a role in creating a separateness between those to be killed or harmed, and those to be kept as citizens. In placing a people outside of the general citizenry and its rules, it both sets them up as 'less than' and allows for their harm. Violence is legitimated when a people is placed outside what Helen Fein has termed the 'sanctified universe of obligation' (Fein 1978: 272).

The Armenians in the Ottoman state already possessed a lesser legal status to their Turkish compatriots – which also contributed to the acceptance of their removal from Turkish society. The means used by the Ottoman state – deportation and accompaniment by released prisoners – was encoded legally, providing another plank of allowability. A similar point can be made with regard to the South African apartheid regime, in which laws of raw separateness already existed, which the apartheid state further enforced through brutal and illegal means, outside of law. The illegality could be ignored by many, as the legality provided a thorough frame. In the case of Cambodia, informal law was both suppressed (the killing of Buddhist monks) and replicated by the Khmer Rouge.

Once law differentiates in this negative way, a space of possibility is opened up. This makes further harm possible, but certainly not inevitable. It is more than the appearance of legitimacy through law (laws discriminating against a particular group, for example). It is the very structure of the legal system – the way in which spaces of difference are created, spaces in which such gross harm can be committed – that is a contributing factor of law to the harm perpetrated. If we view law and the legal system as delineating the boundaries, and the goals, of a particular state, then the use of law in this criminal manner is of importance in not only the acceptance of what is to come, but the structure of what is to come – the way in which laws of difference establish a separateness and hidden spaces for the crimes committed.

South Africa may be described as formally maintaining the rule of law, yet when legislation with criminal intent is introduced, it corrupts the entire system and its operation. These pockets of 'abnormality' transform a legal system. They can characterize an entire state. For what may be seen by external and some internal eyes as 'exceptions' to the law (legislation relating to outsiders in the society) can in effect be the main game for the state executive. This was the case in South Africa and in fact under the National Party leadership the law was increasingly corrupted and law according to many commentators became a tool rather than an arbitrator.

We can observe from the case studies that the use of law at such time is connected to the use and role of law prior to such crime. The position of law as a tool of normative ordering means that the level of law used during will continue to be similar to that used before. It also means that it will be a convenient tool for securing quiescence from the wider, non-targeted population (and the targeted population to some extent).

Law is partner in creating the nation. Yet law stops short of partnering extermination. The way in which Nazi Germany used law, and the way in which the Khmer Rouge used law, can on one level be seen as analogous. Both used law as a tool in laying the foundations of their new states. Law in both cases indicated the tenor of the new regime, the telos of the state. For example, the German Criminal Code (Paragraph 2) referred to 'healthy public sentiment', and the Constitution of Democratic Kampuchea (Article 9) to 'people's justice'.

As a commentator in Nazi Germany wrote at the time: 'We know that the essence and purpose of the criminal law cannot be recognized independently and in isolation. Rather, they have to be seen as emanating from the highest political principle forming the state in question' (Schaffstein, cited in Kirchheimer 1935: 145). Yet while the Nazi state continued with what can be characterized as a deep, though diminishing use of law, the Khmer Rouge used law only at the very beginning, and then no more. Although the Khmer use of law can be attributed to their socialist ideological foundations, this does not explain it all. In Ethiopia, for example, a state along similar ideological lines, there was, unlike Cambodia, a more extensive use of the law. This difference, it is suggested, can be attributed to the use of law prior to the state crime perpetrated. Both Ethiopia and Germany had a long and established formal legal tradition, whereas Cambodia did not.

The differences between Nazi Germany and Democratic Kampuchea can thus be attributed to the different place of law in these societies. Formal law in Germany was deeply embedded in the fabric of Germany society – whereas formal law in Cambodia was on the surface only. The way in which the Khmer Rouge reached the people was through a system of hierarchy and force, both overriding and encompassing informal legal orders, whereas in Germany communication of will was achieved, at least in the beginning, primarily through formal law, backed up by some terror. And whereas in Germany the entire legal system was changed to reflect the new order, in Cambodia the legal system, both formal and informal, was destroyed.

What this can mean is that the very normalcy of law can make the terror seem a necessary exception. Stolleis points this out in regard to the Nazi state:

> The regime's ability to function was based on the fact that the traditional elites in the civil service, the judiciary, the military, and the economy could reassure themselves by looking at the partial 'normality' and justify to themselves and others their involvement through daily collaboration. Terror could thus appear as a regrettable exception – and surely not approved of by the Führer! Thus law that is considered 'normal' and law that is considered terroristic propped each other up.
>
> (Stolleis 1998: 160)

Law can thus provide a connection between the 'ordinary' past and the 'terroristic' present. It can present a continuity that may not in fact exist, but which provides an appearance of normalcy. The very normalcy of law can make the terror seem a 'necessary exception'. It is an effective combination. When formal law may not have previously played a central role, then other factors – the continuation of a certain type of informal ordering, such as in the case of Rwanda and Cambodia – will provide this 'normalcy'.

What is interesting is that it appears that many of these regimes defined themselves peculiarly in *relation to* the law. The political elites maintained a dialogue with law and, to an extent, with the lawmakers. The overt use of law by the Nazi regime, Mengistu, and the Young Turks would appear to support this. Even the limited use of legal rhetoric by perpetrators in Rwanda supports such a hypothesis. Whatever the language of communication previously primarily used, this will be used by the perpetrators. Law as public language mostly continues during state crime. This indicates both the normative role of law and its power.

It appears important that such a dialogue be maintained. It could also be said that the use of law as a means of dialogue fulfils two purposes. The place of law means that it is both a dialogue with the population, an internal dialogue both with the victim group and the rest of the population, as well as a dialogue with the international community. This has important implications for any preventative or rescue measures taken by the international community. If a particular form is maintained, whether formal or informal ordering, this can, as suggested, provide an appearance of 'normalcy'. It could be argued that it even worked for the Khmer Rouge, that their limited use of law may have contributed to their maintaining acceptance from the international community for the duration of their regime (and beyond – the Khmer Rouge occupied the Cambodia seat at the UN General Assembly until 1991). Certainly many within the international community were unconvinced of the brutality of the regime until very late. It worked in Germany, certainly until the declaration of war. It is clear that the use of law can bestow a level of legitimacy on the actions of the perpetrator state. It is a language that is both locally and internationally understood.

Law thus can be an important tool in securing quiescence – from those looking in, for those surrounding, and even from the victims at first. This is the situation in countries in which there is a deeply embedded rule of law tradition, such as Germany. The Jews of Germany saw the Nuremberg Laws as a step towards stability. In countries where formal law has not played such a central role it is less relevant, yet can still play some role. In Rwanda and Cambodia, what became more relevant were other normative orders. In the genocide in Rwanda, the perpetration of genocide was seen as part of the 'communal' work, and in the Khmer Rouge killing fields the Khmer Rouge played the role, at least at first, of the powerful men of Khmer lore.

LIVERPOOL JOHN MOORES UNIVERSITY
LEARNING SERVICES

These observations have implications for the later legitimacy of law as a tool of redress. Any role which law assumes after the perpetration of state crime is intimately connected to the role law may have played during the time of the perpetration of such crime. The state of the legal system post-conflict, its level of legitimacy, the role which may be played for example by international and non-governmental organizations after a legal system has been destroyed, the level of continuity which can be established with the legal system pre, during and post – these are all issues for law post-conflict and entail understanding and knowledge of the role of law during perpetration. That judges could decide differently, for example, as Corder has shown, gives hope to the use of law in post-apartheid South Africa.

The finding that law was not used as a central tool in state murder is an important one for the later legitimacy of law. It gives some hope for the use of law in redress as a tool able to arbitrate fairly and be seen as legitimate in the eyes of both victim and perpetrator groups. However, it still leaves questions as to what this role may be and how in fact law is used in the wake of state crime.

Chapter 3 will focus on the particular forms of law employed in redress in the case studies and how, in the wake of state crime, law continues to partner the state in its nation-building.

Notes

1 The documentary sources for Nazi Germany in this chapter, unless otherwise indicated, are from Arad et al. 1981.
2 In this vein, a document dated 21 September 1939 from Chief of Security Police Reinhard Heydrich to the Chiefs of all Einsatzgruppen (the mobile killing units) of the Security Police reads in its headline 'Subject: Jewish Question in Occupied Territory'. The document begins as follows: 'I refer to the conference held in Berlin today, and again point out that the *planned total measures* (i.e., the final aim – *Endziel*) are to be kept strictly secret' (Arad et al. 1981: 173). SS men involved in the extermination of Jews under Operation Reinhard, that is, the murder of approximately two million Polish Jews in the German-occupied 'Government General', were obliged to sign a statement that they would maintain strict secrecy on the 'evacuation' (extermination) of Jews (ibid: 274). Documented as well is a speech by Heinrich Himmler before senior SS officers in Poznan on 4 October 1943 in which he states:

> I also want to speak to you here, in complete frankness, of a really grave chapter. Amongst ourselves, for once, it shall be said quite openly, but all the same we shall never speak about it in public ... I am referring here to the evacuation of the Jews, the extermination of the Jewish people ... This is an unwritten and never-to-be-written page of glory in our history ...
>
> (Arad et al. 1981: 344)

3 For example, shortly after the introduction of a 'special law' to suppress any political opposition in the occupied Eastern countries, *Verordnung über die Strafrechtspflege gegen Polen und Juden vom 4.12.1941*, Jews were excluded from the application of this law (see Stolleis 1998: 19, fn. 88).

4 I am grateful to Klaus Neumann for his translation of this.
5 Prompted by earlier massacres against the Armenian population in the late nine-
  teenth century and their clearly fragile position, the Armenian Reforms had been
  initiated externally and sought to provide a level of protection to the Armenian
  minority. In the wake of the August–September 1894 Sassoun massacre, the six
  Powers had drawn up the 11 May 1885 Armenian Reform scheme which the
  Sultan finally accepted and signed on 17 October 1895. This did not deter a further series of massacres, with the support of the Sultan, in October 1895, lasting
  through 1896 (Dadrian 1997b: 152–53). At the end of this series of massacres, the
  Sultan declared that 'the Armenian question was closed' (ibid: 163). The Armenian Reforms were resurrected in 1912, with Turkey in a weak position, and
  spearheaded by Russia (contrary to its earlier position of tacit support for the
  Sultan's anti-Armenian policy). On 8 February 1914, the Armenian Reform
  Agreement was signed in Istanbul as a document of international law. It provided
  for foreign Inspectors-General to administer and superintend the reforms. It drew
  a great deal of resentment from many Ittihadist leaders, who felt humiliated by
  such pressure, and at such a weak moment in Turkey's history (in the wake of the
  1912 Balkan war and at a time of internal change – Ittihad was temporarily out of
  power), a feeling which was not to help the Armenians (ibid: 194).

Chapter 3

Cutting off the old, envisaging the new
Law and redress

The political philosopher Otto Kirchheimer in his seminal work, *Political Justice*, asked what the function of courts in political strife is. He answered as follows:

> In the simplest and crudest terms, disregarding for a moment the embellishments, enlargements of function, and safeguards of the age of constitutionalism: the courts eliminate a political foe of the regime according to some prearranged rules.
>
> (Kirchheimer 1961: 6)

The foe these days may well be the past. In legal processes and legal institutions designed to address state crime, we see the attempt to clearly delineate between the previous regime and the new present. Legal processes are designed to create new realities. In the use of law in the wake of state crime we can identify a clear attempt to mark a point between the crimes committed and the present. We cannot say always that a future is imagined, but that the past is separated from.

In this way, law becomes a tool of nation-building in the wake of state crime. What we see in the utilization of law, and the control of law by governments in the wake of mass harm is an instrument designed to separate the old from the new and to define the new polity. Law is called upon to create legacies. In this, it is also called upon to govern. The extent to which it is able to do this, however, is dependent on political and social realities, the place of law and the design of these new legal processes.

In the use, and control, of legal process by governments in the wake of genocide and state crime, we can observe the use of law as a tool in governance and nation-building. Law both signals the direction of the new regime, as well as providing a means of 'moving on'. Law can be critical in establishing new reference points for a society. Law delineates the new borders, what is accepted and what is not. Elimination of the past becomes a core concern of legal and political-legal processes designed to address state crime. This is core to the nation-building function of law, in constituting the new state.

This chapter considers the function and meaning of the varied political-legal responses to state crime, initiated by the state. In so doing it considers the ways in which new realities are established through law and the political-legal processes established in the wake of state crime. We see how the use of law in the wake of state crime is similar to its use during, as a tool in nation-building and in separating out from the 'old', yet still maintaining some continuity. The chapter considers what tools are used in establishing the new polity, the extent to which these are aimed at direct redress of the crime, and the extent to which these may be aimed at a broader societal redress. It begins by outlining what we may see as the uneven 'legal mosaic', the different legal processes for state crime. It then considers the role of law in establishing new reference points and law as a tool of nation-building. It follows with a discussion of the different approaches to state crime – law as focused on direct victim or perpetrator redress, or law directed at a broader more societal redress. The chapter then provides an outline of the main legal redress used for each of the case studies. It concludes with a discussion of a typology of law in the wake of state crime, from its marginalization to its presence.

The legal mosaic

Legal redress takes a variety of forms in the wake of state crime. These include the establishment of government commissions of inquiry and truth commissions, domestic and international prosecutions, domestic and regional or international civil claims, hearings and prosecutions, the enactment of legislation specific to the resolution of the conflict such as lustration and compensation legislation, legislation aimed to remedy at a more institutional level, that addresses causes or consequences of the harm, the passing or amendment of constitutions, and the passing of specific amnesty legislation.

There have been clear absences. State law is rarely used to address state crime against indigenous peoples. While the Canadian Truth Commission process into the Indian Residential School system is an exception, in Australia we see no state legal processes to address state crime against indigenous people, apart from some restitution for stolen wages and isolated reparations processes, and cases brought by victims themselves. Another absence is the crimes committed against the Romani (Gypsies) in Nazi Germany. Subject to the racial laws of Nazi Germany, and targeted for destruction, an estimated seventy to eighty per cent of Romani were killed, yet there has been no reparations and no mention of their fate in legal redress for the crimes of the Second World War.

Responses to genocide and state crime can occur in more than one legal arena, are not necessarily orchestrated and can conflict in their approach. They can be international, national, regional, 'other-state' and purely local. They have occurred directly after the event, or years later (for example, the Extraordinary Chambers in the Courts of Cambodia, established almost three decades after the end of the Khmer Rouge reign). They can take the form of prosecution and the introduction of new legislation, for example, or public inquiry or truth commission. This is rarely an orchestrated legal mosaic.

For example, in Rwanda after the genocide against the Tutsis in 1994, we can identify a wide and conflicting range of official legal and legal-political proceedings. At the same time that the International Criminal Tribunal for Rwanda was held by the United Nations in the African safari town of Arusha in Tanzania, in Rwanda itself there were the criminal trials held by the Rwandan government, the 'gacaca' proceedings held in communities, and new legislation including that which barred marking identity cards with Hutu or Tutsi. In the United States there were cases brought under legislation allowing non-United States citizens to bring civil action for acts committed in violation of international law. In countries such as Belgium, Brussels, Switzerland and France where Rwandans had sought refuge, prosecutions were brought. In Belgium, the families of the ten Belgian soldiers, part of the United Nations mission, who were killed at the start of the genocide, initiated legal proceedings in Belgium against the Rwandans responsible for their deaths. Further, a number of Parliaments outside Rwanda conducted inquiries as to their own roles. Former neo-colonial power France examined its own conduct prior to and during the genocide (the paucity of which prompted a non-governmental organization to launch a French citizen's inquiry), and former colonial power Belgium examined its conduct during the genocide, focused mostly on the killing of the ten Belgian soldiers. The Organization of African Unity (now the African Union) examined the broader international failure to prevent and stop the genocide, and the United Nations looked into its own conduct and response to the genocide. Finally, Rwanda itself conducted its own inquiry into the role of France in the genocide.

Box 3.1 outlines the different types of legal and political-legal proceedings and institutions used to address genocide and state crime.

Box 3.1 The legal mosaic

International level

Legal proceedings held in the international arena are those both convened under the auspices of the United Nations and those initiated by an international body.

Official

United Nations *ad hoc* criminal tribunals
   Permanent International Criminal Court
   International Court of Justice

Non-official or quasi-legal

Non-governmental organization investigatory commissions and inquiries
  International Commission of Jurists reports/rulings
  United Nations Human Rights Commission reports

National

Legal proceedings held in the same nation-state or 'site' in which the crimes were committed.

Official

National criminal prosecutions by the civil legal administration
  National criminal prosecutions by the military legal administration
  Criminal prosecutions sponsored by the United Nations
  Joint United Nations–national criminal tribunal
  Government-sponsored community proceedings (e.g. 'gacaca' in Rwanda)
  Change or amendment of national constitution
  Specific legislation such as lustration or compensation legislation
  Amnesty legislation
  Government truth commission

Unofficial or quasi-legal

Government inquiry
  Non-governmental inquiry
  Non-governmental public (mock) trial

Local (non-official or quasi-legal)

Non-official legal proceedings held within the country in which the crimes have occurred, but not at the state level.

Regional

The regional refers to the region of the country or countries in which the crimes occur. It can also refer to proceedings convened by the European Court of Justice, for example.
  Inter-American Commission on Human Rights/Inter-American Court of Human Rights
  African Commission on Human and People's Rights (African Charter on Human and People's Rights)
  European Court (European Convention on Human Rights)

Other-state

Other-state refers to situations when states other than those within which the crimes were committed hold legal proceedings. This distinguishes between a national arena in which the crimes were actually committed, and a national arena that had little or no connection to the crimes. A trial concerning crimes committed in Rwanda in April–July 1994 which is conducted in a French court is an example of an 'other-state' arena, as is a United States Alien Tort Claims suit conducted in a United States court.

Official

Compensation claims (e.g. Alien Tort Claims in the United States)
　National criminal trials (e.g. war crimes trials in Canada, the United Kingdom, Australia, Italy, France)
　Parliamentary inquiries

Non-official or quasi-legal

Public 'civil society' proceedings (e.g. the Women's International War Crimes Tribunal on Japan's Military Sexual Slavery; the Permanent People's Tribunal)

The new institutions of law

Law 'strains' to cope with the redress for state crime. Mass harm falls outside the scope of 'ordinary' law of the nation-state. Different forms of law may be employed, a combination of the national and the international, or various national remedies, all attempting to address a part of this crime.

Post-conflict legal proceedings can be a mix between the old and the new. They are either new bodies, such as the Truth and Reconciliation Commission of South Africa, a mixture of the legal and the political (not the straight criminal model that had been a companion and collaborator to the apartheid regime), or they include new crimes, such as the charge of 'Crimes against Humanity' at the International Military Tribunal at Nuremberg. They are an attempt to span the dimensions of state crime, yet to maintain a connection to the institution of law.

A key innovation at the International Military Tribunal was that of 'group criminality'. As the Tribunal stated,

> If satisfied of the criminal guilt of any organization or group, this Tribunal should not hesitate to declare it criminal because the theory of 'group criminality' is new, or because it might be unjustly applied by some subsequent tribunals. On the other hand, the Tribunal should make such

declaration of criminality so far as possible in a manner to insure that innocent persons will not be punished.

(International Military Tribunal 1947–49)

These bodies can also provide a firm grounding for other 'spin off' legal procedures, in that they *locate* subsequent trials and proceedings – the International Military Tribunal did this both for the subsequent United States trials as well as local German and other-state trials. Czarnota has observed the development of quasi-judicial bodies, institutions part political and part legal that address this need for new institutions yet that maintain the continuity of law. These bodies, he suggests, ' ... possess institutional structures and characteristics which are able to respond at the same time both to the need for radical change and the need for substantial continuity in dealing with the complicated nature of collective memories' (Czarnota 2001: 127).

In this way, the issue of legitimacy and continuity is resolved in part. Such legal bodies are able to provide a link, and a legitimate role for law, between the past regime and its atrocities and any future affirming role of law and legal process. It is in creating such 'quasi-judicial' institutions that law is able to legitimately address such crimes.

These bodies, however, do not jump too far from established norms. While the International Military Tribunal at Nuremberg did create the new charge of Crimes Against Humanity, it was careful to use this sparingly, preferring to stay with the more established charge of War Crime. And while the Truth and Reconciliation Commission in South Africa did not follow previous legal form in South Africa, it did concur with deep norms of Christianity and African *ubuntu* (a sense of a common humanity), resulting in the path taken by the Commission being thus not totally unfamiliar to most South Africans and consistent normatively, drawing on and appealing to a kind of 'living law'. The Commission also stayed close to the established international law definitions of 'gross violations of human rights' in terms of its mandate, excluding as Mamdani (2000) has noted, the many 'ordinary' violations that took place under apartheid law, that in fact formed the basis of most black South Africans' experiences under apartheid.

In the case of the central legal proceedings after the Armenian genocide and the Holocaust, although the focus was the civilian killings, other acts were also among the charges. The Ottoman State Special Military Tribunal focused on the massacres of the Armenians as well as on 'illegal, personal profiteering' and Turkey's entry into the war. The original motion by the Deputy of the Ottoman Parliament included ten charges, of which only two related to the killing of the Armenians. The Nuremberg Tribunal focused both on the killings of civilians (included in War Crimes and Crimes against Humanity) and on the more general charge of the waging of a war of aggression (Crimes against Peace). In both cases, the legal proceedings included the killings;

however, these were not the sole purpose of the establishment of these legal proceedings.

Law as foundational moment

Law can be core in envisaging a future. The power of law at this time is both in creating a new historical record, and in providing critical Acknowledgment of the harm perpetrated. In this way, in marking out a new normative framework, law creates a 'foundational moment'.

In the use of law during genocide and state crime, law demarcates who belongs. In the use of law after, both in its exclusions and its redress, law does the same thing. The decision not to prosecute or hold inquiries is a statement that the harm is not recognized, and the victims are not full citizens. In the decision to use the law in redress, a statement is made that there is recognition of the harm, and thus that the victims themselves are recognized as having been harmed. In bringing this into the fabric of the state, through the institution of law, the state is clear on who belongs and thus who will be protected. A new constitution can be the clearest statement on this, in its literal constituting of the new state. The 1993 Interim Constitution of South Africa stated:

> This Constitution provides a historic bridge between the past of a deeply divided society characterised by strife, conflict, untold suffering and injustice, and a future founded on the recognition of human rights, democracy and peaceful co-existence and development opportunities for all South Africans, irrespective of colour, race, class, belief or sex.
>
> (*Constitution of the Republic of South Africa* 1993)

Justice Mahomed of the South African Constitutional Court, in the first case heard by the new Constitutional Court, stated that this Constitution,

> retains from the past only what is defensible and represents a decisive break from, and a ringing rejection of, that part of the past which is disgracefully racist, authoritarian, insular, and repressive, and a vigorous identification of and commitment to a democratic, universalistic, caring and aspirationally egalitarian ethos expressly articulated in the Constitution.
>
> (*S v. Makwanyane* 1995, cited in Corder 2004: 253)

Here, law has been key in envisaging a new future, not just a separation from the past but projecting what this future could look like. The Constitution of the new South Africa was designed to be the institution that, as Justice Mahomed noted, 'represents a decisive break from, and a ringing rejection of' the past in its oppressive form.

The approach taken in the wake of the compromise made by the incumbent African National Congress to not prosecute the National Party government and security forces paved the way for the formation of a new South African public normative framework. The establishment of the Truth and Reconciliation Commission and its public exposure of the crimes of the apartheid regime was a clear statement of separation from the past, but one that was also intended, both of necessity and design, to be inclusive.

Another example of envisaging a future was the 'people's tribunals' (*Népbíróság*) established by the new Hungarian government in the wake of the Second World War. Dr István Ries, the first Minister of Justice of post-war Hungary, stated,

> The adjudication of these cases ... is not so much a legal as in the first place a political question. This means that the regular courts are not suitable for these trials and that the current laws are not appropriate. These criminal cases must be tried before courts that represent the conceptions of a democratic Hungary ... and there is a need for corresponding legal rules and regulations to cover all the acts that directly or indirectly brought Hungary to this terrible catastrophe.
>
> (Lévai 1969: 256)

Law is used as the mouthpiece for a new government, articulating its vision and its separation from what has been before. The establishment of these tribunals was one of the Hungarian Provisional National Government's first directives, before the war was even over. That this was a political as well as a legal necessity was clearly stated. These new courts, as publicly pronounced, were to 'represent the conceptions of a democratic Hungary'. Public trials were held where Jewish victims had a chance to provide witness testimony. There was a sense then, that continues today, that the ordinary law cannot deal with this extraordinary crime. That is, that new legal bodies must be developed to address the horrors of the past.

The trial of Adolf Eichmann in 1961 in Jerusalem was a further foundational moment. Hearing the stories of the Holocaust, stories that had not been included in the self-image of the Jewish state, was critical in bringing survivors living in Israel into the national story. Holding one of the key perpetrators on trial, on charges of 'crimes against the Jewish people', was an important statement too in separating out between the old of Nazi Europe and the new of the Jewish state. Elsewhere, post-war denazification processes in Germany were another means of separating out, between the 'new' and the 'old'.

The Ottoman State Special Military Tribunal held at the end of the First World War was also an attempt at a clear break from the previous regime. One of its chief aims was to establish the systematic manner in which the massacres of the Armenians took place, and to allocate institutional as well as individual responsibility. In the Key Verdict on 5 July 1919, the Court found the Cabinet Ministers guilty both of orchestrating the entry of Turkey into the First World War, and of committing the genocide of the Armenians. In establishing the Courts-Martial, as Dadrian has noted, the Sultan's government hoped that this would demonstrate that it was the Ittihadist Party, not the Turkish nation, that was responsible for the Armenian massacres, and that the Allies would be lenient at the Peace Conference (Dadrian 1997a: 31). The Courts-Martial also operated as an attempt at consolidation of power for the Sultan and of marginalization of the Ittihadist party.

As a tool of governance and nation-building, the chosen legal process marks the new regime and its approach. In focusing on a clear break between the old and the new, states can be heavy handed in their means of addressing the crimes of the former state.

The Rwandan government, despite leaning towards a more political settlement early on, decided on a more retributive policy, ending up with over 100,000 persons in jail. The approach taken has meant that rather than the trials being solely a process of accountability for abuses committed during the killings in 1994, they have also become a vehicle of government power and the further exclusion of Rwandan Hutus. Many Hutus have been afraid to return as refugees, and be implicated as *genocidaires*.[1] While the gacaca meetings, designed to hear testimonies and reintegrate offenders back into their communities, have in some cases been an inclusive reconciliatory measure, in others they have been a tool of further division, with, as Human Rights Watch noted in its 2008 report, reports of Tutsi survivors killed (Human Rights Watch 2008).

The consolidation of Tutsi power has been an intended outcome of the legal process, a necessary process initiated for a genocide that claimed over 800,000 lives. As Human Rights Watch has further noted, this has been seen more recently with the use of the genocide denial legislation, with the crime of 'genocide ideology' introduced as a means of silencing opposition: 'Authorities use prosecution, or the threat of prosecution, for "genocide ideology" to silence dissent of many kinds, including calls for justice for RPF war crimes' (ibid). Law here is used as a further tool of governance and nation-building.

The trial of the former members of the ruling Ethiopian military Congress, the 'Dergue', operating through the terror regime of Lieutenant-Colonel Mengistu Haile-Mariam, provides us with another complicated scenario. Article 281 of the *Penal Code of the Empire of Ethiopia*, which defines genocide as a crime against humanity, was viewed as immensely progressive at the time it was drafted. One of the long-held criticisms of the United Nations Genocide Convention has been its failure to include political groups in its scope of protection. This is bearing in mind, as pointed out by Helen Fein, that political groups (together with sexual and class-denominated groups) can have the same kind of enduring characteristics as the groups that are covered in the Convention (Fein 1990: 23). Drafted by Ethiopian and international legal experts in 1957, Article 281 includes political groups, thus making it possible to try the Dergue for the serious crimes committed by the Mengistu regime, and hence expanding the scope of protection beyond national, ethnical, racial and religious groups. Its application in these trials has, however, drawn criticism.

The Ethiopian trials in practice were tainted by their overtly political nature and failure to follow rule of law procedure. Human Rights Watch reported that 'trial lawyers repeatedly complained about due process flaws in that their access to their detained clients was rendered difficult because of restrictions imposed by the government' (Human Rights Watch 1999). Independent reporting on the trials was forbidden, the only allowable reports were by the official government television and newspapers. In the provinces where most of the 'Red Terror Trials' were conducted, the accused had little access to defence lawyers (the defence too was limited at the main Dergue trial) and were subject to lengthy delays, due to the lack of judges available. In a clear separation between the old and the new, the incumbent Ethiopian national government dismissed almost all judges who were a part of the legal system under Mengistu. They later vetted all judges, at all levels of the judiciary, from the Supreme Court down to the local 'woreda' courts, describing this as a necessary 'clearing of the deck' (Elgesem & Girmachew 2009: 45). During the Dergue trial itself the government dismissed a further forty judges due to their perceived independence. It presented difficult problems for the prosecution of the case, with a lack of experienced judges to try the serious crimes that Mengistu and the Dergue stood accused of.

The main Dergue trial ran for twelve years from 1994. Of the seventy-two people originally charged, thirty-three had been in custody since 1991, fourteen others had died in custody and twenty-five were tried in their absence, including the former President who had asylum in Zimbabwe (Amnesty International 2007). The lack of due process followed in these trials and the limitation on public participation, has meant a process focused more on elimination of a foe than any future transformation of the state.

'Show trials' as foundational moments

Law can operate in both crude and sophisticated ways. The first decree passed by the new People's Revolutionary Council of Kampuchea after the overthrow of the Khmer Rouge by Vietnam was Decree-Law No 1, 'providing for the setting up in Phnom Penh of a People's Revolutionary Tribunal to judge the genocide crimes committed by the Pol Pot-Ieng Sary clique' (International Covenants on Human Rights 1979b). The former Prime Minister Pol Pot and his deputy Ieng Sary were tried *in absentia* and found guilty of genocide by the Revolutionary People's Tribunal of the People's Republic of Kampuchea. Genocide was defined in Article 1 of the Decree-law No. 1 of 5 July 1979 as:

> Planned mass killing of innocent people, forced evacuation of the population from cities and villages, concentration of the population and forcing them to work in physically and morally exhausting conditions, abolition of religion, destruction of economic and cultural structures and of family and social relations.
>
> (International Covenants on Human Rights 1979a)

Close to 100 witnesses testified at the Tribunal, and films of mass graves and other atrocities were shown. According to the government, 'Over five hundred delegates from all parts of the country and foreign representatives ... attended the court sittings' (Shawcross 1984: 120). Run as a show trial, its tone can be gleaned from the declaration of the defense counsel for Pol Pot and Ieng Sary:

> I have not come from halfway around the world to give approval to monstrous crime nor to ask for mercy for the criminals. No! A thousand times No!. ... It is now clear to all that Pol Pot and Ieng Sary were criminally insane monsters carrying out a program the script of which was written elsewhere for them.
>
> (People's Revolutionary Tribunal 1979)

The appearance of normalcy in a devastated country was manufactured for the foreigners for the duration of the trial. As the two delegates from the International Red Cross there at the time to coordinate a relief strategy were to note, a fleet of empty cars was driven from Ho Chi Minh City to Phnom Penh, the Vietnamese plates exchanged for Cambodian plates, and Vietnamese girls, dressed in Cambodian sarongs and hair styled according to Cambodian fashion were brought in to be the 'Cambodian' staff of the Hotel Samaki where the foreigners stayed (Shawcross 1984: 120). Twenty-two victim statements were presented, and five witnesses interviewed (People's Revolutionary Tribunal 1979). In addition, reports were presented detailing the harm perpetrated by the Khmer Rouge as well as initiatives established to deal with the victims, for example, the establishment of an orphanage (Witness Statement, ibid). The Tribunal, as its records show, was composed of a President and deputy, and a 'People's Jury' comprising a former judge, a dance teacher, a pediatric doctor, the Minister of Education and Training, the Vice President of the Association of Kampuchean Ladies, and the General Secretary of the Central Committee of Kampuchean Youth (People's Revolutionary Tribunal 1979).

The People's Tribunal was designed to raise the legitimacy of the new regime to the outside world. In this way, the Tribunal can be seen as a key initial part of the new state, designed to signal the end of the Khmer Rouge both to the international community and the local populace. Like the Khmer Rouge before them, who initiated one key piece of legislation, the *Constitution of Democratic Kampuchea*, the incoming Vietnamese government did the same, signalling the telos of the new regime through this one trial, a show trial in the sense of embodying all that was evil about the Khmer Rouge in one sitting, yet of which the crimes were very real.

The trial *in absentia* of Pol Pot and Ieng Sary held in 1979 by the Vietnamese in a newly liberated Cambodia was crudely designed to isolate the new from the old. It was designed to eliminate the Khmer Rouge as a political foe in a situation of continuing civil war and signal the new regime. However, this did not mean that the mass harm perpetrated by the Khmer Rouge was addressed in any sustained manner. While Pol Pot and Ieng Sary were sentenced to death by the Tribunal (although they were not actually held in custody), the Vietnamese spent little time prosecuting other Khmer Rouge leaders, who were still in Cambodia. Rather, many Khmer Rouge cadre were promoted and included within the new regime. The horrors of the past were used as propaganda to endorse the new regime – yet no real measures were taken to bring the perpetrators to account. Elizabeth Becker noted in an article in the *Washington Post* at the time, the discrepancy between the legacy of the Khmer Rouge and the propaganda purposes to which it was put:

> Few official gatherings are complete without a speaker who details how he or she saw children, parents and friends murdered by Pol Pot's henchmen, and other atrocities. It is not unusual for some of the people who carried out such orders to be seated in the audience or even on the podium with the victim recounting the story.
>
> (Shawcross 1984: 359)

Meanwhile, the Khmer Rouge occupied the Cambodia seat at the United Nations long after their overthrow by Vietnam. In fact, the General Assembly voted to keep the Cambodia seat aligned to the defeated government. As Leo Kuper notes, in September 1979, eight months after the ousting of the Pol Pot regime by the Vietnamese, and one month after the trial of Pol Pot and Ieng Sary, in which graphic evidence of atrocities committed by the Khmer Rouge was presented, a majority of seventy-one (thirty-five against, with thirty-four abstentions) in the United Nations General Assembly voted to continue the assignment of the Cambodian seat to the ousted government (Kuper 1981: 173). The People's Tribunal was almost universally condemned, not so much for the fact for its being *in absentia* and thus in violation of international principles of due process, but due to the Cold War context of Vietnam's invasion and subsequent occupation of Cambodia and their place in the geo-political spectrum. Yet, importantly, it was also a forum in which the harm perpetrated was recognized. As John Quigley, one of the Western lawyers invited to attend was to write later, 'Around the auditorium where the trial was held, an overflow audience milled, anxious to talk with anyone who would listen about what they and their families had suffered under the Khmer Rouge' (De Nike et al. 2000: 1).

The complication of what are termed show, or political, trials is that in many cases they are the only attempts at redress. And while they may be conducted as exercises in elimination and containment, for victims they can be important statements, and in fact can turn out to be important official records, sometimes the only one. I observed the importance of this at the Ethiopian trials, with victim after victim recounting their stories. Further, the records of the Rwandan gacaca will, if properly maintained, provide possibly a more comprehensive history of the genocide than the due process run International Criminal Tribunal.

The second action against Pol Pot was the orchestrated local trial of Pol Pot at Anlong Veng, nineteen years later (although it was for turning on his own comrades in an attempted purge in June 1997, not for the atrocities of 1975–79, that he was denounced and imprisoned, according to Nate Thayer's observations of the speakers at his trial) (Thayer 1997a: 15). The 'People's Tribunal of Anlong Veng', held on 25 July 1997, was, it seems, designed to raise the legitimacy of the Khmer Rouge to the outside world, and to increase the chances of their being a partner in Cambodian power-sharing. Observed by one Western journalist, Nate Thayer, it ended speculation of whether or not Pol Pot was dead (Thayer 1997b: 20).[2] Pol Pot was charged with the murder of Son Sen, the detention and attempted murder of Ta Mok and others, and the blocking of negotiations with the Funcinpec party (Marks 1999: 702).

Conducted by the Khmer Rouge against their former leader Pol Pot, whom they sentenced to 'life imprisonment' (translated into house arrest until his death the following year), it was a public act in attempting to create a new reality. Ta Neou, the governor of the area in which the trial was held, declared, 'Our ultimate goal today is that the international community should understand that we are no longer Khmer Rouge and not Pol Potists!' Thayer, the Western journalist who witnessed the trial, writes that individuals in the crowd periodically interrupted leaders offering carefully crafted lectures at the microphone with shouts of 'Long live the emergence of the democracy movement!' (Thayer 1997a: 15).

The 'People's Tribunal of Anlong Veng' had all the trappings of a show trial. Pol Pot was on trial before his cadre, without a defense, on charges that were barely enunciated and without any clear right of appeal. On cue a crowd shouted 'Crush! Crush! Crush! Pol Pot and his clique!' and 'Long live! Long live! Long live! the new strategy!' (ibid: 14–15). It is not known whether this took the 'form' of a Khmer Rouge trial, or whether it was convened in this fashion purely in this instance. It clearly did not follow rule of law norms. Yet should this trial of Pol Pot be dismissed?

A show trial does not necessarily lack legitimacy or meaning. It could be argued that for the Khmer Rouge cadre, the trial of Pol Pot possessed great meaning and legitimacy. It seems that it had great impact, both in helping the Cambodian government to more easily bring certain Khmer Rouge leaders into the political fold, as well as in diffusing the power of the Khmer Rouge. It also could be seen as a way for the Khmer Rouge to purge themselves, in that the Khmer Rouge leadership, also clearly implicated in the 'killing fields', was attempting to lay all blame on Pol Pot and thus to exonerate themselves from criminal liability.

What are perceived to be purely political processes can sometimes have surprising results. The 'people's tribunals' of post-war Hungary have been dismissed as political trials, show trials without legitimacy. Yet Ruth Balint suggests that these trials held in Hungary immediately in the wake of the Holocaust have been too readily dismissed: despite their 'show trial' nature, they were in fact the only forum in which Jewish victims could speak and give their testimony, 'in which survivors could bear witness' (Balint 2010: 291). Under the Communist regime, Jewish victims could no longer be heard. Further, that they played an important role in creating a historical record, which while short-lived, is being unearthed again now.[3] While the people's tribunals clearly fulfilled an ideological function post-war, in implementing a 'people's justice' for the new 'people's state', they created an important record of the Hungarian Holocaust and a space for victims to be heard.

The Indonesia-East Timor 'Commission of Truth and Friendship', set up by the Indonesian government in partnership with the East Timorese government, was widely believed to be a political stunt designed to demonstrate that Indonesia was taking its responsibility to investigate seriously. It was supported by the East Timorese government who were keen to promote an accountability procedure that did not result in criminal convictions and to maintain a good strategic relationship of necessity with their neighbour. The final report, however, did something quite important. It acknowledged the institutional responsibility of the Indonesian state and security forces in the acts perpetrated against the East Timorese people. While this had been established in the East Timor Commission for Reception, Truth and Reconciliation report (mostly dismissed by the East Timorese national leadership), the recognition of the role of institutions and the state in the crime perpetrated by the Indonesians was an important acknowledgement. The criminal trials held by Indonesia through the Ad Hoc Human Rights Chamber were less surprising – just one conviction, overturned on appeal.

The impact of changing political realities

The use of the institution of law, as a core institution of the state, signals that the harm is taken seriously and defined as such. It also means that the harm will enter the institutional memory of that state. This, however, cannot be guaranteed. In defining democratic Hungary, or independent East Timor, or post-war Turkey, even newer political realities can quickly subsume the original break from the past.

The 'people's courts' of post-war Hungary were quickly forgotten as the newer Hungary – Communist Hungary – was entrenched, and in this new worker's polity there was no room for specific redress or even remembering of atrocities particular to one group, namely that of the Jews.

And more recently, while specific trials and inquiries have been held to document and prosecute the crimes perpetrated against the East Timorese under Indonesian occupation, consistent pronouncements by the East Timorese leadership that there must be a focus on reconciliation, not prosecutions, that there must be a legacy of resistance not victimhood, and that the relationship with its Indonesian neighbour is more important than any reckoning with the past, have meant that any consistent efforts at addressing the past are being compromised.

Similarly, what started out as an important set of trials to prosecute the leaders and deputies responsible for the genocide of the Armenians by the Ottoman state during the First World War, turned into a tale of martyrdom and denial with the change of government and international obstruction. The Allies had originally clearly recognized the need for justice. A joint declaration on 24 May 1915 read in part:

> In view of these new crimes of Turkey against humanity and civilization, the Allied governments announce publicly ... that they will hold personally responsible ... all members of the Ottoman government and those of their agents who are implicated in such massacres.
>
> (Dadrian 1997b: 216)

Yet despite these calls for prosecution by the Allies during the war, they ended up thwarting the Courts-Martial. Several articles stipulating the trial and punishment of those responsible for the genocide were originally inserted into the Peace Treaty of Sèvres, signed by the Allies on 10 August 1920. Crimes against Humanity was the original charge (changed to massacres due to opposition from the USA and Japan). Yet the constitution of the court provided for in Article 230 of the Treaty of Sèvres, in which the Allies had 'the right to designate the tribunal which shall try the persons so accused', never eventuated, and in fact the Peace Treaty of Sèvres was abandoned (signed but never ratified). The subsequent Treaty of Lausanne had no mention of war crimes. The British ultimately held no trials for the massacres, despite holding many alleged war criminals hostage. This was despite a beginning which saw the recognition at the Paris Peace Conference by the Commission on Responsibility of the massacre of the Armenians, and which saw serious debate on the manner in which this war crime could be punished (plus great public outrage in Britain as to the treatment of the Armenians). The British Foreign Secretary, Lord Curzon, was to write in 1922, 'I think we made a great mistake in ever letting these people out. I had to yield at the time to a pressure which I always felt to be mistaken' (Willis 1982: 163).

While the trials went ahead locally in the Ottoman State, through the Courts-Martial established by the Sultan's government, they were plagued by political instability within and hostility from without. With the Ittihad party who had committed the atrocities no longer in power, many of those involved began underground offensives. The ascendancy of Kemalism meant the demise of the Courts-Martial, fuelled in part by the occupation by Greece of Smyrna, on the Ottoman coast. Efforts to force Germany to extradite the main 'triumvirate' of Enver, Talat and Cemal were knocked back by the Allies. Meanwhile, with the ascendancy of the Kemalists, and the increasing lack of support locally for the trials, in May 1919 the British seized sixty-seven prisoners (including some of those on trial at the Courts-Martial) and took them to the islands of Mudros and Malta.

As the process of supplanting the Sultan's government and law proceeded, the Courts-Martial became irrelevant. On 29 April 1920, a bill was introduced in the new Kemalist National Assembly in Ankara to declare the official decisions and decrees of the Sultan's Istanbul government null and void. Verdicts were overturned and those convicted declared 'national martyrs'. On 13 January 1921, the full Courts-Martial was abolished. While an estimated twenty-four trials were held that focused on the genocide of the Armenians, and responsibility clearly put on the main perpetrators, this was all to be swept away with the new government. To this day, Turkey has continued to deny the genocide of the Armenians (and other Christian minorities), despite clear evidence to the contrary, including survivor and eyewitness testimony (including from Allied soldiers) and of course the transcripts and judgements of the trials themselves. And while Turkey had hoped the trials may mean more lenient treatment by the Allies, despite the efforts of the Grand Vizier, when he was called to present Turkey's case before the Council of Ten on 17 June 1919, asking for clemency for Turkey, and arguing that 'the great trial of the Unionists at Constantinople has proved the responsibility of the leaders of the Committee [for war crimes committed]', his appeals were rebuffed (*FRUS: Paris Peace Conference* 1919, in Willis 1982: 156).

There are other examples of incomplete national legal proceedings that fell hostage to political considerations. In the wake of the formation of Bangladesh, in which an estimated 1.5 to 3 million Bengalis were killed in the 1971 secession from Pakistan, the new Bangladeshi government passed an Act to ' ... provide for the detention, prosecution and punishment of persons for genocide, crimes against humanity, war crimes and other crimes under international law' (*International Crimes (Tribunals) Act* 1973). Special tribunals were established to try Bangladeshi citizens who had collaborated with the Pakistani armed forces. National prosecutions commenced at the end of January 1972, under the *Bangladesh Collaborators (Special Tribunals)*

Order: International Crimes (Tribunal) Act 1973. A tribunal comprised of
Bangladeshi Supreme Court justices was constituted (Klinghoffer 1998: 106).
Bangladesh also sought to bring charges of genocide under the Genocide
Convention against 195 Pakistani prisoners of war being held in India.
Pakistan then sought an order from the International Court of Justice, to
prevent the case on jurisdictional grounds (*Trial of Pakistani Prisoners of
War* 1973).

Power politics saw the Bangladeshi action being still born, due to a political settlement between the new Bangladesh, India and Pakistan. This
included the recognition of Bangladesh by Pakistan, and the return of prisoners of war to Pakistan by India. On 30 November 1973, a general amnesty
was declared for all convicted under the Act, and in 1975 a presidential
order was issued abolishing the collaborators law and restoring the civil
rights of former collaborators. The extent of harm is still not publicly
recognized, in particular the kinds of harm perpetrated against women
(D'Costa & Hossein 2010). We may now see a reversal of this. In March
2010, the International Crimes Tribunal was established in Bangladesh, using
amended legislation first brought in 1974.[4]

State law and living law

While law is a partner in governing and creating realities, it can only go so
far as a population allows. Due to the public unwillingness to accept Armenian testimony during one of the trials at the Turkish Courts-Martial, that of
the local officials of the province of Yozgat, the Prosecutor-General in his
closing arguments, as Höss notes, told the court that he was intentionally
excluding all evidence supplied by Armenian witnesses, and was concentrat-
ing on documentary evidence and evidence supplied by former government
officials (Höss 1992: 220). The eventual judgement handed down was
still not popular. The execution of Mehmed Kemal (Kemal Bey), former
Inspector of Deportation at Konya, turned into a 'large-scale nationalist
demonstration', after which 20,000 Turkish pounds were raised for his family
(ibid: 219).

The International Criminal Tribunal for the former Yugoslavia provoked
hostile reaction from within Serbia. More of a 'foundational moment' for
the international community in its push for a permanent international criminal court and for defining the core international crimes, it did not have this
effect at one of the sites at which it was targeted. This is despite efforts at
outreach both by the Tribunal and by non-governmental organizations (live
television broadcasts of Tribunal proceedings from the Hague were organized early on by an international non-governmental organization). Its
location away from the site of conflict meant that it had little chance to have
an impact locally and was overridden too by dominant local normative
orders.

In its compromise of due process, and its great length, the Dergue and Red Terror trials in Ethiopia ceased to be central for ordinary Ethiopians. The trials changed from being an important tool of accountability for the state crime perpetrated by the Mengistu regime into another example of political injustice.

In Rwanda, the distrust of the legal process and survivors' own experiences meant that decisions were not necessarily accepted. Survivors will have their own sense of justice that will not always be satisfied by a legal process. This is not unique to Rwanda. In one instance, killings occurred in the wake of a judgement that was seen to be too lenient. In other cases, survivors who have spoken up as witnesses have also been killed. This prompted, early on, the practice of holding trials publicly on hill-tops, to try and clearly show judicial decision making. It was also evident in the way in which prosecutors went about their business, explaining their approach.

What we also see is that when law is absent, or incomplete, individuals and communities step in with their own practices and explanations. Cambodians have also used their own ways to address and understand the harm perpetrated against them, harnessing a kind of 'living law' that was of necessity separate to the inaction of the state and the international community (see Eisenbruch 2007), although not giving up on the need for legal justice (see Lambourne 2004; Chhang 2007). Lia Kent has shown how in the separation of the East Timorese legal processes from the needs of ordinary East Timorese, individuals and communities have begun their own memorial practices (Kent 2010). It can be argued, however, that official law continues to be a critical reference point, and that its absence is keenly felt.

The promise of law as inaction

Prosecution is often used as a promise in lieu of direct action to stop the harms perpetrated. The atrocities committed by the Nazis were known early on in the war. In May 1942 a detailed report was sent by the Polish Jewish organization, the Bund, to the Polish Government in Exile in London, stating that the Nazis had decided upon the mass murder of Polish Jewry and that 700,000 people had already been murdered (Bauer 1989: 103). After not succeeding in galvanizing the Allies into rescue action, Szmuel Siegelbaum, the Jewish delegate in the Polish National Council in London, committed suicide. In August 1942, a telegram was sent by Gerhart Riegner, Secretary of the World Jewish Congress in Geneva to the United States and Britain, with information of a planned massacre of the Jews of Europe by the Germans (ibid: 110). In addition, emissaries were sent to the West, one of the most notable being the young Pole Jan Karski, who in October 1942 was asked by leaders of the Jewish underground of the Warsaw ghetto to be a witness to the horrors of that place. It was to him that the United States Judge Felix Frankfurter replied when confronted by Karski with news of the extermination of Jews in Europe, 'I am unable to believe what you say'. He did not think Karski was lying, he was unable to believe. It was a full year later that the Allies made a formal pronouncement on the need for later prosecution – not for immediate action.

The first Allied pronouncement against the crimes of Nazi Germany came in October 1943, at the Moscow Conference. The United Kingdom, the United States and the Soviet Union, in a Declaration on German Atrocities (30 October 1943) jointly declared:

> At the time of the granting of any armistice to any government which may be set up in Germany, those German officers and men and members of the Nazi Party, who have been responsible for, or have taken a consenting part in [the above] atrocities, massacres and executions, will be sent back to the countries in which their abominable deeds were done in order that they may be judged and punished according to the laws of these liberated countries and of the free governments which will be created therein.
>
> (Moscow Declaration on German Atrocities 1943)

This followed a declaration in the British Parliament, endorsed by the Allies, on 17 December 1942. As Yehuda Bauer relates, at the proposal of one of its members, the whole British parliament stood up, for the first and only time in its history, in honour of the Jewish victims. But once the members had stood up in silence for one minute, they sat down again (Bauer 1989: 113–14).

Much was known about the Rwandan genocide. The International Criminal Tribunal for Rwanda was clearly established with the realization of the ineffectual role of the United Nations in preventing and stopping the genocide. It was, as one Deputy Prosecutor put bluntly, set up by the international community to 'ease its conscience of the failure that happened there'. The United Nations investigation began *during* the genocide – the Special Rapporteur began his work on 9 June 1994. Prior to this, as was publicly revealed during the investigation of the Belgian Senate into the Rwandan genocide, there had been communication between United Nations representatives in Rwanda and the United Nations New York office regarding evidence of preparation of a genocide (Senat de Belgique 1996–97).

A facsimile was sent on 11 January 1994 by General Romeo Dallaire, then Commander of the United Nations Assistance Mission for Rwanda (UNAMIR) force in Rwanda, to Major-General Baril, then second-in-command to Kofi Annan in the Department of Peace-Keeping Operations at the United Nations in New York. The fax notified Baril of the existence of an informant, a 'top level trainer in the cadre of interhamwe-armed militia' [sic], and that 'Interhamwe has trained 1,700 men in RGF [Rwandan Government Forces] military camps outside the capital'. Information given by the informant included the following (as summarized by Dallaire in the fax):

Principal aim of Interhamwe [sic] in the past was to protect Kigali from RPF [Rwandan Patriotic Front]. Since UNAMIR mandate he [the informant] has been ordered to register all Tutsi in Kigali. He suspects it is for their extermination.

(Dallaire 1994)

Cables went back and forth between Rwanda and New York right up to the start of the genocide, as well as throughout. On 8 April, when the killings began, a cable from the UNAMIR force stated, in part, ' ... sheltering of civilians terrorized by a ruthless campaign of ethnic cleansing and terror'. Rather than describing what was happening as the beginning of a genocide, the United Nations Security Council spoke of the 'breakdown of a ceasefire'. Rather than increasing the United Nations force on the ground, and revising its mandate, the United Nations withdrew its peacekeeping force, authorizing a skeleton force of just over 200 men.[5] Extra troops were brought in by France, Belgium and Italy for the sole purpose of rescuing white expatriates. Black Tutsis were left to die. Meanwhile, the Rwandan ambassador at the United Nations, with Rwanda by chance having its rotating turn on the Security Council, was allowed to speak unhindered. Internal State Department documents are said to speak of a genocide – external communication was notable in its absence of the word genocide.

There was knowledge too of the genocide of the Armenians by the Ottoman state during the First World War, with reports sent from eyewitnesses. The Allies made a joint pronouncement on 24 May 1915, which read in part:

In view of these new crimes of Turkey against humanity and civilization, the Allied governments announce publicly ... that they will hold personally responsible ... all members of the Ottoman government and those of their agents who are implicated in such massacres.

(Dadrian 1997b: 216)

Yet this promised action by the Allies did not eventuate.

The international community did not believe in the crimes that had been committed by the Khmer Rouge while they were being perpetrated. It took some time afterwards for there to be recognition of what became known as the 'Killing Fields', the 1.8 million Cambodians killed by Pol Pot and the Khmer Rouge between April 1975 and January 1979 which ended with the invasion by Vietnam. Even with recognition it took many more years for action to follow. The geo-political location of Cambodia meant prosecutions were not supported.

At the start of the Khmer Rouge atrocities, in 1975, the United Nations Commission on Human Rights was requested to investigate allegations of mass killing in Cambodia. Its findings were tabled in 1978, and nothing done. It took until 2006 for an international criminal tribunal to be established to address the crimes of the Khmer Rouge. This is despite the efforts of activists and scholars Hurst Hannum and David Hawk who, in the 1980s, prepared a 200-page draft model dispute to take to the International Court of Justice under the provisions of Article IX of the Genocide Convention that nominates the International Court as the place to take disputes, and tried to persuade a country to take it (Hannum 1989). No government was willing to take the case on. Earlier, Greg Stanton's Cambodia Genocide Project sought to persuade a government to bring a case against the Khmer Rouge exile regime, the Coalition Government of Democratic Kampuchea, while the Khmer Rouge still represented Cambodia at the United Nations. In 1986 they specifically approached Australia, who refused, on the grounds this would require recognition of the 'Democratic Kampuchea' government (Stanton 1993: 149).

Possibly the most harrowing case of law as inaction is the application made by Bosnia and Herzegovina to the International Court of Justice in March 1993 asking the Court to intervene in the killing of Bosnian Muslims by Serbia and Montenegro. The Court ordered that the Federal Republic of Yugoslavia (Serbia and Montenegro) take measures to 'deter and stop acts of genocide', yet they continued (*Application of the Convention on the Prevention and Punishment of the Crime of Genocide* 1993). In its judgement 14 years later, the Court found that the acts at Srebrenica (although not elsewhere) did constitute genocide, yet that Serbia was not in fact responsible, denying any link between the crimes perpetrated by the 'Republika Srpska' and the Serbian state leadership.

Looking forward and looking backward – patterns of legal redress

In the legal redress employed by states in the wake of mass harm, we can identify those that 'look backward' and those that 'look forward'. That is, those focused on the harm itself, on perpetrators and on victims, and those focused on a more future-oriented societal or preventative redress. Of course, it cannot be said that in focusing on perpetrators and victims one is only 'looking backward', as this can play an important role in establishing the new regime and can be a critical foundation for victims. Likewise, any broader societal redress is of necessity focused on the harm in identification of causes and solutions. We can observe two categories of redress in terms of legal process:

- Perpetrator and victim redress: legal process aimed at direct remedy of the crime
- Societal redress: legal process aimed at a broader institutional or societal redress

Both perpetrator and victim redress and societal legal redress have a norm-fashioning role, and both are critical to the telos of the new state, yet are differently targeted in terms of addressing state crime.

Perpetrator and victim redress

These legal proceedings aimed at perpetrator accountability and victim redress, address what may be termed the mechanics of the crime – what was done, who did it, who was harmed. Perpetrator and victim-specific legal proceedings are aimed at providing contained legal redress for that situation only. As such, they attempt the 'minimum' of order and of redress of that genocide or state crime.

The attempt to immediately 'contain' the situation and create order is the first stage of legal redress. This is where we first see perpetrator redress proceedings. Perpetrator redress proceedings include criminal prosecution (civil and military trials), truth commissions, lustration legislation. Perpetrator redress is generally the first wave of legal proceedings. This redress aims at immediate redress of the situation, through identification and penalization of the individual key perpetrators of the crime. It seeks an immediate closure to the situation, a level of containment, through removal of the key perpetrators from the wider society.

Victim redress is generally accorded a lower priority than perpetrator redress. In some national legislatures, compensation legislation is dependent upon criminal prosecution. Rwandan criminal trials have a civil component that was designed to award compensation. Victim redress outcomes include monetary compensation, restitution arrangements (property for example), the establishment of institutions to help the victims or victims' families (for example, pension plans or continuing payments), and reparations measures. Such arrangements can be organized for individuals, or an amount given to groups (Germany's payment of a lump sum to the State of Israel, for example). Compensation can, and often is, at a minimum level. The South African Truth and Reconciliation Commission's compensation section (the Reparations and Rehabilitation Committee) was much criticized for the limited compensation it delivered to victims.

Victim redress need not always be monetary. Other arrangements may include the provision of participation in state institutions (a representative from a victim group for example). It may also include provision for 'rebuilding' – the new Trust Fund of the International Criminal Court is an example of this, focused not on individual compensation but on enabling victims to establish themselves again. Naomi Roht-Arriaza has termed this form of reparations, 'reparations as development' (Roht-Arriaza 2004). She also suggests the concepts 'reparations as community-level acknowledgement and community service', and 'reparations as preferential access' (ibid). Reparations can also include forms of community work for victims by perpetrators, or the building of memorials (Pritchard 1998).

While a specific remedy, victim redress generally occurs later, often resulting from sustained pressure. Rwandan compensation has still not eventuated, despite being part of the national criminal proceedings. South African compensation was far lower than that recommended by the Truth and Reconciliation Commission. Compensation for Nazi-related crimes is only now being completed, many schemes having only started some years ago after many of the survivors had passed away. Austria, for example, only activated its scheme in 2001, fifty-six years after the end of the Second World War. It is only since the collapse of communism that restitution is occurring within former communist countries, both for property taken during communist and during Nazi times.

Societal redress

Societal redress refers to processes aimed at remedying the general situation in that society, which may have contributed to the crimes committed, and which aims at prevention of any future harm. This can be understood as a more 'maximum' role for law. This forward looking approach also has a role in establishing accountability, in recognizing institutional responsibility, as well as a role in structural transformation – the writing of new Constitutions, the establishment of Human Rights Ombudsmen, for example. The impetus to draft societal redress legislation is generally in the immediate period after a conflict, when there is a political climate of change, of separating from the past.

Societal legal redress is concerned with looking beyond the particular state crime, and, in encompassing what has occurred, envisioning a future society where such events are not an option. This redress can be found in general legislation, such as new citizenship legislation and the drafting of new constitutions, and new international treaties or conventions. Legislation that bans particular political organizations (the banning of the Communist and Nazi Parties by the Czech Republic, and the banning of the Nazi Party by the German Basic Law) falls within societal redress. Such legislation aims at providing a stable future base for the society. Societal redress is generally the second wave, after perpetrator and victim redress. It also may occur simultaneously with perpetrator and victim redress, supporting these. There is, however, a longer time frame within which societal and institutional reform may sit on the national agenda.

Within societal legal redress, we can also place what could be considered *crisis* legislation: the establishment or activation of legal institutions and/or legislation to deal immediately with the socio-political crisis resulting from a conflict. Currency reform in post-Nazi Germany is an example of this.

We can identify some overlap between societal redress and perpetrator and victim legal redress. The Interim South African Constitution of 1993, designed to signal the new South Africa, included a section titled 'National

Unity and Reconciliation' regarding the establishment of the Truth and Reconciliation Commission. The Truth and Reconciliation Commission of South Africa is an example of a legal process incorporating elements of both perpetrator and victim redress together with societal redress. Legal proceedings aimed dominantly at perpetrator and victim redress can also include elements of societal redress. The Turkish Courts-Martial that examined both how the Ottoman state entered the war and perpetrated genocide, as well as laying specific charges against individuals is an example of this.

The following examples of past major state crime legal proceedings show a mosaic covering both perpetrator and victim redress and societal redress.

Legal proceedings for the Holocaust 1933–45

Legal proceedings in the wake of the crimes committed by the Third Reich under Hitler constitute the most varied mosaic of legal proceedings for state crime. The proceedings have been interconnected as well as fragmented. The Soviet Union began its trials in mid 1943, targeting those who collaborated with the Nazis and charging them with treason and killing Soviet citizens. Other early legal proceedings began in November 1944, with the trial before a Polish Special Tribunal in Lublin of six SS men who were guards at Majdanek concentration camp. Legal proceedings continue to this day, with war crimes trials being conducted in different countries, and reparations agreements still being formulated.

Post-Holocaust proceedings have operated in the national, regional, other-state and international arenas. They have taken the form of criminal trials (civil and military), legislation (denazification process and compensation/restitution) and constitution-making. The audience of these legal proceedings has been varied, both national and international. The type of legal proceedings has included perpetrator redress (trials and denazification process), victim redress (compensation and restitution) and societal redress (new West German constitution, currency reform legislation, denazification process). Whereas the focus in the immediate aftermath of the Second World War was on perpetrator redress (criminal trials), while criminal proceedings continue, the more recent focus, due to intensive representations by community organizations, has been on victim restitution. This has also manifested itself through class actions taken in 'other state' courts, namely the United States, to push for compensation from banks and industries. Most proceedings to address this period have been perpetrator or victim based – trials for perpetrators, and reparations programs for victims. New legislation in (then) West Germany banning Nazi organizations and the denial of the Holocaust may be construed as 'forward looking' but can also be seen as insufficient in considering the causes of the harm, and applying to new situations.

Apart from the International Military Tribunal, trials held for atrocities committed during the Second World War in the immediate aftermath used 'ordinary' legal procedures – military tribunals and criminal courts. Either the charge of war crimes was used, or charges such as murder, ill-treatment and illegal arrests found in the ordinary criminal codes of prosecuting courts. One exception for this was the State of Israel with its use of 'crimes against the Jewish people', developed in the wake of the Holocaust and in the wake of the establishment of the state. *The Nazi and Nazi Collaborators (Punishment) Law* 1950 defines three principal crimes: Crimes against Humanity, War Crimes, and Crimes against the Jewish People (see Wenig 1997). The *Eichmann* trial, which used this formulation, was very specifically a trial that sought perpetrator redress, brought by the victims against a former perpetrator.

Three main periods can be identified: the direct aftermath of the Holocaust 1945–58, the intermediate period 1958–78 and the current period 1978–present. 1958 marks the establishment of a Central Office of State Administration of Justice for the Investigation of Nazi Crimes in West Germany. 1978 marks the passing by the US Congress of the Holtzmann Amendment to the Immigration and Naturalization Act of 1952, signifying a new emphasis on finding alleged war criminals. The collapse of communism can be seen to mark a fourth era – with access to new documents through the opening up of archives, new countries now accessible for victim reparations and with rapidly ageing perpetrators, a new era of post-Holocaust legal proceedings commenced.

Immediately post-war legal proceedings were conducted essentially simultaneously, and were both national and international. They included the well-known *International Military Tribunal to Prosecute the Major War Criminals of the European Theatre* held at Nuremberg, 20 November 1945 to 1 October 1946, as well as the subsequent military and civil prosecutions carried out by the Allied signatories to the London Agreement (British, US, French, Soviet), denazification proceedings in the four Zones, and civil and military trials in other former occupied European countries. The new West German constitution was also introduced during this period, and internal German war crimes trials conducted. These proceedings were all established in the direct aftermath of the crimes committed by the Nazi regime. Their aim was specifically to punish the perpetrators, to separate out 'Germans' and 'perpetrators' and to establish a new foundation for (ultimately West) Germany.

The 1958 trial of former Einsatzgruppen members in Ulm, Germany demonstrated to German officials that many of the perpetrators had yet to be tried. In 1958, the Central Office of the Land Judicial Authorities for the Investigation of National-Socialist Crimes was established. Its focus was the crimes of murder and manslaughter carried out by the operational groups and units of Security Police and Security Service men as well as those perpetrated in concentration and labour camps or in the ghettos. In addition, the criminal liability of members of the Reich Security Office was investigated. The Central Office initiated 400 judicial inquiries in 1959, including crimes committed by the operational groups and units of the Security Police and Security Service in Russia and in the extermination camps of Auschwitz, Belzec, Sobibor, Treblinka and Chelmno. It was at this time that the problem of a statute of limitations became apparent. Under German law of the time, the statute of limitation of crimes liable to a life sentence was twenty years; for criminal acts liable to a term of imprisonment of more than ten years, fifteen years; and for other criminal acts ten years (Article 67 of the Penal Code, in Rückerl 1979: 52). This meant that post-1960, many crimes would be unable to be tried or receive an adequate sentence. The ability to prosecute the crime of murder was to expire on 8 May 1945. In 1965, the West German Parliament (*Bundestag*) voted to extend the statute of limitations for Nazi crimes involving murder. In 1968 the United Nations General Assembly voted in the *Convention on the Non-Applicability of Statutory Limitations to War Crimes and Crimes against Humanity*, which provided post-Nuremberg legal proceedings with an important international legal framework (despite the West German government not signing the Convention). In June 1969, the West German parliament approved a bill providing for the annulment of the statute of limitations on murder and genocide.

We have no absolute number of criminal legal proceedings conducted, or individuals indicted. One estimate is that 70,000 German nationals have been brought to trial both in and outside Germany (ibid). As Rückerl noted, between 8 May 1945 and 31 December 1978, German public prosecutors opened a total of 85,802 proceedings. With the increased age of perpetrators, there was an increased push to prosecute in the West, although these trials number in the tens. Trials in Germany have substantially slowed down: between 1987 and 1997, there were only fourteen trials held against fifteen defendants.

While post-Holocaust proceedings have been mostly perpetrator and victim-directed, we can identify some more directed at institutional and societal change. In the context of the cessation of the Second World War, 'emergency legislation' promulgated by the Allies included measures for providing adequate housing, rationing food, gas and electricity. It also included legislation for currency reform as well as the decartellization of mammoth industrial concerns. It included the revival of the federal character of Germany, as well as the replacement of the Reich organization, including the replacement of the old legal order (Krawinkel 1949: 250–51). These were measures aimed primarily at state (and institutional) reconstruction.

Such legislation certainly had a broader societal impact. In particular, as Krawinkel notes, the currency reform legislation had a great impact both morally and physically, including a reduction in criminality (ibid). However, such legislation can be separated out from legislation and legal proceedings aimed specifically at societal reconstruction, for example, institutional recommendations arising out of the South African Truth and Reconciliation Commission.

Parallel initiatives included the denazification legislation, a crude tool aimed both at the 'purging' of former Nazi officials and the restructuring of the public service. The genesis of the denazification procedures was the Yalta conference of February 1945 at which Roosevelt, Churchill and Stalin declared their determination to wipe out all vestiges of the Nazi party and its influence. In a joint statement they declared:

> We are determined to ... wipe out the Nazi party, Nazi laws, organizations, and institutions, remove all Nazi and militarist influences from public office and from the cultural and economic life of the German people, and take such other agreed measures in Germany as may be necessary for the future peace and safety of the world.
>
> (Yalta Agreement, February 1945)

It was at Potsdam in July 1945 that this was clarified. The Potsdam Agreement, signed on 2 August 1945 by the leaders of the United States, Britain and the Soviet Union, contained the following declaration:

> All members of the Nazi party who have been more than nominal participants in its activities and all other persons hostile to Allied purposes are to be removed from public or semi-public office and from positions of responsibility in important private undertakings. Such persons shall be replaced by persons who, by their political and moral qualities, are deemed capable of assisting in developing genuine democratic institutions in Germany.
>
> (Potsdam Agreement, August 1945)

A list of persons subject to 'mandatory arrest' had been drawn up by the Supreme Headquarters of the Allied Expeditionary Forces prior to the end of the war: 178,000 persons were placed under arrest by the three Western allies, with the Soviets detaining 67,000 more (Gutman 1990: 359). In each of the zones of occupation, the denazification policy differed widely. The Americans were the strictest. Their denazification law, enacted on 5 March 1946, was administered in the three states (*Länder*) of the American zone (Bavaria, Greater-Hesse and Württemberg-Baden) through 545 tribunals which classified persons according to whether they were 'major offenders', 'offenders', 'lesser offenders', or 'followers' (Tutorow 1986: 7–8). The law was designed to remove former Nazis from public service. Tutorow outlines it as follows: 13 million Germans in the American zone were required to register. The basis for the classification was a questionnaire that had to be filled in by the person to be 'denazified', in which personal data, a record of activities during the Nazi regime, and associations with Nazi organizations were recorded. Three million persons were found subject to classification under the denazification law, and over 930,000 persons were tried by denazification tribunals (some amnesties were granted by the Military Governor). The penalties imposed ranged from fines (500,000 persons), to restrictions on employment (122,000 persons), to confiscation of property (25,000 persons), to a declaration of ineligibility to hold public office (22,000 persons), to a requirement to perform special labour (30,000 persons), to prison sentences of a maximum of ten years (9,000 persons).

These tribunals (consisting of one professional jurist as chairman and two lay judges) operated, according to the Control Council regulation, on a presumption of guilt, and it was up to the individual to prove his or her innocence (Gutman 1990: 361). With the departure of the Americans, however, a law was enacted in 1951 allowing some who lost positions due to denazification to return to their official positions. There have also been compensation payments to some of those who suffered through denazification.

Britain and France did not follow denazification with the same zeal as the Americans. The British were concerned with the potential total breakdown of German life if Germans familiar with local conditions were excluded from employment in responsible posts (noting that the British occupied the heavily damaged, densely populated and highly industrialized Ruhr district). They pursued a more pragmatic policy. The goal of the French was to weaken Germany. Its policy followed this creed, subscribing to the principle that Nazi elements must be removed, yet sometimes engaged German experts from outside their zone of occupation who had been dismissed through denazification as well as retaining in their posts persons who were incriminated by activities in Nazi organizations (ibid: 360). In the Soviet zone, denazification measures were designed to serve the Soviet's main objective, restructuring society according to Communist principles. Hence, most rank and file Nazis were not affected by denazification measures due to their joining the Communist party (ibid).

What was absent in post-Nazi Germany was legislation addressing the underlying causes of the conflict. Legislation that outlawed the Nazi Party and other related organizations can be considered a necessary and immediate reform, and one aimed at future prevention on one level, yet not a broader restructuring of that society. Reform to citizenship legislation, what may be considered a broader redress, came much later. In January 2000, Germany's citizenship provisions were changed, allowing for those born in Germany, not only those descended from those considered 'German' to gain German citizenship (albeit still with limitations). Such a change allows for a more inclusive understanding of who is and can be part of the German nation. In allowing for the political inclusion and recognition of those who had previously not otherwise been considered properly 'German', this goes some way to addressing the underlying causes of the state crime in a way that the mostly perpetrator and victim redress proceedings do not.

Legal proceedings for Cambodia under the Khmer Rouge 1975–79

Legal redress for the crimes perpetrated by the Khmer Rouge in Cambodia from April 1975 to January 1979 has been perpetrator focused. It cannot be said that this has been an immediate redress. While Vietnam after its invasion of Cambodia in January 1979 established a military tribunal, the People's Revolutionary Tribunal, and there was a local 'trial' of Pol Pot shortly before his death, a joint international-national criminal tribunal, the 'Extraordinary Chambers in the Courts of Cambodia' was only established in 2006, under a 2004 law for the prosecution of crimes committed during the period of Democratic Kampuchea. Only some years earlier, in 1999, lawsuits were filed in Belgium by Cambodian survivors. The lack of any sustained legal redress for the crimes of the Khmer Rouge is despite international and national non-governmental organization effort over the years to have a case brought to the International Court of Justice and a Tribunal established.

In July 1998, pursuant to General Assembly resolution 52/135, United Nations Secretary-General Kofi Annan established a Group of Experts, with the following mandate:

> To evaluate the existing evidence with a view to determining the nature of the crimes committed by Khmer Rouge leaders in the years from 1975 to 1979; To assess, after consultation with the Governments concerned, the feasibility of bringing Khmer Rouge leaders to justice and their apprehension, detention and extradition or surrender to the criminal jurisdiction established; To explore options for bringing to justice Khmer Rouge leaders before an international or national jurisdiction.
>
> (*Report of the Group of Experts for Cambodia* 1999)

In its final report, the Group recommended that a Tribunal be established, to focus on genocide and crimes against humanity during the Khmer Rouge period. It recommended that due to 'the level of corruption in the court system and the routine subjection of judicial decisions to political influence', and 'the consequent lack of confidence of the Cambodian public in its judiciary', 'domestic trials organized under Cambodian law are not feasible and should not be supported financially by the United Nations' (ibid: 132–34). The Group 'reluctantly concluded that trials in Cambodia are fraught with too many dangers and that a United Nations tribunal should be located elsewhere' (ibid: para 168) and recommended the establishment of an ad hoc international criminal tribunal by the United Nations, to be held in a city in the Asia-Pacific region (ibid: para 171).

Despite the recommendations of the Group of Experts, a memorandum of understanding between the United Nations and the Cambodian government, agreeing to cooperate in the establishment of a Cambodian court, was drafted and presented to the Cambodian government on 7 July 2000 (*Tribunal Memorandum of Understanding* 2000). The *Law on the Establishment of Extraordinary Chambers in the Courts of Cambodia for the Prosecution of Crimes Committed During the Period of Democratic Kampuchea* was passed by both Houses of the Cambodian Parliament in January 2001. While its implementation was subsequently blocked by Prime Minister Hun Sen, after its final passage through the Cambodian National Assembly and the Cambodian Senate in June and July 2001, Cambodia started saying that it would go ahead with a tribunal with or without United Nations support. After much negotiation and stalling, a final law, the *Law on the Establishment of the Extraordinary Chambers* 2004, in accordance with the original United Nations agreement, was struck in October 2004.

The government had not been active in pursuing former Khmer Rouge. This only changed with the establishment of the Tribunal. Former Foreign Minister Ieng Sary had been pardoned in 1996 by King Norodom Sihanouk after leading mass defections from the Khmer Rouge to the government (Dunlop & Thayer 1999: 20). He is now indicted and in detention to face trial at the Extraordinary Chambers.

The arrest of former senior Khmer Rouge leader Ta Mok by the Cambodian Hun Sen government in March 1999 on charges of genocide, and the arrest of Kaing Guek Eav ('Duch'), head of the Khmer Rouge secret police and director of the S-21 Security Prison, on 7 May 1999, had appeared initially calculated to limit any further criminal proceedings. As reported in the *Far Eastern Economic Review*, Prime Minister Hun Sen had been non-committal on the issue of arresting others implicated in the crimes of 1975–79, saying the government couldn't tell the judicial branch what to do (ibid). Other key leaders, Khieu Samphan, Nuon Chea and Ke Pok had lived in freedom, their whereabouts known by the Cambodian government. The passage of anti-Khmer Rouge legislation in 1994, as Steven Ratner and Jason Abrams write, while indicating some domestic pressures for accountability, when put together with the 1996 amnesty of Ieng Sary suggested more of a political manoeuvre than a genuine step toward accountability (Ratner & Abrams 1997: 268).

This seems to have changed with the establishment of the Tribunal. In 2010, the Tribunal had in its custody Nuon Chea, 'Brother No. 2', Ieng Sary, 'Brother No. 3' and former Minister for Foreign Affairs, Ieng Thirith, wife of Ieng Sary and former Minister of Social Affairs, Khieu Samphan, former President of Democratic Kampuchea, and Kaing Guek Eav ('Duch'), former director of the detention and torture center S-21 at Tuol Sleng in Phnom Penh.

Legal proceedings for the war in the former Yugoslavia 1992–94

In regard to the former Yugoslavia, we can identify at least ten instances of legal proceedings to address the conflict. These include the International Criminal Tribunal for the former Yugoslavia held in the Hague by the United Nations, the case brought by Bosnia-Herzegovina to the International Court of Justice against Serbia-Montenegro, national criminal trials held in Bosnia-Herzegovina, Croatia and Serbia (including the establishment of War Crimes

Chambers), the establishment of a Human Rights Chamber in Bosnia-Herzegovina, two failed truth commissions, one in Bosnia-Herzegovina and one in Serbia, trials held in Austria, Switzerland and France among others, and claims brought under the United States Alien Torts Claims Act.

This mosaic of legal proceedings is simultaneously international, national and other-state, with an early emphasis on the international. The legal proceedings are mostly perpetrator and victim-directed legal redress and have been mostly external. Legal proceedings began while the main perpetrators were still in power (Slobodan Milošević only ceased to be President of Serbia in October 2000). Work on the Hague Tribunal first began in October 1992 with the creation of a Commission of Experts established in 1992 by the United Nations Security Council Resolution 780.[6] Following the submission of the Commission's *Interim Report* (1992), the Security Council on 25 May 1993 in Resolution 827 voted to establish an ad hoc tribunal – *The International Tribunal for the Prosecution of Persons Responsible for Serious Violations of International Humanitarian Law Committed in the Territory of the Former Yugoslavia since 1991* (Statute of the International Tribunal for the Former Yugoslavia 1993).

Bosnia and Herzegovina had begun their criminal investigations already in June 1992, in particular into Radovan Karadžić, Ratko Mladić, and Mićo Stanišić, through both the Higher Court in Sarajevo and the District Military Court in Sarajevo. In 1995, they were requested by the Hague Tribunal to defer to the Tribunal in regard to these investigations. The International Court of Justice only gave its judgement in the case brought by Bosnia and Herzegovina in 2007, in which it found that while the acts at Srebrenica constituted genocide under the Genocide Convention, Serbia was neither directly responsible nor complicit in it (*Application of the Convention on the Prevention and Punishment of the Crime of Genocide* 2007).

The focus has been more on implementation of norms from outside, rather than any change to the internal situation. As Cotic observed, while Milošević was still President there was great internal opposition, with the establishment of the Tribunal viewed as an assertion of political supremacy (Cotic 1996: 13). In fact, a survey conducted by the Belgrade weekly *NIN* in October 2000 found that more than half of the 2,000 people questioned said Milošević should not stand trial for war crimes anywhere. Thirty per cent said he should face charges in Serbia and only nine per cent favoured extraditing him to the Hague tribunal (Radio Free Europe/Radio Liberty 2000).

This is in contrast to the great deal of international interest the Tribunal initially generated, as the new Nuremberg and a potential blueprint for the then yet to be established permanent International Criminal Court. Both the Tribunal and the International Court of Justice case have had different audiences and different roles to the usual central proceedings in the wake of state crime and genocide. Their role has not been containment, rather global institutionalization of some norms, the further development of international criminal law, and the hope for more effective regulation of such conflicts. The length, and some aspects of the Tribunal's procedures (in particular, allowing defendants to represent themselves, meaning that former victims have been cross-examined by their former perpetrators), together with the death of Milošević without substantial conclusion of his trial, yet a substantial body of new international criminal law for genocide, crimes against humanity and war crimes, mean a mixed legacy for the Tribunal.

Where both a broader and more locally directed legal redress may be found is in the Human Rights Chamber of Bosnia and Herzegovina established through the Dayton Peace Agreement. The Human Rights Chamber (*Dom Za Ljudska Prava*), together with the Office of the Ombudsman, operated through to the end of 2003 until it was merged with the Constitutional Court of Bosnia and Herzegovina. The Chamber was established in order that the parties to the Dayton Peace Agreement, The Republic of Bosnia and Herzegovina, the Federation of Bosnia and Herzegovina and the Republika Srpska, 'secure to all persons within their jurisdiction the highest level of internationally recognized human rights and fundamental freedoms ...' (*General Framework Agreement for Peace in Bosnia and Herzegovina 1995:* Ch 1, Art I. Agreement on Human Rights, Annex 6).[7]

The Chamber was not designed to directly address acts committed during the war, but to provide redress for their continuing effect. So, as noted in its Annual Report, in March 2003 the Chamber issued its decision in the 'Srebrenica cases', directed against the Republika Srpska, which dealt with the rights of family members to be informed about the fate and whereabouts of their loved ones (Human Rights Chamber for Bosnia and Herzegovina 2003: 5). Further, it has also examined employment discrimination on the grounds of ethnic and national origin, as well as claims of maltreatment in custody and the right to a fair trial. Housing and property claims were the most frequently heard matters, in particular cases that address the refusal or delay in allowing refugees or displaced persons to return to their pre-war homes. Compliance, however, turned out to be difficult.

One of the first cases was brought by the Islamic Community in Bosnia and Herzegovina against The Republika Srpska (*The Islamic Community in Bosnia and Herzegovina v. The Republika Srpska*). The community sought a ruling with regards to the killing, expelling and displacement of Muslims in Banja Luka and the destruction of its fifteen mosques. The Chamber found that it was not competent to rule on this due to its having occurred prior to 14 December 1995 (prior to the entry into force of the Dayton Peace Agreement). The Chamber could, however, rule on the other claims brought by the Islamic Community, namely the subsequent removal of the remains of those mosques, the desecration of adjacent graveyards, the destruction of a further building, the municipality's ongoing refusal to permit the construction of seven mosques and the erection of fences around the remains of the sites, the inability for Muslim believers to worship on adequate premises, the local authorities' failure to protect believers during worship and funerals, and the refusal to allow the burial of the late Mufti in the Ferhadija mosque (all events which occurred after 14 December 1995). The Chamber found that this constituted discrimination on the grounds of religion and national origin in the enjoyment of their right to freedom of religion and the right to peaceful enjoyment of their possessions. They ordered a series of remedies, including the swift granting of permits for reconstruction of seven of the destroyed mosques and permission to erect enclosures around the sites of the fifteen destroyed mosques (see Human Rights Chamber for Bosnia and Herzegovina 1999).

Yet while the City of Banja Luka Department of Urban Planning granted approval to the Islamic Community to reconstruct the Ferhadija mosque and other facilities on the site of the former mosque in the centre of the city, construction of the mosque only began in 2008.

Legal proceedings for the genocide in Rwanda 1994

The redress for the 1994 genocide in Rwanda has been mostly perpetrator focused. The main proceedings have been the International Criminal Tribunal for Rwanda, the national criminal trials, and the nationally directed yet communally based 'gacaca' proceedings. Victim compensation that was promised is yet to eventuate. Other proceedings have included civil claims brought in the United States using the Alien Torts Claims Act, and criminal trials in Belgium, Brussels, Switzerland and France among others. Neo-colonial power France and former colonial power Belgium conducted inquiries as to their conduct in the genocide, as did the United Nations. The Organization of African Unity established an 'International Panel of Eminent Personalities' to conduct an inquiry, which recommended the payment of reparations to the government and people of Rwanda by the international community, and full cancellation of the national debt. The Rwandan government conducted its own inquiry, the Mucyo Commission. These inquiries can be considered as aimed at both an institutional and societal redress as well as victim redress. Rwanda has also introduced new legislation that bars identity cards marked with either Hutu or Tutsi. This is legislation aimed at societal redress.

Unlike the former Yugoslavia, in Rwanda there has been a strong set of national legal proceedings. At the end of the genocide, the new transitional Rwandan government, sworn in on 19 July 1994, and prior to this, the Rwandese Patriotic Army and Rwandese Patriotic Front, began rounding up suspects and putting them in jail. Many others were detained in military camps. It was a time of great instability, both internally and on the borders of Rwanda. Hutu extremists, former perpetrators of the genocide, were attempting to establish a 'government in exile' in the refugee camps (see Terry 2002). The Rwandese Patriotic Front were attempting to establish control internally.

From October to December 1996, 1.3 million Rwandan refugees returned to Rwanda from the camps in Zaire and Tanzania. Many of these would be put in jail, as genocide suspects. At this stage the government appears to have been split over what to do with regard to the alleged *genocidaires*. The moderates favoured a more political settlement,[8] the hardliners (who were to win power in mid-1995) a more retributive policy. Already in August 1994 the new Prime Minister, Faustin Twagiramungu, declared that it would be necessary 'to try 30,000 people' to punish the genocide adequately (cited in Prunier 1995: 305). This number was to prove too low.

A framework for national prosecution with civil damages was one of the first laws passed by the new Parliament, two years after the genocide had ended, under Organic Law No. 8/96 (30 August 1996): *Organic Law on the organization of prosecutions for offences constituting the crime of genocide or crimes against humanity committed since 1 October 1990*. This was one of the first pieces of legislation passed by the new Parliament. As outlined by the Rwandan Ministry of Justice at the time, there had been debate as to whether the trials should be conducted by the courts which existed prior to 1994, or whether a new court should be established to deal solely with the genocide. The decision was taken to create specialized chambers within the existing structure. These chambers would be established in the Court of First Instance, the court with civil and criminal jurisdiction over the prefectures (provinces) of Rwanda. The first trial began in the prefecture of Kibungo, on 27 December 1996. Held throughout Rwanda, in all ten prefectures, they were public and broadcast on national radio.

The trials, however, were plagued by resource problems – lack of judges, of lawyers, of bad roads to even get to the trials, plus the extraordinarily large numbers waiting for trial. This is not so extraordinary if one considers the nature of the genocide, that while it was state directed, it also was perpetrated within communities, often one-on-one. Yet it has meant for a country devastated by genocide a real problem in terms of how to try this number of people. Six years after the genocide, there were an estimated 130,000 genocide suspects in Rwandan jails, comprising about 90 per cent of all prisoners in Rwanda. Yet the capacity of national detention centres prior to 1994 was 18,000. In the first year of trials, there were 300 tried. In the second year, in 1998, there were 250 tried.[9] This was an incredibly rapid pace, yet still one, that if they had continued in that manner, would have meant taking 100 years to try all those in detention. This led to the government introducing 'gacaca' legislation to address the slow progress and large numbers, in overcrowded Rwandan jails, with the elections of the gacaca judges for the first level held on 4 October 2001.

The gacaca process, drawing on the old communal adjudication system of 'agacaca', has been both perpetrator and victim focused. In its being located communally, and with its focus on reconciliation and forgiveness, it can also be seen to have a broader remit of future-oriented prevention. It has also been a means to get through large numbers of alleged *genocidaires* still in prison over a decade and half since the end of the genocide. Its progress, however, has been uneven, with Human Rights Watch and others reporting concerns as to the conduct of these proceedings, with some survivors coerced into accepting former perpetrators back into the community, and in other instances survivors killed (see Human Rights Watch 2008). The traditional agacaca were based on a high level of trust. In the wake of the genocide, the use of the gacaca raises questions as to whether this trust exists for the system, albeit refashioned, to work.

The Rwandan national legal proceedings have had to tread a fine line between all kinds of pressures: internal pressures between hardliners and the moderates, including from the survivor organization *Ibuka* who have pressed for strict retributive justice, and the external pressure from the international community who favour the international tribunal in Arusha in Tanzania. Yet informal mechanisms pose their dangers too – the former agacaca system was itself based on inequality, with Tutsi leaders being the primary adjudicators. It was in fact not commonly used prior to the genocide. Even for those cases which could conceivably fit within the agacaca framework, people often preferred to go to court.

The most challenging issue in the wake of state crime can be the lack of legal and other resources. This has particularly been the case in Rwanda. In the wake of a genocide that claimed an estimated half to three quarter of a million lives, and that while orchestrated centrally, included many one-on-one killings in communities, the reality is that there will be thousands of perpetrators of heinous crimes, in a country destroyed.

Four years after the genocide, and with over 100,000 in jail, there were only forty-five lawyers in the country, with an estimated ten Rwandan lawyers doing defence work for the genocide trials. Most of the lawyers, however, could not bring themselves to do this work. The non-governmental organization *Avocats sans Frontieres* had a Belgium mission in Rwanda primarily for the provision of defence lawyers, but also for the provision of victims' representatives. The central Prosecution Office in Kigali that focused on the investigation of Category One offenders had only four lawyers early on, and no investigation team. All other case files, thousands of them, were handled by the resident state attorneys in each province – with few resources.

One trial in the province of Kibungo was adjourned twice due to the lack of any legal representation for the victims. It was a trial of thirteen accused, twelve of whom had pleaded guilty. The victims filled the benches in the courtroom – some sixty of them. This was the second time they had attempted to hold the trial. Previously the victims had no legal representation. The court had adjourned so they could obtain some. Knowing this, *Avocats sans Frontieres* had sent a lawyer to this trial, a lawyer from Burundi, to represent them. However, the victims declined him as their representative, because he worked for *Avocats sans Frontieres* who had been supplying the defence lawyers for the trials, and who were supplying a defence lawyer in this trial as well, and as he was not Rwandese. This was not uncommon.[10] The victims thus told the court again that they had no legal representation, that they had sent a letter to the Rwandan Bar for assistance, but had as yet heard no reply. The court adjourned again for a month, with the agreement of all. The judges warned, however, that this was the last adjournment they would sustain.

In another instance, bad roads meant that a trial could not be held. One trial in the commune of Murambi, in the province of Byumba, was held as an 'itinerant trial' mainly due to the fact that the thirty-six accused, who were from this commune, were being detained in a prison at the other side of the province, and the road between the prison and the commune, where the witnesses lived, was so bad that it was physically impossible to convene a continuing trial with both witnesses and defendants. The solution was the itinerant trial, where the three judges, the Public Prosecutor, the two defence lawyers and the victim's representative heard witness testimony *in camera* in the commune itself. Prior to this the defendants had entered their pleas: four had pleaded guilty, the others not guilty. They planned to bring the victims and the defendants together for a few final days of hearing once all witness testimonies had been heard. It was envisaged that this would take a number of months.

The national proceedings have had some international support, but most support has been focused on the International Criminal Tribunal for Rwanda in Arusha. The Tribunal was established by United Nations Security Council Resolution 955, on 8 November 1994. It arose out of the recommendation of the Commission of Experts established in July 1994 to 'examine and analyse ... the evidence of grave violations of international law committed in the territory of Rwanda, including the evidence of possible acts of genocide' (Preliminary Report of the Independent Commission of Experts 1994). This was also the conclusion of the Special Rapporteur of the Commission on Human Rights in Rwanda, who supported the initiation 'as soon as possible' of the 'International Court for Rwanda' set up by the Security Council, as well as the initiation of the 'local courts that are to be established in order to try persons charged with genocide, so as to stop, or at least reduce, acts of reprisals' (Report of the Special Rapporteur 1995). Rwanda had also requested that an international tribunal be established, and decried the 'evident reluctance' of the international community to set up an international tribunal, stating in a letter to the United Nations Security Council from the Permanent Representative of Rwanda to the United Nations, that this is 'tantamount to diluting the question of genocide that was committed in Rwanda' (Permanent Representative of Rwanda 1994: 3–4). It later became less enthusiastic when it realized it would not have the control it desired over such a tribunal, and that the death penalty would not be an available penalty. It eventually voted against the resolution establishing the Tribunal.

A number of points of contention have led to an often strained relationship between the Rwandan government and the Tribunal. On 1 May 1998, the first executions of Rwandans found guilty of genocide and crimes against humanity under Organic Law 08/96 were carried out. The Rwandan criminal code had included the death penalty in punishment (this has now changed), whereas the Tribunal, in compliance with international law, has life imprisonment as its most severe penalty. The treatment that these different groups of defendants receives is also contentious: the overcrowded jails of Rwanda compared with the relative luxury of the detention facility in Arusha.[11] The Tribunal too has been plagued by resource problems and slow processing of cases. Arusha, dusty and small, is better known as a safari town, a place for tourists to stop over en route to game parks and Mount Kilimanjaro. It is five hours by potholed road from Nairobi, and over nine hours from Dar-es-Salaam. The nearest airport, Kilimanjaro, is not on major airline routes. Few people in the town are greatly interested in the Tribunal, and most do not even know that the hearings are public. Stories abounded in the beginning of a lack of basic facilities (phone lines, email, paper supply). While the location of the Tribunal was clearly symbolic (it was in Arusha that the Arusha Peace Agreement, the power-sharing arrangement between the government and the Rwandan Patriotic Front which was meant to end the civil war, which brought the UNAMIR force into Rwanda, and which preceded and indeed triggered the genocide was signed after a year-long negotiation on 4 August 1993) the Tribunal has not been properly resourced. The Secretary General of the United Nations at the time of the Tribunal's establishment, Boutros Boutros-Ghali, wrote of his being guided by the Security Council's preference for an 'African seat' (*The United Nations and Rwanda 1993–1996* 1996: 65).

Most of the evidence has been oral, coming from eyewitness accounts from persons still living in Rwanda. The eyewitness focus presents its own difficulties. The use of phrases such as 'to do the work', and 'to clean out the underbrush' have to be interpreted, as noted by a former head of Prosecution, in light of ideological use and specific cultural allusions. Those documents which exist possess the same ambiguity as other documents used in other genocides, such as the genocide of the Armenians and the Holocaust. The word genocide is never specifically used. Rather, the use of terms such as 'road blocks' and 'self defence', as one Judge of the Court noted, need to be interpreted contextually.

While criticized for its slow progress and small numbers of prosecutions, and in many ways having been treated as the 'poor cousin' of the Yugoslav Tribunal, the Rwandan Tribunal has been important for international law and understandings of genocide. For example, in one of its first judgements, in the trial of Jean-Paul Akayesu, the former mayor of Taba commune, the court found that the acts of rape and sexual violence committed by Akayesu were acts of genocide (*The Prosecutor v. Jean-Paul Akayesu* 1998). This was the first time that rape and sexual violence had been described as a tool of genocide in an international court. Further, the trial and judgement of Kambanda (*The Prosecutor v. Jean Kambanda* 1998) was the first prosecution of a former head of state for genocide, and together, the Akayesu and Kambanda judgements, the first two judgements of the Tribunal, were the first convictions of genocide by an international court.

Legal proceedings for Ethiopia under Mengistu and the Dergue 1974–91

Ethiopia in the wake of the 'Dergue' and the Mengistu regime is an example of almost exclusive perpetrator redress. The arena is dominantly national. Two sets of national criminal legal proceedings were conducted to address the abuses committed during the period of rule by Lieutenant-Colonel Mengistu Haile-Mariam and the Dergue Coordinating Committee of the Armed Forces from 1974 to 1991. These were the 'Dergue trials' covering the seventeen-year military dictatorship, and the 'Red Terror' trials covering the Red Terror period, a concentrated period of abuse that lasted for a few years from 1977 to 1980. In addition there has been at least one Alien Torts Claim conducted in the United States.[12] There has been little international involvement in the national trials which have been largely marginalized by the international community.

In the wake of the defeat of Mengistu by the Ethiopian People's Revolutionary Democratic Front and the Ethiopian People's Liberation Front in 1991, a Special Prosecutor's Office was established under existing national genocide legislation (Article 281 of the *Penal Code of the Empire of Ethiopia* 1957).[13] The Special Prosecutor's Office was established by Proclamation No. 22/1992 on 8 August 1992, to 'conduct investigation and institute proceedings in respect of any person having committed or [been] responsible for the commission of an offence by abusing his position in the party, the government or mass organization under the Dergue-WPE regime' (*Proclamation establishing the Office of the Special Prosecutor* 1992). Theft of property constituted a major part of this investigation.

This, as Greenfield notes, constituted a significant departure from the conclusion to previous changes of power – for example, the massacre of government officials following an attempted coup d'etat against Emperor Haile Selassie in 1960 (Greenfield, in Haile-Mariam 1999: 679). On capturing Addis Ababa, the Ethiopian People's Revolutionary Democratic Front arrested and detained an estimated 2,000 persons believed to have participated in various human rights violations – the Special Prosecutor later characterized his task as being the largest investigation and prosecution of human rights abuses since Nuremberg (Office of the Special Prosecutor, Press Release November 1993, in ibid: 680).

The main Dergue trial began in December 1994. The Dergue trial included the policy-makers, the top government officials, the official Dergue ministers, who later became key provincial leaders. The Dergue trial accused those who were members of the Dergue, the military Congress during the Red Terror period who had seized power in the lull after the revolt against Emperor Haile Selassie I and who took collective decisions on matters including extra-judicial executions. It also charged field commanders, those who gave and received orders. There were approximately 100 members of the Dergue. Forty-four former members were put on trial – the indictment itself contained over 100 names, some of whom were dead when the indictment was prepared, and most of whom were tried *in absentia*. Mengistu himself was given sanctuary in Zimbabwe. In addition to the Dergue trials, the 'Red Terror' trials indicted thousands who were instrumental in implementing these decisions and policies. These were the 'foot soldiers', the rank and file.

The Dergue members were on trial as a group (there was a single indictment document), yet charged separately. They appeared every sitting day as a group. The trial of the Dergue military council began in December 1994 and was conducted every Tuesday and Thursday in Addis Ababa Federal High Court (on the other days, the other Red Terror trials were held). The former military council faced charges of genocide, war crimes and crimes against humanity. The indictment listed 211 charges against the over 100 defendants. In book form, it ran to 268 pages. Dergue members also were charged and appeared in the Red Terror trials. In addition, there were seven trials held outside of the capital, held in the State supreme courts of the different regions delegated by the Central Federal High Court (Haile-Mariam 1999: 691). Many prisoners on trial in the provinces were without files, a claim denied by the Chief Prosecutor. The trials were often adjourned, particularly outside the capital, where prisoners would turn up to be told that their trial is again adjourned – usually due to a lack of judges. A Chamber ruling prohibited critical commentary of these trials. The only public reports of the proceedings were by government journalists who recorded daily proceedings, for newspaper reports as well as broadcasts for the evening news.

Many of the judges were inexperienced. After dismissing almost all judges who were part of the legal system under Mengistu, to fill the vacancies level 8, 9 or lower grade staff members or students from the Civil Service College were chosen to undertake a short 'crash course' of between three to six months in order to take positions as judges. The shortage of judges meant frequent adjournments. It also meant a great lack of experience on the bench. Four years after the trial began, in the three-judge Chamber in the main Dergue trial, the President held a two-year law diploma, which contained no international law subjects, one judge was a fairly recent law graduate, and the other judge, picked from the civil service and put through a three- to six-month judge-training course, did not graduate from high school.

The lack of attention which this set of proceedings was given is striking. It was marginalized by the international community, with international involvement comprising some funding at the beginning and the use of international consultants. As a national attempt to prosecute state crime, it was an important set of proceedings, yet marred significantly by a failure to follow due process. The Dergue trial concluded on 12 December 2006. All but one were found guilty of genocide, all but nine guilty of aggravated homicide, all but one guilty of public incitement to commit genocide, all but twelve found guilty of abuse of power, and all but one guilty of unlawful arrest and detention (Tronvoll et al. 2009: 137–38). The verdict was passed by two judges to one, with the dissenting judge arguing that the defendants should not have been convicted of genocide, as the law of the Dergue allowed for the elimination of political groups (ibid: 138–39).

Legal proceedings for the genocide of the Armenians 1915–18

The central legal proceeding for the Armenian genocide was the Special Military Tribunal ('Courts-Martial'), established on 16 December 1918, which conducted four sets of proceedings until it was disbanded by the new Kemalist government on 11 August 1920. These were national criminal prosecution proceedings. These trials were focused on both immediate perpetrator accountability and in refashioning the Ottoman state through an examination of the institutions that had both brought Turkey into the First World War and committed genocide against the Armenians in Turkey. The Grand Vizier was to point to the truncated but continuing trial of Young Turk leaders as proof of the 'rehabilitation of the Ottoman nation' (Willis 1982: 156). In a post-war session (4 November 1918) of the Turkish Parliament, the Temporary Law of Deportation, used to 'legitimate' the deportations (and thus killings) of the Armenians, was repealed, due to its 'unconstitutionality'. The Courts-Martial was the sole state-conducted legal procedure for the genocide. Since its demise shortly after its establishment, and despite having conducted an estimated twenty-four trials, it was buried due to the denialist stance taken by Turkey which has been supported by much of the world.

The only other proceeding, a non-governmental proceeding, was conducted by the Permanent People's Tribunal in Paris in 1985. More recently, reparations cases have been brought against Turkey on behalf of the Armenian community for property taken, and restitution claimed against insurance companies and banks for non-payment of life insurance policies and for holding money and assets belonging to victims of the genocide.

The Turkish Courts-Martial trials were established and conducted around the view that the Armenians had been intentionally massacred. This is important to note in light of contemporary Turkish denials that such massacres occurred and that any killings were the result of civil war. In fact, as Höss points out, the court in the Yozgat trial rejected the Prosecutor-General's wish to prosecute the accused under Article 56 of the Ottoman Penal Code which 'pertains to ethnic or other groups pitted against each other through atrocities involving mutual slaughter' (Höss 1992: 220). Höss notes that not only did this preclude the prosecution of the Armenian population of Yozgat, but it negated the myth that the Armenians were involved in an insurgency and that the massacres could be classified within the context of justifiable civil war (ibid).

The process of establishing some kind of trial began through the Ottoman parliament. This was in part due to the public outcry at the escape from Istanbul of seven key leaders of the Young Turks, including the 'triumvirate' of Talat Paşa, Enver Paşa and Cemal Paşa, and others including the police and security chiefs. On 2 November 1918, a Deputy in the Chamber of Deputies of the Ottoman Parliament, Fuad, introduced a motion for a trial of the Ministers of the two wartime Cabinets. The motion included as an attachment ten charges against the Ministers. Charges No. 5 and No. 10 related to the killings of the Armenians. The others included aggression, military incompetence, political abuses and economic crimes. No. 5 challenged the enactment of the Temporary Laws, with their associated 'orders and instructions' and subsequent 'disasters' being 'completely contradictory to the spirit and letter of our Constitution'. The Deputy, notes Dadrian, invoked 'the rules of law and humanity' (Dadrian 1997b: 319). Charge No. 10 indicted the Ministers for the creation of 'brigands [çetes] whose assaults on life, property and honour rendered the Ministers guilty as co-perpetrators of the tragic crimes that resulted' (ibid).

Simultaneously, the Senate, the upper chamber of the Ottoman Parliament, also debated the matter of investigating and prosecuting the wartime crimes. Çürüksulu Mahmud Paşa, former Minister of Public Works, submitted a motion, proposing in subsequent debate that investigation of the abuses be related to 'the conduct of internal affairs policy (dahiliye siyaseti) and governance' (ibid: 337).

Two inquiries were subsequently established – the Fifth Committee of the Chamber of Deputies, and what was known as the Mazhar Inquiry Commission. The Fifth Committee conducted hearings, in which Ministers were interrogated. They also gathered key documents, demonstrating the collusion between the military and the executive in the genocide of the Armenians. The Mazhar Commission was charged with investigating the conduct of government officials and also found key documents, in particular telegraphic orders from twenty-eight provinces identified as centres of deportations and massacres. These were all handed over to the Courts-Martial.

The Courts-Martial was established by Imperial authorization on 16 December 1918. On 8 January 1919, the Extraordinary (or Special) Courts-Martial was declared operational. By mid-January 1919, the Inquiry Commission had compiled 130 separate dossiers of suspects, which it forwarded to the Courts-Martial. Its recommendation, as stipulated in the Criminal Procedure Code, was that the evidence was incriminating enough to warrant the commencement of criminal proceedings against the suspects (Dadrian 1997b: 320–21). On 8 March 1919, the statute of the new Courts-Martial was introduced.[14]

All the trials took place in the building of the Ottoman Parliament in Istanbul, in the Great Hall of the Ministry of Justice. Unusually for a courts martial, the proceedings were public. As noted by the presiding judge, this was 'In order to demonstrate the intent of the Court to conduct the trials impartially and in a spirit of lofty justice [*kemali adil ve bitaraf*]' (*Takvimi Vekâyi*, No 3540, cited in ibid: 322). Abstracts were also published daily in the official government newspaper.

The basis of legal proceedings was Ottoman law. The Courts-Martial prosecutors relied on the Ottoman Penal Code for the charges laid. The key charge was 'deportation and massacre'. The indictment as a whole empha-sized that 'the investigation of massacres and illegal, personal profiteering, is the principal task of this Tribunal' (*Takvimi Vekâyi*, No 3540, cited in ibid: 324). Although the charges came from the existing Ottoman Penal Code, their application (to the charge of massacres of the Armenians) was new. One of its chief aims was to establish the systematic manner in which the massacres of the Armenians took place, and to allocate institutional as well as individual responsibility – this can be seen in the organization of the trials.

There were four main series of trials, within the framework of the Courts-Martial: Ittihadist Leaders and Central Committee Members; Ministers of the two Wartime Cabinets; Responsible Secretaries and Delegates (who organized and supervised the deportations) and the 'Special Organization' (those who did the killings); and Officials in provinces where the massacres took place. The first two series of trials were merged after the British took sixty-seven of the prisoners to the islands of Mudros and Malta.

The first series of trials focused on the 'principal co-perpetrators' – the Cabinet Ministers and the leaders of the ruling Ittihad party – Enver, Cemal and Talat. The indictment also focused on institutions – the Ittihad party (particularly its Central Committee – namely Drs Nazim and Şakir), the General Assembly and the two provincial control groups. The Defence Ministry, the War Office (particularly the Special Organization) and the Interior Ministry were also targeted. Importantly, as Dadrian notes, the Young Turk Ittihad party's objectives and methods were declared criminal by the Procuror-General (ibid: 323). In the Key Verdict on 5 July 1919, the Court found the Cabinet Ministers guilty both of orchestrating the entry of Turkey into the First World War, and of committing the genocide of the Armenians. Sentences were handed down on 8 January 1920. Former leaders Talat, Enver, Cemal and Dr Nazim (and Dr Şakir in a separate prosecution on 13 January 1920) were given the death penalty *in absentia* (Willis 1982: 156). Other ministers were given prison sentences of fifteen years. In trials of atrocities perpe-trated in the provinces, Trabzon, Yozgat, Harput, Erzinjan (also known as Erzincan), Baiburt (also known as Bayburt) and Mosul, a handful were executed.

Dadrian estimates that two dozen trials were held. Over 200 files had been prepared on individuals – government, military and Party officials alleged to be participants in the genocide. Yet only twenty-four or so trials were held. As explained earlier in this chapter, with the ascendancy of Kemalism and the change of government, the proceedings were abandoned.

The Allies had promised an international tribunal, and in fact had completed an investigation. The 'Commission on Responsibilities and Sanctions' was established in January 1919 at the Preliminary Peace Congress in Paris, concluding, ' … all persons belonging to enemy countries … who have been guilty of offences against the laws and customs of war or the laws of humanity, are liable to criminal prosecution' (Dadrian 1997b: 305). Despite this, no international trials were held, despite the British holding the sixty-seven alleged war criminals on Mudros and Malta. Rather, the Allies gave little support to the Courts-Martial conducted by Turkey, instead obstructing its progress. What had started as a solid attempt at accountability for crimes perpetrated, ended up, through lack of international will and internal change, marginalized and turned into a denial that the genocide had even occurred.

Legal proceedings for apartheid South Africa 1948–91

At the end of the apartheid regime in 1991, four sets of political-legal proceedings were initiated. The African National Congress conducted two internal non-state inquiries in 1992 and 1993. The South African Truth and Reconciliation Commission was established, with three components – the Human Rights Violations Committee which heard from victims as well as conducting hearings into institutional responsibility for apartheid, the Reparation and Rehabilitation Committee which was the least active of the three, and the Amnesty Committee which heard and decided on applications for amnesty for those involved in 'political' crimes. Limited national criminal trials were held. Further, a new inclusive Constitution for South Africa was drafted. More recently, we have seen a United States Alien Tort Claim proceeding initiated against businesses in South Africa under apartheid. What distinguishes the South African approach has been its dominant focus on societal redress. While the Truth Commission was seen to incorporate victim redress through its ability to disclose information that may otherwise not be available (for example, where individuals were buried, or how they were killed), its focus was consciously on providing a basis for a new South Africa.

South African legal proceedings, apart from the Tort Claim, have been wholly national. The Truth and Reconciliation Commission was an internally initiated national process, although, as its Report notes, the process which led to its formation 'took place within an international framework, which increasingly emphasized the importance of human rights and the need to deal with past human rights violations' (Truth and Reconciliation

Commission of South Africa 1999a: 50). It drew on existing principles, yet formulated them anew.

Despite the existence of an international text under which the former apartheid government could have been prosecuted, the United Nations *Convention on the Suppression and Punishment of the Crime of Apartheid*, this international route was not taken. South Africa decided against criminal trials as the main route. In the main this was a compromise for a peaceful transition, yet as Archbishop Desmond Tutu stated in his introductory remarks to the Final Report, 'Another reason why Nuremberg was not a viable option was because our country simply could not afford the resources in time, money and personnel that we would have had to invest in such an operation' (ibid: 5).

Those criminal trials that were held were not a success. The 'de Kock' trial secured one conviction after a lengthy eighteen-month trial. The 'Malan' trial found General Malan not guilty. The Goniwe inquest examined the death of the Cradock Four, yet according to the authors of the Commission Report, 'failed to answer the numerous questions concerning the death of the "Cradock Four"' (Truth and Reconciliation Commission of South Africa 1999a: 123). Another set of prosecutions came out of the judicial inquiry chaired by Judge Richard Goldstone into the April 1990 Sebokeng Massacre (eleven people were killed and more than 400 injured when South African police fired on a crowd of about 50,000 African National Congress (ANC) supporters in a township outside Johannesburg). However, as Goldstone notes, the criminal trial came to an end when the policemen applied to the Truth and Reconciliation Commission for amnesty (Goldstone 2000: 14–16).

Prior to the establishment of the Truth and Reconciliation Commission there had been two ANC-led commissions (see Hayner 2001: 60–64). These were pushed for by twenty-three former members of the ANC, the Returned Exiles Committee, who had been detained in the ANC camps accused of being agents of the state. In March 1992 ANC President Nelson Mandela appointed the Commission of Enquiry into Complaints by Former African National Congress Prisoners and Detainees, also known as the Skweyiya Commission, for its Chair, T. L. Skweyiya. Its focus was events at ANC detention camps located throughout Southern Africa, including Angola, Tanzania and Zambia. Although initially publicly released, the report, which documented what it termed 'staggering brutality' in ANC camps, was later withdrawn from wider circulation, due to ANC concerns about its accuracy.

A second commission was immediately put together. It ran differently to the first – the hearings were public, they were styled as formal court hearings, with counsel involved, witnesses and the opportunity for defense by the accused. Unlike the first commission, in which two of the three commissioners were ANC members, the new Commission of Enquiry was seen to be independent, with the three commissioners coming from the United States, Zimbabwe and South Africa. The Commission of Enquiry into Certain Allegations of

Cruelty and Human Rights Abuse against ANC Prisoners and Detainees by ANC members was also known as the Motsuenyane Commission, after the President of the commission, retired business leader Dr Samuel M. Motsuenyane. Its report, submitted in August 1993, reached similar conclusions to the first commission, however formatted differently, with a description of each case brought before it, including the names of specific individuals, something the first report did not include. The ANC response was to congratulate the commission on its work, accept its general conclusions (while, as Hayner notes, denying that 'there was any systematic policy of abuse'), and to call for a truth commission to be set up to cover abuses on both sides of the conflict in South Africa since 1948: 'We regard the Skweyiya and Motsuenyane Commission Reports as a first step in a process of national disclosure of all violations of human rights from all sides' (ibid: 64).

The Truth and Reconciliation Commission of South Africa was based on the final clause of the Interim Constitution of 1993 in which it is written, 'The pursuit of national unity, the well-being of all South African citizens and peace require reconciliation between the people of South Africa and the reconstruction of society', to 'transcend the divisions and strife of the past', of the 'need for ubuntu ["community, in the sense of restoring right relationships between people"] but not for victimisation' (*Constitution of the Republic of South Africa* 1993). The then South African Minister of Justice, Dullah Omar, summarized the mandate of the Commission as follows:

> Establishing as complete a picture as possible of the causes, nature and extent of the gross violations of human rights which were committed during the period from 1 March 1960 to the cut-off date including the antecedents, circumstances, factors and context of such violations, as well as the perspectives of the victims and the motives and perspectives of the persons responsible for committing such violations, by conducting investigations and holding hearings.
>
> (Omar 1995)

The Act subsequently passed in Parliament was titled the Promotion of National Unity and Reconciliation Act, No 34 of 1995 (26 July 1995), which provided for the establishment of a Truth and Reconciliation Commission, a Committee on Human Rights Violations, a Committee on Amnesty and a Committee on Reparation and Rehabilitation.[15] The investigation of apartheid was a clear aim of the Commission. In choosing a path of provision of amnesties, a choice was made that would elicit the most information. As it stated in its Final Report, presented to President Nelson Mandela on 29 October 1998:

> The issue is not ... a straight trade-off between amnesty and criminal or civil trials. What is at stake, rather, is a choice between more or less full

disclosure; the option of hearing as many cases as possible against the possibility of a small number of trials revealing, at best, information only directly relevant to specific charges.

(Truth and Reconciliation Commission of
South Africa 1999a: 122)

Yet it was also clearly a choice of political necessity, to avoid civil war. As Dumisa B. Ntsebexa notes, the amnesty provision came at the end of a four-year-long negotiation process that itself was a consequence of a political compromise between the contending parties (Ntsebexa 2000: 158). The process was marked by compromise in the hope of orchestrating a peaceful transition. It was known, for instance, that members of the apartheid security establishment would impede such a transition if 'Nuremberg-style' trials were held.[16]

The provision of amnesty was contested, with a number of legal challenges to the Commission. The first of these was filed jointly by the Azanian People's Organisation (AZAPO), the Biko, Mxenge and Ribeiro families, challenging the constitutionality of the amnesty provision of the Truth and Reconciliation Commission. They sought an order from the Constitutional Court declaring the amnesty provision (s 20(7)) of the Promotion of National Unity and Reconciliation Act 34 of 1995 unconstitutional (*Azanian Peoples Organisation (AZAPO) and Others* 1996). They were unsuccessful, with Chief Justice DP Mahomed noting the following in judgement:

> Much of what transpired in this shameful period is shrouded in secrecy and not easily capable of objective demonstration and proof ... Secrecy and authoritarianism have concealed the truth in little crevices of obscurity in our history. Records are not easily accessible; witnesses are often unknown, dead, unavailable or unwilling. All that often effectively remains is the truth of wounded memories of loved ones sharing instinctive suspicions, deep and traumatising to the survivors but otherwise incapable of translating themselves into objective and corroborative evidence which could survive the rigours of the law.
>
> (*Azanian Peoples Organisation (AZAPO) and Others* 1996,
> *Judgment*: para 17)

Yet it also saw itself doing something more than pure investigation of apartheid. It saw itself as a vehicle for societal reconstruction. This was a critical part of its mandate. It was orchestrated both through the individual human rights violations hearings, where individuals had a chance to tell their story, and through the institutional hearings, which heard submissions from individuals and organizations as to the behaviour of a range of government and non-government institutions in apartheid South Africa, from the medical and legal professions, to the Church.

In this, it can be seen as both encompassing perpetrator and victim redress – finding out what was done, who did it, who was harmed – as well as an institutional and societal redress, through both its sets of recommendations aimed at institutional change that came out of its final report as well as its mandate to 'bring South Africans together'.

Law addressing state crime: a typology

We can establish a typology of law in the wake of state crime and genocide, ranging from the marginalization or absence of law, to the utilization of law in the wake of the harm committed:

- Law marginalized at the national and the international levels (Cambodia legal proceedings until recently, Turkey after demise of Courts-Martial);
- Law marginalized at the national, active at the international (former Yugoslavia legal proceedings);
- Law active at the national, marginalized at the international (Ethiopia legal proceedings; Turkey post-First World War; South Africa legal proceedings);
- Law active at the national and at the international (Rwanda legal proceedings; Holocaust legal proceedings).

Law marginalized at the national and the international levels

The use of law in addressing the crimes of the Khmer Rouge has not been a strong one at the national level. While Vietnam engaged in immediate legal redress, the trial was in the main a show trial, designed to herald the end of the Khmer Rouge regime, rather than provide any sustained accountability. This was demonstrated through the inclusion of Khmer Rouge soldiers at all levels, as well as the trial being held without Pol Pot and Ieng Sary actually in attendance. The weak use of law nationally combined with the absence, until recently, of action at the international level in establishing a joint Cambodia-United Nations criminal tribunal, has meant the marginalization of law in addressing this state crime. Political changes in Turkey in the wake of the First World War meant the marginalization of the key legal proceedings to address the genocide of the Armenians, the Courts-Martial. What had been largely recognized as a crime became subject to denial until today the fact that there was a legal proceeding to address the state crime perpetrated by the Ottoman state has been mostly forgotten.[17]

Law marginalized at the national, active at the international

The use of law in addressing the conflict in Yugoslavia, has, mostly, been weak at the national level. The action has been at the international level, yet at such a distance, and with little national cooperation, that it has mostly failed to change norms nationally. Law here is a reference point for the international community, but not for the national community. As mostly perpetrator and victim focused, it has also failed to substantially change institutional structures nationally.

Law active at the national, marginalized at the international

The addressing by the incumbent Ethiopian government of the crimes of the Mengistu regime was a strong one, yet weakened through its lack of adherence to due process, resulting in a compromised and slow process. This is in contrast to almost complete disinterest internationally. Turkey started a strong response to the genocide against the Armenians, yet due to the change of regime and lack of international support and in fact, obstruction, this changed to a lack of redress nationally, as well as internationally, with the promised tribunal of the Allies not eventuating. South Africa had an active response nationally, with its truth commission. The international played no role in redress, however, despite international instruments such as the Apartheid Convention.

Law active at the national and at the international

Legal responses to the genocide in Rwanda and to the Holocaust are both examples of active national and international legal responses to state crime. In Rwanda, we have both a sustained national programme of criminal trials and community reconciliation proceedings, however, these have been marginalized by the international community due to the challenges of putting such large numbers on trial, as well as a sustained legal process at the international level through the International Criminal Tribunal for Rwanda, which has been weakened also due to small numbers of defendants and long time periods. In the wake of the Second World War we have had a strong international response that began immediately, the International Military Tribunal at Nuremberg, together with the military trials run by the United States, Britain, France and the Soviet Union. This was coupled with a somewhat delayed national response at the national level, yet which picked up in the late 1960s with a change to the statute of limitations and which has been coupled with some 'other-state' criminal trials throughout the world as well as increased civil proceedings which have resulted in delayed victim redress initiatives.

Conclusion

We see different strengths and weaknesses in approaches to law addressing state crime – but we do see law as a tool of governance, a break between the old and the new. It is a choice to use law. Law is subject to political realities and to its place. Law's impact is dependent on these.

We also see a mix of perpetrator and victim initiated redress and a broader institutional and societal redress. There is clearly more of the former, yet in the drafting of new Constitutions, and of some legislation, and in larger and more holistic inquiries such as the Truth and Reconciliation Commission of

South Africa, we see attempts to reshape a society in the wake of state crime. The following chapter considers the extent to which these legal processes address the parameters of the state crime and what accountability for state crime looks like. It considers the key challenge to law – to address these crimes as crimes of state. It argues for a more specific approach to these crimes of the state, an approach that recognizes the particular parameters of mass harm and works towards full accountability and towards prevention.

Notes

1 In the wake of the genocide, Cyprian Fisiy noted that for most refugees and returning Hutu, especially men, there was the constant threat of arrest based on the assumption that they were guilty of massacres; otherwise they would have been killed during the genocide (Fisiy 1998: 23–24).
2 Until July 25, 1997, Pol Pot had not been seen by foreign journalists since 1979, when he was filmed by Naoki Mabuchi, a Japanese photographer with close ties to the Khmer Rouge (Thayer 1997b). The Khmer Rouge defense minister Son Sen had been negotiating with Prince Norodom Ranariddh for a face-saving way to bring the remaining rebels into an alliance with Ranariddh's Funcinpec party. Pol Pot had ordered the execution of Son Sen and about a dozen family members on June 9 – this is believed to have led to his trial. Ta Mok subsequently concluded the Funcinpec deal on July 4 (Hajari 1997).
3 Randolph Braham has noted that the 'tragedy of individual Jewish communities in Trianon Hungary was exposed in the war crimes trials held between 1945 and 1948 under the auspices of people's tribunals in Budapest and various country seats' (Braham 1996: 208, cited in Balint 2010: 291).
4 In 1991 a citizen's movement, with a mandate of 'eliminating the Killers and Collaborators of 1971', demanded a trial of Golam Azam, the head of the Jamaat-e-Islami Party for complicity in the 1971 killings. With no official response, a public non-official trial was held (Ganguly 1995: 167–78; Jahan 1995; Ahmed 1996).
5 Dallaire and his deputy Brigadier Henry Kwami Anyidoho were to defy the United Nations Security Council on this, keeping 456 men in Rwanda (Dallaire gave everyone the option of leaving). Dallaire had asked for a force of 1,200 but the United Nations had agreed to only 270. See Melvern 2000: 174.
6 The Commission was given extremely limited resources, and was terminated early, all factors which pointed to the political context in which some of the main perpetrators, namely Serbian leader Slobodan Milošević, and Bosnian Serb leaders Radovan Karadžić and Ratko Mladić, were deemed necessary partners in a peace deal. For further discussion of the Commission's work and difficulties, see Bassiouni 1996.
7 The Chamber and the Ombudsman were mandated to consider [the Chamber through public hearings], all alleged or apparent violations of human rights as provided in the European Convention for the Protection of Human Rights and Fundamental Freedoms and the Protocols thereto [Article II. 2 (a)], or alleged or apparent discrimination on any ground such as sex, race, colour, language, religion, political or other opinion, national or social origin, association with a national minority, property, birth or other status arising in the enjoyment of any of the rights and freedoms provided for in the international agreements listed in the Appendix to this Annex, where such violation is alleged or appears to have

been committed by the Parties, including by any official or organ of the Parties, Cantons, Municipalities, or any individual acting under the authority of such official or organ [Article II. 2 (b)]. Agreement on Human Rights, Annex 6, General Framework Agreement 1995.

8 As evidenced in part by discussions had by Mahmood Mamdani with Rwandan officials in July 1995 (Mamdani 1996). The situation however rapidly changed with the removal from the government of Hutu leaders, and the subsequent consolidation of hardliner policy.

9 Not all those tried were found guilty. Of the 550 people tried in 1997 and 1998, twenty per cent were acquitted of charges of genocide, twenty per cent were given the death penalty, twenty per cent sentenced to a short period of imprisonment, and forty per cent sentenced to life imprisonment (*Avocats sans Frontieres Annual Report* 1998).

10 The non-governmental organization *Avocats sans Frontieres* developed a poster in conjunction with the Rwandan government. It depicts an ordinary Rwandan courtroom, with the defence lawyer standing before the three-judge Bench, and the room full of victims and observers. The writing around the picture reads (in Kinyarwanda): 'The defence lawyer is not a friend of the accused. He is a friend of justice'.

11 This was highlighted in one notable motion which had the defence counsel of one accused asking the Chamber to order the Commander of the detention facility to provide his client with a particular type of yoghurt milk, which led to a series of exchanges: Chamber to the defence counsel: 'Point out in Article 20 [of the Statute] the exact obligation whereby the Commander of the Facility must buy yoghurt milk for your client.' Chamber to the Commander of the detention facility: 'Can a decision by the Chamber help in regard to your procuring the second type of yoghurt milk?'. International Criminal Tribunal for Rwanda, Arusha, 11 December 1998.

12 There has been a successful United States Alien Tort Claim: *Abebe-Jira v. Negewo* (1996) in which US$500,000 was awarded to each of three plaintiffs for injuries suffered in the late 1970s under the Dergue military dictatorship.

13 Art. 281. Genocide; Crimes against Humanity. *Penal Code of the Empire of Ethiopia* (1957):

> Whosoever, with intent to destroy, in whole or in part, a national, ethnic, racial, religious or political group, organizes, order or engages in, be it in time of war or in time of peace:
>
> 1. Killings, bodily harm or serious injury to the physical or mental health of members of the group, in any way whatsoever; or
> 2. Measures to prevent the propagation or continued survival of its members or their progeny; or
> 3. The compulsory movement or dispersion of peoples or children, or their placing under living conditions calculated to result in their death or disappearance, is punishable with rigorous imprisonment from five years to life, or, in cases of exceptional gravity, with death.

14 There was debate in the Parliament, the press, and during the first two sittings of the military tribunal, as to whether the defendants should be prosecuted before the High Court, before the Military Tribunal, or regular criminal courts. It was concluded by the prosecution that as martial law as implemented by the Ittihadists on April 12/25 1909 was still in force (and according to Article 113 of the Ottoman

Constitution this meant that civil laws are suspended), the Courts-Martial were the only option (see Dadrian 1997b).

15 The Act was subsequently amended: Promotion of National Unity and Reconciliation Amendment Act, No. 87 of 1995 (linguistic changes); Promotion of National Unity and Reconciliation Amendment Act, No. 18 of 1997 (increasing the size of the Amnesty Committee); Promotion of National Unity and Reconciliation Second Amendment Act, No. 84 of 1997 (again increasing the size of the Amnesty Committee).

16 Alex Boraine writes that in a private interview with Nelson Mandela, Thabo Mbeki made clear that senior generals of the security forces had personally warned Mandela of dire consequences if members of the security forces had to face compulsory trials and prosecutions following the election. According to Mandela, they threatened to make a peaceful election totally impossible (Boraine 2000: 143–44).

17 This is compounded by the lack of access to complete transcripts of the Courts-Martial. Information about the Courts-Martial is taken from excerpts published at the time in the official government paper, *Takvim-i-Vekâyi,* the 'Official Gazette'. These excerpts have been read and translated by Vahakn Dadrian, upon whose work I primarily rely for information on the Courts-Martial.

Chapter 4

Accountability and responsibility

Addressing the state and institutions

The Truth and Reconciliation Commission of South Africa hearings into the role of the media during the apartheid regime confirmed, through testimony given by Sampie Terreblanche, a former South African Broadcasting Corporation board member, the use of the Broadcasting Corporation as an instrument of government, through its being the 'propaganda arm' of successive National Party governments (Truth and Reconciliation Commission of South Africa 1999b: 172). It was also shown, through evidence given by former State agent Major Craig Williamson, that a 'special relationship' existed between the Broadcasting Corporation and the intelligence community (ibid: 173). Most importantly, the Final Report concluded that 'the former state was the major violator' (Truth and Reconciliation Commission of South Africa 2003: 615). As it showed, through testimony given at the Commission:

> patterns of abuse manifested themselves throughout South Africa in much the same way. These were not isolated incidents or the work of mavericks or 'bad apples'; they were the product of a carefully orchestrated policy, designed to subjugate and kill the opponents of the state.
> (Truth and Reconciliation Commission of South Africa 2003: 617)

State crimes, that is, gross and systematic human rights violations by the state, are committed as part of state policy and using state and non-state institutions. These crimes are not committed by a loose configuration of individuals who conspire to commit such a crime. While perpetrated by individuals, they are committed within the framework of the state, or the emerging state, which has harnessed core institutions to carry out this policy.

Carried out 'in the name of the state', they involve the use and transformation of a state structure and its institutions, both civil and state.

Head of State Hitler never signed his name to documents regarding the deportation and extermination of Jews; however, it is known, through knowledge of the command structure of the German state 1933–45, that such documents had Hitler's implicit approval. Central decisions were made by a small group of individuals, the elite at the top of the SS (Schutzstaffel) hierarchy, and carried out by a wider group of German and non-German functionaries, also individuals. However, they were carried out in the name of the German state and according to its ideology, National Socialism. Importantly, they were also carried out within the framework of the institutions of the German state. Without such involvement and without such a framework, the scope of the killing would not have been so great. The murder of civilians was state policy, and as such, although perpetrated and orchestrated by individuals, constituted an act of state.

The genocide against the Armenians by the Turkish state under cover of the First World War can be compared. The instructions as to the deportation and killing of the Armenians were sent directly from Head of State Talat Paşa (and the others in the ruling 'triumvirate', Enver Paşa and Cemal Paşa) to deputies in the provinces. These instructions were in the form of telegrams, and most were somewhat coded. A few, however, are explicit and bear his signature as head of the Turkish state at the time. The Courts-Martial proceedings acknowledge this: one witness spoke of 'doing government business' (Höss 1992: 220). It is clear that the destruction of the Armenians was a policy of the Turkish state at the time. It was integral to the pan-Turkish ideology of the state, a 'mystical vision of blood and race' that sought a Greater [homogenous] Turkey and was a repudiation of Ottomanism (Astourian 1992: 69). As Stephan Astourian notes, the *Aghed* [the genocide of the Armenians] is an essential part of Kemalist Turkey's birth certificate (ibid). It was carried out by individuals, yet not just any individuals, but soldiers and officers in the Turkish army. As such, it was carried out within the framework of the institutions of the state.

Apartheid South Africa, the genocide of the Armenians, and the Holocaust of European Jewry are the clearest examples of an entire state structure being mobilized in order to commit state crime. However, all systematic state crime is committed as part of state policy and using state institutions. Perpetrated by individuals, state crime is committed 'in the name of the state'. The word used in criminal tribunals is 'conspiracy' or 'common plan'. Whether implicit or explicit, it is a crime that bears the 'letterhead' of the state, emerging or existent. Despite this, there has been little conceptualization of state crime in the law of international crime. Our approaches are still mostly individual. While there has been an attempt to locate individuals within their organizational structures, we are still largely using models of individual accountability to address state crime. This is despite the particular character of state crime – the involvement of institutions, the co-opting of populations – incurring a broad spectrum of responsibility not usually engaged with by the mechanism of the criminal trial of individuals or truth commissions that rely on individual testimony.

This is not a new criticism. Hannah Arendt and Judith Shklar both raised it, questioning how it is that the ordinary criminal trial, even those at

Nuremberg with their 'extraordinary' characteristics, could address institutional crime (Arendt 1954: 310; Shklar 1964: 192). Both found fault with the mechanism of a criminal trial, arguing that this vehicle could not encompass the breadth of what had been perpetrated.

This chapter considers this issue of state crime as involving institutions, both state and non-state, and the challenge this poses to law and accountability. In legal redress for state crime we can observe some attempts at a broader addressing of its institutional parameters. These range from 'grouping' individuals responsible into their organizational affiliation and the criminalization of institutions at the International Military Tribunal at Nuremburg, to the non-criminal examination of institutions at the Truth and Reconciliation Commission of South Africa. These cases, and others, are covered in detail later in this chapter. Yet while we may see individuals placed according to institutional affiliation, the institution itself, and the state, is rarely specifically addressed.

Institutions may be religious institutions, the institutions of business, and other institutions of civil society and public governance. For example, we see both state and non-state involvement in the apartheid regime in South Africa. Some of these institutions were indeed targeted by the South African Truth and Reconciliation Commission in its institutional hearings, for example the role of the Dutch Reform Church. The role of the Catholic Church in the deeper acceptance of discrimination against and exclusion of Jews in Germany from 1933 has been explored by many scholars (see Lewy 1964). So too the horrific participation of the medical profession, particularly during the Holocaust and the Armenian genocide (see Dadrian 1986; Lifton 1986).

In considering current approaches to addressing the institutional dimensions of state crime and the challenge to law, the chapter charts a relationship between causation, responsibility and liability, and proposes a distinction between individual criminal liability and institutional civic liability. The first section considers the relationship between individual and institutional accountability. The different legal approaches to state crime are then charted in terms of their individual and institutional focus, with a discussion of the emerging practice of addressing structural causes. Four approaches that address the institutional parameters are discussed – the International Military Tribunal at Nuremberg, the 'associations' of the United States Military Trials at Nuremberg, the lustration processes in post-communist Europe, and the investigation of institutions at the Truth and Reconciliation Commission of South Africa. The chapter concludes with a discussion of the concept of 'civic liability', aimed at the redress and transformation of institutions in the wake of state crime.

State crime, individual crime and the law

The parameters of state crime are structurally different to those of ordinary domestic or national crime. These are crimes, drawing on the genesis of the international legal concept of 'crimes against humanity', that are violations of human rights on a sufficiently savage or systematic scale. When systematic violations are committed by the state or emerging state, this requires the participation and potential transformation of some if not all of the institutions of the state, including the development of institutions by the state or branches of the state for this purpose. We see this in the formation of the *Interahamwe* 18 months prior to the genocide in Rwanda, and its transformation into an armed militia by the ruling post-independence party, the MNRD (National Revolutionary Movement for Democracy and Development). The *Interahamwe*, mainly comprised of youth, did much of the killing in the genocide in Rwanda.

What makes these crimes particular is not necessarily the numbers of individual perpetrators, but rather their place in the life of a nation: these are crimes committed 'in the name of the state' (the existing state or state to be), utilizing state or state-like institutions, and committed as part of state or emerging state policy. Individuals killing individuals is not what identifies this kind of crime. They are not rape plus murder plus displacement, but crimes committed as a whole package of destruction and displacement of nations, groups and peoples. They of necessity harness and transform institutions and engage and are rooted in particular ideologies and structural inequalities and histories.

State responsibility already exists for certain acts. Namely, for failing to honour a treaty, for violating the territorial sovereignty of another state, for damaging the territory or property of another state, for employing armed force against another state, for injuring the diplomatic representatives of another state, and for mistreating the nationals of another state (Harris 2004: 505). It is also a principle of international law, as articulated in the 2001 International Law Commission's Draft Articles on State Responsibility, Article One, that 'every internationally wrongful act of a State entails the international responsibility of that State'. According to the International Law Commission's Commentary to the Draft Articles on State Responsibility, this principle is one most strongly upheld by State practice and judicial decisions and most deeply rooted in the doctrine of international law. It is also understood, as the 2001 International Law Commission's Draft Articles note in their commentary to Article 31, that failure to meet convention obligations, and thus commit a 'wrongful act' involves an obligation to make reparations – that this is the indispensable complement of a failure to apply a convention.

What we do not have in law, however, is a concept of state crime. The discussion in the international law literature has focused on whether a state can be criminally liable, the legal conclusion from certain acts of states being labeled 'international crimes'. The idea of state crime, as discussed in Chapter 1, had originally been considered by the International Law Commission. It considered this in its deliberations on creating a framework of state responsibility. Rapporteur James Crawford noted the 'reality that State structures may be involved in wholesale criminal conduct – in genocide, in attempts to extinguish States and to expel or enslave their peoples' (Crawford 1998: 7). The principle of state criminal responsibility and the recognition of state crime was, however, abandoned.

Individual and institutional responsibility

The inclusion of individual responsibility for international crimes had been viewed by the international law community as immensely progressive. As Otto Triffterer notes, international law, particularly since the Second World War, has emphasized exercising jurisdiction over individuals rather than states (Triffterer 1986: 101). It thus may appear paradoxical that after the fight to have individual responsibility accepted, the argument is now being made that a strong principle of state and institutional responsibility is just as important. Acceptance of both, however, need not be contradictory. An argument for recognition of state institutional parameters of state crime is not an argument for the abolition or the tempering of individual responsibility.

It is irrefutable that certain key leaders were primarily responsible for particular state crime – Hitler for the Holocaust, Pol Pot for the killings in Cambodia, Mengistu for the killings and repression in Ethiopia, and so on. It has been established in international law that the three core crimes of genocide, crimes against humanity and war crimes, as well as torture, in both times of war and peace, are international crimes which have risen to the level of *jus cogens* (of which no violations are permitted), and that there exists therefore an inderogable obligation to prosecute or extradite. This was confirmed with the decision of the House of Lords that crimes committed by Augusto Pinochet while presiding over a repressive military regime as President of Chile are extraditable crimes.

A move to recognition of state responsibility does not cancel out individual liability. The International Law Commission in its deliberations on this topic explicitly stated that state responsibility should not replace individual responsibility. It is clear that in order to investigate institutions one must deal with the individuals within these institutions: otherwise, for example, the institution may well be dismantled in form but be reassembled under another guise. This appears to be the result of the policy of lustration in some former Communist countries, whereby, as in the case of post-communist Poland, former leaders established new networks outside of the political sphere, and continued to exercise substantial influence (see Łoś & Zybertowicz 2000).

A kind of collective liability is not what is sought; the 'responsibility of all and hence the responsibility of none' as Dwight MacDonald put it in his scathing analysis of American responsibility for crimes in the Vietnam War (Macdonald 1957: 33). Rather, it is to point to the particular characteristics of such crime, and thus to a different remedial path to that ordinarily taken with individual crimes or of international crimes such as bribery of foreign public officials or drug offences which are not necessarily crimes of state in a way that genocide and apartheid are. It is a path that asks that we look to the multi-layered components of the crime, individual and institutional, and to remedies that allocate accountability, criminal and non-criminal. It is a path that has been taken and suggested with regard to corporate crime (see Fisse & Braithwaite 1993).

Both institutions and individuals, according to their placement, role and activity bear differing levels of responsibility and potential liability. However all three levels (state, institutional and individual responsibility) are of importance in addressing state crime. Addressing the state means addressing both the individuals and the institutions. The scope of these crimes could not have been as large without harnessing and transforming key societal institutions. In order to address state crime in its totality, the individual participants and the state and its institutions, as well as other large institutional bodies, must all be addressed. This is both in order to address the crime as a whole, as well as to provide for reconstruction and prevention. An individual focus alone fails to acknowledge the particular parameters of state crime and to unravel the many layers of responsibility, accountability, knowledge and complicity.

Individuals and institutions: legal approaches to state crime

We can identify the dominant approaches to legal redress for state crime as follows:

Addressing individual perpetrators as individuals and in their organizational capacity. Examples are the International Criminal Tribunal for the former Yugoslavia, the International Criminal Tribunal for Rwanda, Rwandan national criminal trials, the Extraordinary Chambers in the Courts of Cambodia, and the Revolutionary People's Tribunal of the People's Republic of Kampuchea.

Addressing individual perpetrators as members of groups or organizations. Examples are the International Military Tribunal at Nuremberg, United States Military Trials at Nuremberg, the Ottoman State Special Military Tribunal, Lustration processes in post-communist Eastern Europe, the trial of the Dergue military council in Ethiopia, and some joinder indictments at the International Criminal Tribunal for Rwanda.

Addressing the state as the state. An example is the International Court of Justice case: *Bosnia and Herzegovina v. Serbia-Montenegro.*

And the approaches we see emerging are:

Addressing institutions, institutional responsibility and individuals. Examples are the Truth and Reconciliation Commission of South Africa, the East

Timor Commission for Reception, Truth and Reconciliation, and the Indonesia-Timor Leste Commission of Truth and Friendship.

Addressing individual perpetrators as members of communities. Examples are the Rwandan Gacaca proceedings, and the Community Reconciliation Process within the East Timor Commission for Reception, Truth and Reconciliation.

Addressing structural dimensions to state crime. Examples are the Truth and Reconciliation Commission of South Africa Final Report recommendations and institutional hearings, the Guatemalan socio-economic accord, the Timor-Leste Commission for Reception, Truth and Reconciliation Final Report recommendations, the Final Report of the Truth and Reconciliation Commission of Peru, the Final Report of the Commission on Historical Clarification of Guatemala, the Truth and Reconciliation Commission of Liberia institutional hearings and recommendations, and the Truth and Reconciliation Commission of Sierra Leone recommendations. This is in addition to general societal-based redress such as new constitutions, new legislation and new citizenship frameworks.

As we have seen, it is individual perpetrators and individual victims who are heard and spoken about in criminal trials or truth commissions. Even so, there is often some attempt to place individual perpetrators within their organizational role – as heads of states, as army commanders and as state officials. In this way, it could be argued, there have been attempts to get to the institutional nature of this kind of crime. Further, there have been attempts to note, if not fully address, the structural dimensions of state crime, the causal factors that can directly contribute to mass harm.

Slobodan Milošević was brought to trial as a former head of state, and his charges (for Kosovo, Bosnia-Herzegovina and Croatia) were deliberately joined (see *The Prosecutor v. Slobodan Milošević*). In this way, the breadth of what had been perpetrated was designed to be illustrated, including his decision making as head of state. The first two judgements of the International Criminal Tribunal for Rwanda, the trial of former mayor Jean Paul Akayesu (*The Prosecutor v. Jean-Paul Akayesu*) and the former Rwandan Prime Minister Jean Kambanda (*The Prosecutor v. Jean Kambanda*), illustrate clearly the manner in which the genocide was perpetrated as state-directed, and locate the crimes committed by these two officials within the wider context of the genocide. Similarly, the charges of both direct and public incitement to commit genocide and crimes against humanity against former editor in chief of the *Kangura* newspaper, Hassan Ngeze, at the International Criminal Tribunal, were directly linked to his position as editor.

In the first trial at the criminal tribunal for the crimes perpetrated by the Khmer Rouge, the 'Extraordinary Chambers in the Courts of Cambodia for the Prosecution of Crimes Committed During the Period of Democratic Kampuchea', the prosecution of Kaing Guek Eav (alias 'Duch') focused on his role chairing the headquarters of the Khmer Rouge Special Branch of the secret police, running the Tuol Sleng prison in Phnom Penh.

At the Ottoman State Special Military Tribunal, the 'Courts-Martial', the defendants were grouped according to their position in the state, their institutional affiliation, and their role in the genocide of the Armenians. This was explicit recognition of the connection between individuals and the institutions with which they were affiliated. Individuals were grouped and put on trial in the following categories – Ministers of the two Wartime Cabinets, Ittihadist Leaders, Central Committee Members, Responsible Secretaries and Delegates, and various local officials (the Trabzon Officials case for example).

This was the situation too at the International Military Tribunal at Nuremberg, in which the main group of defendants was linked to a list of organizations and institutions of Nazi Germany, yet still tried as individuals. The indictment of the International Military Tribunal against twenty-four former Nazi officials was directed against them 'Individually and as Members of Any of the Following Groups or Organizations to which They Respectively Belonged' (International Military Tribunal 1947–49: 27). A further innovation of the Tribunal was the criminalization of the organizations of which the individuals on trial had been members. This was a specific tactic, devised by the United States in the pre-Nuremberg meetings, partly in order to get through the thousands of potential accused and to address the 'common plan' of the Nazi crimes.

At the separate United States Military Trials at Nuremberg, defendants were grouped into significant 'associations', with a further three trials held that addressed corporations that collaborated with the Nazi state – I.G. Farben, Krupp and Flick. In all of these, individuals were put on trial. Further, members of groups or organizations declared criminal at the International Military Tribunal at Nuremberg could automatically be brought to these military trials.

Similarly, the former members of the Dergue military council of the Mengistu regime in Ethiopia were indicted as a group, appearing every day together, yet charged separately. As stated in the indictment, this was to demonstrate their functioning as a group.

At the Ottoman State Special Military Tribunal, the Dergue trials in Ethiopia, the Extraordinary Chambers in the Courts of Cambodia, the International Military Tribunal at Nuremberg and the United States Military Trials at Nuremberg, the procedural organization was based around the official position of the actors in the conflict. However, indictments were brought against defendants as individuals first, and as members of particular organizations second. Their institutional affiliation was an important statement, and legitimized their individual prosecution, yet in terms of their trials was used primarily as an organizational tool. At the International Military Tribunal at Nuremberg, criminalization of institutions was a mechanism to gather more evidence against individuals and to secure individual convictions: the institutions themselves were examined, however only in the context of individual criminalization.

The 'joinder' indictments at the International Criminal Tribunal for Rwanda that brought individuals together in one trial can be placed in the same category, as both an organizational tool for the prosecution of these individuals, yet also one that painted a picture of the genocide. As noted by officials at the Tribunal, midway through the Tribunal's investigations it became apparent that the evidence implied a structured and systematic plan of genocide, both by government and non-governmental institutions. There was evidence of a conspiracy from the top down to the militia groups. Teams were then formed to investigate the units responsible for the genocide, and to identify the individuals responsible in these particular institutions. The investigation teams, which formed the basis of the 'joinder' indictments submitted by the Prosecution to the Chamber included ones that examined the military, political parties and extremists, government senior officers, sexual assaults, and media and propaganda in the genocide in Rwanda. The evidence collected by the Tribunal of meetings between senior government officials, of machetes distributed throughout regions from top to regional military commanders, the evidence of incitement in radio and print from the top, all collected by the Tribunal, pointed to a clear government plan.

Yet in the above examples, while the individual is placed according to institutional affiliation and institutional role in the perpetration of the state crime, what we see little of is a specific addressing of the institutions involved, both state and non-state. Nor do we see the allocation of state responsibility. While an individual judgement may provide an important account of a particular conflict, the form of the criminal trial means that any accountability will rest only with the individual – there is no possibility of the allocation of a wider accountability.

The only legal forum where states, not individuals, can be held legally accountable for state crime is the International Court of Justice in the Hague. This court, established in 1945 (the successor to the League of Nations' Permanent Court of International Justice) is an avenue for state liability, a body of arbitration designed to settle legal disputes brought to it by states. Importantly, it was nominated as the place to bring cases of genocide in the Genocide Convention. It is, however, despite being the self-proclaimed principal judicial organ of the United Nations, rarely used to address state responsibility for state crime.

Apart from an advisory opinion issued by the Court in 1951 allowing reservations to the Genocide Convention, there has been only one genocide case heard at the International Court of Justice, brought in 1993 by Bosnia and Herzegovina against Serbia and Montenegro – *Application of the Convention on the Prevention and Punishment of the Crime of Genocide (Bosnia and Herzegovina v. Serbia and Montenegro)*. The now permanent International Criminal Court cannot find responsibility for a state, only individuals.

Critically, only states can bring cases to the International Court of Justice or be parties to cases at the Court. The genocide case brought by Bosnia and Herzegovina against Serbia and Montenegro was unusual. States rarely bring actions against other states for actions of genocide or other state crime, as shown by the failure to bring proceedings against Cambodia in the 1980s. Further, victim communities are rarely in a position to bring an action for state crime. The International Court of Justice case brought by Bosnia and Herzegovina was only possible due to the nation-state status Bosnia-Herzegovina now holds, a status due only to the war in the former Yugoslavia, which is the reason Bosnia-Herzegovina brought an action to the Court.

The other approach currently available is a political-legal one that engages the community. In these newer approaches to state crime, we see a broader identification of state crime perpetrators and conspirators. This can range from core individuals to institutions and states. We also see new ways of addressing state crime that move away from the traditional prosecutorial model and towards initiating broader structural change.

An example of this was the South African Truth and Reconciliation Commission which held hearings that focused on the institutions that supported apartheid and suggested recommendations for structural change. The Timor-Leste Commission for Reception, Truth and Reconciliation also held thematic hearings and gave recommendations.[1] The Indonesia-Timor Leste Commission of Truth and Friendship allocated broad and institutional responsibility for the conflict. Recently, the Truth and Reconciliation Commission of Sierra Leone, and the Truth and Reconciliation Commission of Liberia held institutional hearings and generated recommendations for structural change.

At the Timor-Leste Commission for Reception, Truth and Reconciliation, the actors in the oppression of Timor-Leste were identified as state, institutional and individual. For example, the Commission report found that Portugal, both as colonial power and while Timor-Leste was under Indonesia occupation, held responsibility for the harm perpetrated. It concluded, in particular, that 'Portugal took insufficient steps to ward off an Indonesian invasion that was clearly imminent' and that it 'fell short' in 'its obligation to protect the people of Timor-Leste from harm' (Timor-Leste Commission 2005: Part 8, 90). Further, the Report found that the support given by Australia and the United States of America to Indonesia made them complicit in the denial of self-determination to the people of East Timor. In regards to the responsibility of Australia, the Report concluded that ' … during the

Indonesian occupation successive Australian governments not only failed to respect the right of the East Timorese people to self-determination, but actively contributed to the violation of that right' (ibid: Part 8, 91). In regards to the responsibility of the United States of America, it found that they 'failed to support the right of the East Timorese people to self-determination, and that its political and military support were fundamental to the Indonesian invasion and occupation' (ibid: Part 8, 91). The Commission also found the United Nations to hold responsibility in its taking 'inadequate action', in particular the Security Council, which, while condemning the Indonesian invasion, did not find 'a violation or threat to international peace and security' (ibid: Part 8, 93).

The Indonesia-Timor Leste Commission of Truth and Friendship, to the surprise of many observers, allocated responsibility for the conflict to the Indonesian state and security forces, and thus allocated institutional responsibility.

The South African Truth and Reconciliation Commission held both institutional and individual hearings on human rights violations committed during apartheid. In its institutional hearings for example, the Commission found that the South African media, in failing to report adequately on gross human rights violations, 'helped sustain and prolong the existence of apartheid' (Truth and Reconciliation Commission of South Africa 1999b: 189). A gap thus identified by the South African commission was the institution, and its role in the perpetration of harm.

As part of the 2003 Comprehensive Peace Agreement, in the wake of its fourteen-year conflict Liberia established both a truth commission and a process of army and police reform. From 2006, the Truth and Reconciliation Commission of Liberia heard both thousands of individual testimonies as well as holding over 500 thematic and institutional hearings. Simultaneously, measures were put in place to transform the police and army, including the disbanding of the army and the training of new soldiers, and the vetting of the police force and retraining of police. Sierra Leone had done the same as part of its peace agreement, signed in Lomé in 1999; *Peace Agreement Between the Government of Sierra Leone and the Revolutionary United Front of Sierra Leone.* From 2002, the Truth and Reconciliation Commission of Sierra Leone held both individual victim hearings and thematic hearings, and gave recommendations for structural change, including the establishment of a National Human Rights Commission, judicial independence, inclusion of women and children in political decision making, and greater political and economic autonomy for the provinces.

As Lisa Laplante outlines, the 1999 final report of the Commission on Historical Clarification of Guatemala examined 'the systemic causes of state violence, including economic exploitation, racism and political exclusion' (Laplante 2008: 335). Further, the final report of the Truth and Reconciliation Commission of Peru, as Laplante notes 'speaks of an "evident relation"

LIVERPOOL JOHN MOORES UNIVERSITY
LEARNING SERVICES

between poverty and social exclusion and political violence that "ignited" and then became the "backdrop" of the war' (ibid: 336).

While implementation of recommendations coming out of many of these commissions has been compromised, these approaches give us frameworks that address prevention as well as attempt to establish a broader responsibility.

In these new processes too we are seeing the introduction of measures that address communities as well as individuals. The gacaca proceedings in Rwanda addressed perpetrators as members of their communities, in hearings that were held locally on 'hilltops' in local communes where the genocide was perpetrated. In holding hearings throughout the country, the Truth and Reconciliation Commission of South Africa aimed to make the process accessible and communally based.

In East Timor, the Community Reconciliation Process within the Timor-Leste Commission for Reception, Truth and Reconciliation was designed, as Lia Kent has noted, to 'support the reintegration of individuals who had committed minor criminal offenses back into their communities', not, she emphasizes, as 'an individual reconciliation process between victims and deponents [former perpetrators]' (Kent 2004: 8). An engagement with community was seen as a core element of the commission process. Thus, 'in many cases the "victims" with whom the deponents are seeking to be reconciled are not "individuals" but entire *suco's* (villages) and *aldeia's* (neighbourhoods)' (ibid).

These are different approaches to centralized trials or inquiries in that they include the community as actor and locate redress within the communal structure and not solely at the state or individual level. Further, they consider a range of actors as responsible for state crime, in particular institutions and states. It is through identifying responsibility at both the individual and the institutional level, that we may see a broader and more sustained approach to dealing with the past. The question of distributive justice has been increasingly raised, with both survivors and commentators arguing for more attention to be made to ongoing inequities and inequalities. In her study of community views of the East Timor truth commission's community reconciliation process, Kent found that many victims were frustrated with the lack of attention to continued economic inequalities. As she noted, several victims expressed the view that the deponents are still 'living well' (i.e. prosperously); working in civil service positions, as teachers and for the police; while those who were pro-independence continue to be *aat nafatin* (still living poorly) (ibid: 26). As one man stated, 'Economic issues need to be resolved before anything else. We can't just leave the problems of justice but we can't talk about justice if we are hungry' (ibid: 27). How to address ongoing inequalities is being recognized as a necessary factor in doing justice.

In identifying the state and its institutions, together with non-state institutions, as responsible perpetrators and collaborators, there is a chance for these issues to be integrated structurally into the response by the state. With a more directed attribution of liability, we may see a clearer link to 'making things right' by the state.

It is here that the follow-up of recommendations for structural change, such as those in the reports of the truth commissions of South Africa and East Timor, become critical. Socio-economic accords, like that struck in Guatemala in the wake of the civil conflict there, have the potential to create that balance between accountability and institutional liability as well as structural change. This emerging approach, as we will see in the discussion of the institutional hearings of the Truth and Reconciliation Commission of South Africa below, has the potential to make an important contribution to ways of addressing state crime, in identifying key actors and key causes that may allow law to play a role both in later prevention and current redress.

Institutional approaches to state crime

The institutional dimensions and the complexity of state crime have been recognized in a number of legal proceedings and political-legal institutions. Both the South African Truth and Reconciliation Commission's institutional hearings and the declaration of criminality of institutions by the International Military Tribunal at Nuremberg addressed institutions directly. The 'joinder' indictments of the International Criminal Tribunal for Rwanda, the 'joint criminal enterprise' doctrine of the International Criminal Tribunal for the former Yugoslavia, the main joint indictment of the International Military Tribunal at Nuremberg with its recognition of a 'common plan', the grouping of individuals in the United States Military Trials at Nuremberg, and the main joint indictment of the Dergue military leadership in Ethiopia confronted state crime through a recognition that it requires a level of coordination and institutional capture. The lustration legislation in parts of post-communist Eastern Europe, discussed below, addressed individuals within particular institutions and according to institutional affiliation.

We can see that institutional responsibility for state crime has been addressed through five main approaches:

Criminalization of institutions through collections of criminal individuals. International Military Tribunal at Nuremberg.

Institutions as groups of individuals with a 'common plan'. International Criminal Tribunal for Rwanda, the 'joint criminal enterprise' of the International Criminal Tribunal for the former Yugoslavia, the 'common purpose' in the Statute of the International Criminal Court, and the Ethiopian 'Dergue' trial.

Organizations engaged in criminal purpose. Addressing of corporations at the United States Military Trials at Nuremberg.

Institutions and organizations made up of criminal individuals. Lustration and denazification processes, United States Military Trials at Nuremberg.

Institutions addressed in a non-criminal manner. Truth and Reconciliation Commission of South Africa.

The following section will discuss four of these approaches: the criminalization of institutions at the International Military Tribunal at Nuremberg, the grouping into 'associations' at the United States Military Trials at Nuremberg, the broad lustration processes in post-communist Eastern Europe, and the investigation of institutions at the Truth and Reconciliation Commission of South Africa.

International Military Tribunal at Nuremberg

The indictment of the International Military Tribunal (IMT) against the twenty-four former Nazi officials was directed against them 'individually and as members of any of the following groups or organisations to which they respectively belonged' (International Military Tribunal 1947–49: 27). These groups were Die Reichsregierung (Reich Cabinet), Das Korps der Politischen Leiter der Nationalsozialistischen Deutschen Arbeiterpartei (Leadership Corps of the Nazi Party), Die Schutzstaffeln der Nationalsozialistischen Deutschen Arbeiterpartei (commonly known as the 'SS') and including Der Sicherheitsdienst (commonly known as the 'SD'), Die Geheime Staatspolizei (Secret State Police, commonly known as the 'Gestapo'), die Sturmabteilungen der NSDAP (commonly known as the 'SA'), and the General Staff and High Command of the German Armed Forces (International Military Tribunal 1947–49: 27).

The Chief Prosecutors requested the Tribunal:

1. To find that certain of the defendants were members of the above groups, and
2. To declare that said groups and organizations were criminal organizations.
   (International Military Tribunal 1947–49: 97)

This was pursuant to Article 9 of the Charter of the International Military Tribunal that provided as follows:

> At the trial of any individual member of any group or organization the Tribunal may declare (in connection with any act of which the individual may be convicted) that the group or organization of which the individual was a member was a criminal organization …
> (Charter of the International Military Tribunal: Article 9)

Thus, any finding of criminality of a group or organization had to be in conjunction with a ruling on an individual.

The inclusion and criminalization of organizations was designed to have a twofold effect. Firstly, as noted in the Minutes from the International Conference on Military Trials in London on 2 July 1945, to 'utilize these closely knit voluntary organizations as evidence of a conspiracy' (an integral part of the conspiracy theory was the demonstration of a 'common plan', rendering everyone who participated liable for the acts of every other). Secondly, to make it a criminal offence to have been a member of those organizations declared criminal (International Conference on Military Trials 1945).

The first effect was thus to help demonstrate a 'common plan', through demonstrating the existence of organizations which were engaged in achieving criminal aims. The second effect was to criminally implicate others for future trials. As Justice Jackson explained at the International Conference on Military Trials in July 1945:

> These organizations constitute the means through which, under the American proposal, a large number of people can be reached with a small number of long trials – perhaps one main trial. The difficulty in our case is that we have in the neighborhood of perhaps 200,000 prisoners. We don't want to have 200,000 trials. Some of them perhaps ought to be tried individually on charges of individual criminal actions; but also they should be tried for their part in the planning of the extermination of minorities, the aggressive warfare, the atrocities against occupied nationals, and offenses of that character.
>
> (International Conference on Military Trials 1945)

Having convinced the Soviet Union on this, it was a ruling designed to have enduring effect. According to Article 10 of the Charter, members of groups or organizations declared criminal could be brought to 'national, military or occupation courts' by signatories to the Charter.

The judgement of the Tribunal found the following organizations to be criminal: part of the Leadership Corps of the Nazi party, the Gestapo, the SD and the SS. The Tribunal found the SA, the Reich Cabinet, and the General Staff and High Command not to be criminal in character.

1. *The Leadership Corps of the Nazi party.* The Leadership Corps of the Nazi party for which a declaration of criminality was sought included the Führer, the Reichsleitung, the Gauleiters and their staff officers, the Kreisleiters and their staff officers, the Ortsgurppenleiters, the Zellenleiters and the Blockleiters. This group contained at least 600,000 people (International Military Tribunal 1947–49: 258). The prosecution later excluded from its declaration all members of the Ortsgruppenleiters (who had no discretion in following orders, acting under definite instructions), and all assistants of the Zellenleiters and Blockleiters. The judgement held that the machinery of the Leadership Corps was used for the widespread dissemination of Nazi

propaganda and to keep a detailed check on the political attitudes of the German people (International Military Tribunal 1947–49: 258). The judgement declared such activities not to be criminal. What was, however, found to be criminal was their operations in countries occupied by Germany, which in their role in elimination of local custom and detection and arrest of persons who opposed German occupation was found to be criminal under Articles 6(b) and 6(c) of the London Charter. The Leadership Corps played a role in the persecution of the Jews – the Gestapo and SD coordinated with Gauleiters and Kreisleiters with regard to the 'Kristallnacht' of 9 and 10 November 1938. They were also employed to disseminate information to the wider German population with regard to the necessity of 'ruthless severity' against the Jews. They played an important role in the Slave Labor Program, and in the mistreatment of prisoners of war.

In finding that the organization of the Leadership Corps participated in 'War Crimes and Crimes against Humanity' connected with the war, the Tribunal found the Leadership Corps, with the exception of its lower rungs, to be criminal. The group comprised those members who 'became or remained members of the organization with knowledge that it was being used for the commission of acts declared criminal by Article 6 of the Charter, or who were personally implicated as members of the organization in the commission of such crimes' (International Military Tribunal 1947–49: 262).

2. *Gestapo and SD.* Due to their close working relationship, the Gestapo and the SD were considered together by the Tribunal, although each had made separate submissions. The Tribunal concluded that the Gestapo and the SD 'were used for purposes which were criminal under the Charter involving the persecution and extermination of the Jews, brutalities, and killings in concentration camps, excesses in the administration of occupied territories, the administration of the slave labor program, and the mistreatment and murder of prisoners of war' (ibid: 267). Excluded from their judgement on the Gestapo were all persons employed by the Gestapo for purely clerical, stenographic, janitorial or similar unofficial routine tasks. Excluded from their judgement on the SD were 'honorary informers who were not members of the SS, and members of the Abwehr who were transferred to the SD' (International Military Tribunal 1947–49: 268). The Tribunal thus declared to be criminal the group:

> composed of those members of the Gestapo and SD holding the positions enumerated … who became or remained members of the organization with knowledge that it was being used for the commission of acts declared criminal by Article 6 of the Charter, or who were personally implicated as members of the organization in the commission of such crimes.
>
> (International Military Tribunal 1947–49: 268)

3. *The SS*. The SS was meant to comprise the elite of National Socialism, organized along highly disciplined lines, with the express object of assisting 'the Nazi government in the ultimate domination of Europe and the elimination of all inferior races' (ibid: 272). The head of the SS, Heinrich Himmler, indicated that the SS was concerned with 'perpetuating the elite racial stock with the object of making Europe a Germanic continent' (ibid). The Tribunal concluded that the SS was utilized for purposes which were criminal under the Charter involving the persecution and extermination of the Jews, brutalities and killings in concentration camps, excesses in the administration of occupied territories, the administration of the slave labour programme, and the mistreatment and murder of prisoners of war (ibid: 273).

In its judgement on the SS, the Tribunal included all persons who had been officially accepted as members of the SS, with the exception of the so-called SS riding units. The Tribunal declared to be criminal:

> the group composed of those persons who had been officially accepted as members of the SS as enumerated in the preceding paragraph who became or remained members of the organization with knowledge that it was being used for the commission of acts declared criminal by Article 6 of the Charter, or who were personally implicated as members of the organization in the commission of such crimes, excluding, however, those who were drafted into membership by the State in such a way as to give them no choice in the matter, and who had committed no such crimes.
>
> (International Military Tribunal 1947–49: 273)

The basis for the finding was the participation of the SS in the organization of 'War Crimes and Crimes against Humanity' connected with the war.

4. *The SA*. Membership in the SA was generally voluntary, notwithstanding the transfer of various veterans groups into the SA in 1933, and the political and economic pressures put on civil servants after 1933 to join. Prior to the killing of the Chief of Staff of the SA, Ernst Julius Röhm, and the general purge of the SA leadership in 1934, the SA had played an important role in establishing control by terror of the Nazi party, particularly in the 'Kristallnacht' burning of synagogues and looting. After 1934, the SA was removed as a central force, and although isolated units participated in 'War Crimes and Crimes against Humanity' (notably the ill-treatment of Jews in the ghettos of Vilna and Kaunas, and the guarding of prisoners in Danzig, Posen, Silesia and the Baltic States), the Tribunal found that the SA after the purge had been 'reduced to the status of a group of unimportant Nazi hangers-on', and that it had not been shown that the atrocities committed prior to 1934 were 'part of a specific plan to wage aggressive war, and the Tribunal therefore cannot hold that these activities were criminal under the Charter' (ibid: 275). They concluded:

although in specific instances some units of the SA were used for the commission of War Crimes and Crimes against Humanity, it cannot be said that its members generally participated in or even knew of the criminal acts. For these reasons the Tribunal does not declare the SA to be a criminal organization within the meaning of Article 9 of the Charter.

(International Military Tribunal 1947–49: 275)

5. *The Reich Cabinet.* The Reich Cabinet comprised members of the ordinary Cabinet after 30 January 1933, members of the Council of Ministers for the Defense of the Reich, and members of the Secret Cabinet Council. The Tribunal stated that it is of the opinion that no declaration of criminality should be made with respect to the Reich Cabinet for two reasons: (1) because it is not shown that after 1937 it ever really acted as a group or organization; (2) because the group of persons here charged is so small that members could be conveniently tried in proper cases without resort to a declaration that the Cabinet of which they were members was criminal. According to the Tribunal, 'from the time that it can be said that a conspiracy to make aggressive war existed the Reich Cabinet did not constitute a governing body, but was merely an aggregation of administrative officers subject to the absolute control of Hitler'. Further,

> Not a single meeting of the Reich Cabinet was held after 1937, but laws were promulgated in the name of one or more of the Cabinet members ... A number of the cabinet members were undoubtedly involved in the conspiracy to make aggressive war; but they were involved as individuals and there is no evidence that the Cabinet as a group or organization took any part in these crimes.
>
> (International Military Tribunal 1947–49: 275–76)

What the Tribunal appears to be saying is that while the Reich Cabinet may have been used instrumentally as a framework for the perpetration of the crimes of Nazi Germany, it did not act as an effective and functioning organization in the pursuit of the implementation of these policies. As stated in the judgement, various laws authorizing acts criminal under the Charter were circulated among the members of the Reich Cabinet and issued under its authority signed by the members whose departments were concerned. As they concluded, however, this does not prove that the Reich Cabinet, after 1937, ever really acted as an organization (ibid: 276).

6. *General Staff and High Command.* The General Staff and High Command comprised an approximate 130 officers, who had held the highest positions in the military hierarchy in the Nazi regime. The Prosecution had argued that this conglomeration of persons was a 'group', rather than an 'organization'. The Tribunal found this not to be the case. Rather, it found them to be 'an aggregation of military men, a number of individuals who

happen at a given period of time to hold the high-ranking military positions' (ibid: 278). That is:

> in the case of the General Staff and High Command [as compared with the SS for example], he could not know he was joining a group or organization for such organization did not exist except in the charge of the Indictment. He knew only that he had achieved a certain high rank in one of the three services, and could not be conscious of the fact that he was becoming a member of anything so tangible as a 'group'.
>
> (International Military Tribunal 1947–49: 278)

The Tribunal found that the military officers in the General Staff and High Command as a defined group did not participate in the planning and waging of aggressive war and in committing 'War Crimes and Crimes against Humanity': they may have participated as individuals, and this, it suggested, would be brought out in individual trials.

If the Tribunal had found the General Staff and High Command to be criminal, then it would have had to find the equivalent in other countries, namely the Allies' bombing of Dresden, for example, criminal as well. This was politically unacceptable. As it was, the Tribunal argued that,

> their planning at staff level, the constant conferences between staff offi-cers and field commanders, their operational technique in the field and at headquarters was much the same as that of the armies, navies, and air forces of all other countries. The over-all effort of OKW (High Com-mand of the German Armed Forces) at coordination and direction could be matched by a similar, though not identical, form of organiza-tion in other military forces, such as the Anglo-American Combined Chiefs of Staff.
>
> (International Military Tribunal 1947–49: 277)

The declaration of criminalization for certain institutions of Nazi Germany resulted in four outcomes:

1. It banned the continuing existence of these organizations;
2. It made it a criminal offence to have been a member of such an organi-zation after 1 September 1939 in conjunction with individual criminal acts (International Military Tribunal judgment);
3. It allowed this to be used as evidence of criminal activity in future trials: Law Number 10 of the Control Council of Germany made 'Membership in categories of a criminal group or organization declared criminal by the International Military Tribunal' a crime;
4. It made membership grounds for indictment in future trials for signa-tories to the London Charter (Britain, the US, the USSR) before

national, military or occupation courts (Article 10, Charter of the International Military Tribunal).

There is a clear question as to the worth, and dangers, of criminalizing institutions. A declaration of criminality of an organization by the IMT resulted in the ability by national signatories to put on trial those belonging to these institutions (Article 10 of the London Charter), and in Germany, to make membership in these institutions a criminal offence (Law Number 10 of the Control Council of Germany). It ran the risk, however, of authorizing a principle of 'collective responsibility', and, as the Tribunal itself noted, producing 'great injustice' (ibid: 255). Yet it also ran the risk of absolving certain institutions, notably the Wehrmacht, of their responsibility. In particular, it put no great onus on them to institute change.

  The IMT in its judgement stated clearly that the principal organizations of the former Nazi regime could not be judged separately from its members. Importantly, the judgement stated that the mind of the organization was bound up with the mind of its members. It sought to identify particular institutions of the Nazi regime which were established for criminal purposes, or which carried out criminal purposes. Awareness of these criminal goals, and participation in them, would contribute to an individual's criminality. Knowledge that the organization was 'being used for the commission of acts declared criminal by Article 6 of the Charter' was a key factor in each decision. The groups declared criminal could not include 'persons who had ceased to hold the positions enumerated ... prior to 1 September 1939'. These crimes were linked to the declaration and subsequent conduct of war within the IMT context of a 'conspiracy to make aggressive war'.

  The reasoning of the Tribunal confuses itself between organizations established for criminal purposes, and organizations which did achieve criminal purposes. In criminalizing institutions, this would seem to be of importance. There would appear to be more reason to declare criminal an organization established purely for criminal purposes, than one which did achieve criminal purposes. An organization which did achieve criminal purposes could have a chance of transformation and internal change, compared with one solely established for a particular criminal purpose. It appears that the criminalization of organizations was very much for organizational purposes: a way, as Justice Jackson put it, of indirectly criminalizing '200,000 potential criminals' (International Conference on Military Trials 1945).[2]

United States military trials at Nuremberg

These trials by United States military prosecutors were held in United States military courts following the joint International Military Tribunal at Nuremberg. They were established pursuant to the London Agreement of

8 August 1945, Article 6,[3] and the Charter of the International Military Tribunal, Articles 10[4] and 11,[5] and derived their legitimacy from the amalgamation of these documents, Control Council Law No. 10, in particular Article III (1)(a).[6]

Two groups of defendants were targeted: the leaders of the European Axis powers and their principal agents and accessories (aside from those already sentenced by the International Military Tribunal), and members of organizations which the International Military Tribunal had declared criminal (Buscher 1989: 31). Twelve trials were held: the Medical Case, the Milch Case, the Justice Case, the Pohl Case, the Flick Case, the I.G. Farben Case, the Hostage Case, the RuSHA Case, the Einsatzgruppen Case, the Krupp Case, the Ministries Case and the High Command Case (Trials of War Criminals before the Nuremberg Military Tribunals 1949–53).

It is the way in which the trials were organized that demonstrates an explicit recognition of institutional parameters. Many of the twelve war crimes trials were based around significant associations in Nazi Germany. For example, in the Medical Case, twenty of the twenty-three defendants were doctors, and the charges related principally to medical experimentation on human beings. The Justice Case focused on officials from the Reich Ministry of Justice and German prosecutors and judges, charged with implementing the racial laws. The Einsatzgruppen Case heard charges of mass murder against officers of the mobile killing units responsible for murdering over a million Jews and others in occupied Europe. The Ministries Case grouped together officials from Ministries in Nazi Germany. The High Command Case tried Generals of the Wehrmacht and High Command.

Some of those on trial were also charged with membership in a criminal organization. For example, in the first trial, known as the Doctors Trial or Medical Case, ten of the defendants were charged and found guilty of membership in a criminal organization through their membership after 1 September 1939 of the SS. Significantly, the judgement in the Justice Case stated the following:

> Control Council Law No. 10 provides that we are bound by the findings as to the criminal nature of these groups or organizations. However, it should be added that the criminality of these groups and organizations is also established by the evidence which has been received in the pending case.
>
> (Trials of War Criminals before the Nuremberg Military
> Tribunals 1949–53: 1031)

This can be read as an attempt to move away from a notion of collective punishment.

The findings against the defendants' membership in a criminal organization focused on their knowledge of its criminal character. For example, in respect to the charges in the Justice Case against defendant Günther Joel, the former Chief Public Prosecutor, and holder of other significant positions such as liaison officer between the Reich Ministry of Justice and the SS (including the SD), and the Gestapo, and eventual senior positions in the Reich Ministry of Justice, the judgement stated that 'concerning Joel's membership in the SS and SD, a consideration of all the evidence convinces us beyond a reasonable doubt that he retained such membership with full knowledge of the criminal character of those organizations' (ibid: 1142).

One clear difference between the United States Nuremberg trials and the International Criminal Tribunal for Rwanda 'joinder' indictments was the political context. As an occupying force, the United States, unlike the United Nations through the International Criminal Tribunal, was in a position to physically dismantle some associations (one consequence of the I.G. Farben Case was the breaking up of the corporation into smaller entities). The principle behind the 'joining' nevertheless appeared the same: that in grouping individuals of a similar position together, more information could be gathered, with a greater likelihood of proving the offences charged. Undoubtedly, the trials served to prove another point: the 'penetration' of Nazism through all layers of German society and the responsibility for state crime within both state and other organizations within Germany.

Lustration processes in post-communist Eastern Europe

The process of 'lustration' demonstrates another method by which institutions and organizations have been addressed within the legal process. The word lustration is derived from the Latin *lustratio*, which means purification by sacrifice or by purging. This has also been called 'decommunization' in the post-communist context, or 'denazification' in the post-Second World War context.

In the post-communist context, as Jirina Siklová has noted, it is the process of screening individuals in positions of political or economic influence in order to determine whether they once had ties to the former state security service (Siklová 1999: 248). It is an attempt both to 'cleanse' institutions and to penalize individuals for belonging to certain organizations, declared criminal. In its practice it includes the removal of certain persons from public positions, as well as the barring of certain persons from holding public office in the future.

Whom does the lustration law affect? Writing in regard to screening laws of the Czech Republic, Siklová notes that it does not affect high-ranking Communist Party members, or StB (the former state security service) officers for whom spying was a job description (ibid: 255). Additionally, the high-ranking Communist Party members generally did not seek employment in the public sector – rather they have entered the private sector, and have moved from the old privileged *nomenklatura* network under communism to form the present *nomenklatura* network, as illustrated by Maria Łoś and Andrzej Zybertowicz (Łoś & Zybertowicz 2000).

The policies of lustration in post-communist Eastern Europe purport to be mechanisms to address institutional complicity. Yet these policies operate on an individual basis. The language of the Czech screening laws speaks of those who acted 'immorally' (Siklová 1999: 255). Individuals who were key players in institutions that played a role in the perpetration of these crimes will be 'purged' from the organizations themselves and in this way penalized, but only if they attempt to remain in these or other public institutions (see Ellis 1997). In its focus on individuals, lustration does not address these institutions as a whole, rather censures certain persons if they attempt to remain in the public sphere. Moreover, it presupposes guilt rather than innocence. In remaining at the individual, rather than the institutional level, the policy of lustration as practised in the post-communist context does not get us that much closer to a fuller addressing of state crime.

Truth and Reconciliation Commission of South Africa

The Truth and Reconciliation Commission chose not to follow a policy of lustration. After commenting on the meaning of lustration, the Commission decided not to recommend lustration because it was felt that it would be inappropriate in the South African context (Truth and Reconciliation Commission of South Africa 1999c: 311). Desmond Tutu, in his introductory statement, did state, 'It is suggested, however, that when making appointments and recommendations, political parties and the state should take into consideration the disclosures made in the course of the Commission's work' (Truth and Reconciliation Commission of South Africa 1999a: 3).

The Human Rights Violations Committee was the section of the Truth and Reconciliation Commission designed to hear the story of apartheid. The bulk of the hearings were individual hearings; however, the Human Rights Violation Committee also established 'institutional', 'group' and 'special event' hearings. These hearings were designed to illustrate and examine the structure of apartheid – to examine the main state and non-state institutions in apartheid South Africa, to illustrate those groups particularly affected by apartheid or who were not well enough highlighted in the individual hearings, as well as to focus on particular 'special' areas or events, which may be seen as a microcosm of the functioning of the apartheid system and/or which were seen as warranting special attention. As such, the hearings were designed to identify the structure of apartheid, both internally (as identified within particular institutions and particular 'events') and externally (putting all these institutions, groups and events together to establish 'the whole picture'). The Commission invited submissions from particular groups and institutions, and in part wished to establish a dialogue between those who benefited and those who lost under the apartheid system.

The institutions selected were those the Commission Report termed 'influential sectors of the apartheid society'. These were all sectors, the Report noted, which had come under attack for what was seen by some as their complicity with the apartheid system (Truth and Reconciliation Commission of South Africa 1999b: 2). The aim of this was (1) to 'paint the backdrop against which such human rights violations occurred', and (2) to find some level of understanding as to how 'people who considered themselves ordinary, decent and God-fearing found themselves turning a blind eye to a system which impoverished, oppressed and violated the lives and very existence of so many of their fellow citizens' (ibid: 1). It was another way of asking, how was it humanly possible? The decision to investigate some of the key institutions in South Africa under apartheid entailed a recognition of the framework within which such dehumanization and oppression was possible. It involved a recognition of apartheid as a crime formulated by the state executive, implemented by the state legislature, and complied with by a number of state institutions such as the judiciary, the armed forces and the police, and supported by a number of non-state institutions (albeit with strong links to the State) such as the Church.

The institutions and sectors identified by the Commission, and made the subject of hearings by the Human Rights Violations Committee, were the media, business, prisons, the faith community, the legal system, political parties, the armed forces, the State Security Council and the health sector. These institutions and sectors were both state and non-state. Not all the institutional hearings were given separate treatment in the Final Report. The media, business, prisons, faith community, legal system and health sector hearings were, and each of these hearings was reported on separately and particular recommendations made.

The Commission also convened hearings on three areas that they believed warranted special attention: compulsory military service, children and youth, and women, as well as what were termed 'special event' hearings: the Trojan Horse Hearings (covering the 1985 attack on schoolchildren by non-uniformed police officers in Athlone township), the Caprivi Hearings (covering the training of Inkatha hitsquads in then South West Africa in the 1980s), and the Mandela United Football Club Hearings (covering the group responsible for assaults on Soweto residents, under the guidance of Winnie Mandela). In addition, there were a number of special focuses of the Commission. Volume Two, Chapter Six included reports on Special Investigations: The Death of President Samora Machel, the Helderberg Crash, Chemical and Biological Warfare, Secret State Funding, and Exhumations.

Over 500 individuals, groups and organizations made formal submissions for these institutional hearings to the Commission. These included those requested by the Commission, and those submitted voluntarily. A number of organizations refused to take part in the institutional hearings; for example, the management of the Afrikaans press refused to participate, and while judges sent submissions, they refused to appear. The submissions were requested to focus on a number of issues, primarily the conduct of these institutions during the apartheid era, but also including recommendations for the future. As such, the hearings were designed to contribute to the Commission's mandate, which included:

> recommendations to the President with regard to the creation of institutions conducive to a stable and fair society and the institutional, administrative and legislative measures which should be taken or introduced in order to prevent the commission of human rights violations.
>
> (*Promotion of National Unity and Reconciliation Act*
> 1995: Section 4 [h])

The Commission mandate was broad, and the institutional, group, and special event hearings were designed to investigate the functioning of the apartheid system and to determine accountability within it, with a view to transformation of these groups and institutions. They were also designed to establish the extent to which these institutions as a whole or in part 'collaborated' with the apartheid system, and the extent to which the apartheid system relied on their compliance and proactivity.

A key issue in the institutional hearings was the extent to which these particular institutions, to use the terminology applied in submission to the media hearing, provided a 'cloud of cover' under which gross human rights violations were possible. In the media hearings, this crystallized as an examination of the relationship between the media and the state, within a context of heavy state media regulation. Evidence was given of 'a "macro-continuum" from the owners of the media, to the editors who controlled the newspaper, right down to the dustbin cleaners who cleaned the dustbins at night and stuffed material in an envelope to be collected by agents' (Truth and Reconciliation Commission of South Africa 1999b: 180). Even the 'English press' which saw itself as separate to government, despite individual acts of anti-government reporting, according to the Media Monitoring Project, and as supported in the conclusions of the Commission, 'continued to report within the political, social, and economic discourse defined by the apartheid state' (ibid: 186).

This seemed to be a common theme in institutional behaviour in the apartheid era: the anticipation of what the government would wish, and the internal compliance, or self-monitoring, of this. It led to a critical response to two questions posed by the Commission prior to the media hearings: 'Could the media under apartheid be held responsible for the perpetration of gross human rights violations? Moreover, to what extent could they be held responsible for creating a climate in which violations occurred unhindered?' (ibid: 187–88).

Most damningly, the report of the Media hearings concluded with a quotation from the former editor of the anti-apartheid Afrikaans newspaper *Vrye Weekblad*, Max du Preez:

> If the mainstream newspapers and the SABC [South African Broadcasting Corporation] had reflected and followed up on all these confessions and revelations, every single one subsequently proved to have been true, the government would have been forced then to stop, to put a stop to the torture, the assassinations and the dirty tricks. It would have saved many, many lives.
>
> (Truth and Reconciliation Commission of
> South Africa 1999b: 191)

The Commission's findings as to the media's responsibility for apartheid and its violations were that 'With the notable exception of certain individuals, the mainstream newspapers and the SABC failed to report adequately on gross human rights violations. In so doing, they helped sustain and prolong the existence of apartheid' (ibid: 189).

The African National Congress in its submission to the business hearings had asked that 'Historically privileged business as a whole must ... accept a degree of co-responsibility for its role in sustaining the apartheid system of discrimination and oppression over many years' (ibid: 22). The hearings, however, questioned the extent to which 'business' could be considered a homogeneous entity. Not surprisingly, it was demonstrated that 'overwhelming economic power resided in a few major business groupings with huge bargaining power vis-à-vis the state' (ibid: 30). They also raised the interwoven nature of apartheid and labour exploitation; that without the system of apartheid many businesses would not have been as financially successful as they were. As the Congress of South African Trade Unions' submission pointed out, 'apartheid's labour laws, pass laws, forced removals and cheap labour system were all to the advantage of the business community' (ibid: 24). That is, 'capitalism in South Africa was built and sustained precisely on the basis of the systematic racial oppression of the majority of our people' (ibid: 22). At the same time, as raised in a number of submissions to the business hearings, the system of apartheid also raised the costs of doing business. This in turn raised the question as to why then business did not protest more about apartheid, if it were harming them so directly.

A spectrum from active involvement to profiting from the system of apartheid was drawn up in the conclusions to the business hearings of the Truth and Reconciliation final report. The conclusions were divided into three sections: first-, second- and third-order involvement. First-order involvement was described as direct involvement with the state in the formulation of oppressive policies or practices that resulted in low labour costs (or otherwise boosted profits). The mining industry was singled out as belonging to this category. Second-order involvement was described as knowledge of the oppressive use to which services would be applied. The provision of covert credit cards by banks to death squads fell into this category (although it was pointed out that the same banks were involved in the movement of funds from overseas donors to organizations resisting apartheid). Third-order involvement was described as ordinary business activities that bene-fited indirectly by virtue of operating within the racially structured context of an apartheid society (ibid: 26). Most businesses fitted into this last category. As the Report noted, the current distribution of wealth (which is sub-stantially concentrated in white hands) is a product of business activity that took place under an apartheid system that favoured whites (ibid).

Various strategies for redress and as a contribution to reconstruction were suggested at the business hearings. These included social responsibility investment programmes, support for non-governmental organizations, and improved employment equity programmes. They also included proposals such as the cancellation of all apartheid debt, the introduction of a 'wealth tax' and the establishment by business of a reparations fund. These were all to be later refused by President Thabo Mbeki. As the final report noted, an alarming gap between rich and poor existed in South Africa, one aggravated by the fact that wealth and poverty were very largely defined in racial terms (ibid: 57). The final set of recommendations in the report of the Commission highlighted the importance of economic justice in achieving a strong and meaningful human rights culture in order to ensure no repetition of the past. Recognizing that it is impossible for the public sector alone to find the resources required to expedite the goal of economic justice, it urged 'the private sector in particular to consider a special initiative in terms of a fund for training, empowerment and opportunities for the disadvantaged and dispossessed in South Africa' (Truth and Reconciliation Commission of South Africa 1999c: 308). The wealth tax was mentioned in the recommen-dations; however, the report noted that it does not seek to prescribe one or other strategy, rather recommends that urgent consideration be given by government to harnessing all available resources in the war against poverty. It did recommend 'a scheme be put into place to enable those who benefited from apartheid policies to contribute towards the alleviation of poverty' (ibid: 308). As such, it urged that consideration be given to the most appro-priate ways in which to provide restitution for those who have suffered from the effects of apartheid discrimination. These were listed as: 'a wealth tax; a once-off levy on corporate and private income; each company listed on the Johannesburg Stock Exchange to make a once-off donation of 1 per cent of its market capitalization; a retrospective surcharge on corporate profits extending back to a date to be suggested; a surcharge on golden handshakes given to senior public servants since 1990; the suspension of all taxes on land and other material donations to formerly disadvantaged communities' (ibid: 319).

The lack of access to central institutions by non-white South Africans was emphasized in all the hearings. The use of an alternate broadcast media by the African National Congress, Radio Freedom, broadcasting from five 'friendly' countries in Africa, was demonstrated. Alternative media were constantly harassed, banned, closed down, and staff detained and tortured. The business and labour hearings heard from the National African Federated Chambers of Commerce how 'discriminatory legislation, the application of the Group Areas Act, and the allocation of licenses, among other ways' systematically undermined the black business sector (Truth and Reconciliation Commission of South Africa 1999b: 32). The hearings found that Afrikaner capital was actively favoured by the state (through access to contracts, licenses and subsidies for example) (ibid: 30).

The institutional hearings focused too on the institutional culture of these different institutions. Evidence was given as to the strict racial hierarchy imposed, from black staff members at the South African Broadcasting Corporation being given the worst equipment, and being summarily dismissed or whipped, *sjambokking*, to black prisoners being treated that much worse than white prisoners in the state prisons.

'As an institution of the state, prisons – together with the police, the judiciary and the security apparatus – were an integral part of the chain of oppression of those who resisted apartheid' (ibid: 199). This opening sentence in the Report's introduction to the prison hearings outlines the rationale for such a hearing. The summation in the final report also justified the hearing, noting that the 'prisons were a microcosm of the society outside' [in terms of the apartheid structure] (ibid: 199). The opening sentence also heralds what appears to be an important omission: the absence of any hearings into the police or the security apparatus.

The prison hearings focused on political prisoners in prisons inside South Africa, although evidence on the ANC detention camps in Angola outside the country was also heard. The Commission's decision that pass laws and their effects fell outside the Commission mandate meant that the experiences of the one in four prisoners who were 'pass law offenders' were not a part of the hearings. Those who were subject to detention without trial were also not a part of the two-day hearing, although it was noted that their experiences had been heard through the victim hearings, particularly the case of Steve Biko. Another area on which there were no submissions was the 'farm prison' system. This was the system whereby those who did not produce their 'passes' would 'volunteer' at farms in order to have charges against them dropped.

The Department of Correctional Services, although involved in preliminary discussions with the Commission, declined to participate in the hearing, which the Commission Report noted was 'unfortunate as it excluded the possibility of an official response to the testimonies and of an authoritative perspective on changes in prison policy during the years under review' (ibid: 204).

Evidence was heard on the link between prisons and apartheid, racial segregation, special treatment of political prisoners, health in prisons, particular treatment of women in prisons, solitary confinement, capital punishment, media reporting on prisons, African National Congress detention camps, and, in relation to the experience of common law prisoners and their falling outside the mandate of the Commission, 'the need to emphasise that continuing vigilance and care in running all prisons is necessary at all levels' (ibid: 218). The hearing found, among other conclusions regarding the ill-treatment of prisoners, that 'the Department of Prisons co-operated with the former state in the use of imprisonment or the threat of imprisonment in the chain of control and oppression of opponents of apartheid' (ibid: 218). Recommendations in the final report focused on the necessity of increased training of prison personnel, and an emphasis on rehabilitation of prisoners (Truth and Reconciliation Commission of South Africa 1999c: 314). A special set of recommendations under the health sector focused on health care services in prisons (ibid: 335). It also made the observation that the bureaucratic organization of the Department of Correctional Services made it particularly difficult to institute the appropriate initiatives to promote transformation.

The location of the institutional hearings was designed to be symbolic. For instance, the prison hearings were intended to be held on Robben Island, the site of the prison where anti-apartheid activists had been held, notably Nelson Mandela. Due to logistical problems, they were held at the Johannesburg Fort, 'an equally appropriate symbol of political resistance' (ibid: 199). The media hearings were held at the offices of the South African Broadcasting Corporation in Johannesburg, 'chosen as a strong symbol of state control of media in the apartheid era' (ibid: 166).

The legal hearings focused mainly on the judges. The Commission had requested that individuals and organizations in the legal field address a number of issues: to focus on the role of the legal system in all its parts, on ways in which the legal system may be evaluated, and on recommendations for the future. The Commission stated:

> It is not the purpose of the hearing to establish guilt or hold individuals responsible; the hearing will not be of a judicial or quasi-judicial nature. The hearing is an attempt to understand the role the legal system played in contributing to the violation and/or protection of human rights and to identify institutional changes required to prevent those abuses which occurred from happening again. We urge all judges both serving and retired to present their views as part of the process of moving forward.
>
> (Truth and Reconciliation Commission of South Africa 1999b: 95)

As it happened, no judge did appear in person, and none of the magistracy, which was 'lamentable' according to the Report, 'especially when it is considered that this is the level at which most South Africans engage with the courts' (ibid: 3). Prior to the legal hearings, the Commission issued a press release noting, 'The appearance of judges would be of immense symbolic value, which would in turn be greatly enhanced by apologies by members of the Bench for the past' (Truth and Reconciliation Commission 1997a). According to the judges, however, in their written submissions, 'it would have been improper, both in form and substance, for judges to appear in person at the hearing, for this would affect their independence, which was guaranteed under the Constitution' (Truth and Reconciliation Commission of South Africa 1999b: 96). According to alternative legal bodies such as the Black Lawyers Association (BLA), Lawyers for Human Rights (LHR), The Legal Resources Centre (LRC) and the National Association of Democratic Lawyers (NADEL), it was just such a 'public reckoning and apology by the "old-order" lawyers which was essential' (ibid: 97). How does one address the 'law bearers', the judges in this system, portrayed by Hugh Corder with reference to members of the Appellate Division as 'while formally independent from political influence, manifestly incorrupt, and consciously impartial, were integral parts of the very structure which had created and now maintained injustice' (Corder 1984: 240)?

Submissions from the legal establishment argued that the doctrine of parliamentary sovereignty under the Westminster system required of legal professionals to defer to the will of Parliament, and that where there was a level of ambiguity or room for manoeuvre, 'lawyers argued for, and judges mostly adopted, an interpretation which favoured liberty and equity' (Truth and Reconciliation Commission of South Africa 1999b: 96). On the other hand, submissions from non-establishment legal bodies, such as the BLA, LHR, the LRC and NADEL, argued that lawyers and the courts under apartheid, as too the practising and teaching legal profession, 'with very few and notable exceptions, had co-operated in servicing and enforcing a diabolically unjust political order'. They noted several empirical studies since the mid-1970s which had demonstrated a judicial partiality towards the legislature and executive (ibid: 97).

In its summary of the legal hearings, the Commission found that 'part of the reason for the longevity of apartheid was the superficial adherence to "rule of law" by the National Party'. It also noted that acquiescence in this ranged from '*qui tacet consentire* (silence gives consent)', to more active participation in the 'entrenchment and defence of apartheid through the courts' (Truth and Reconciliation Commission of South Africa 1999b: 101). 'The Pretoria Bar, for example, refused to admit black members and only passed an apology for its racism in October 1997' (ibid). Other examples are discussed by David Dyzenhaus in his coverage of the legal hearings (Dyzenhaus 1998).

The recommendations of the final report with regard to the legal system focused on what it termed 'access to justice' issues: codes of practice for police and prosecutors, increased access to legal representation, witness protection, law student education, and increased training of legal professionals (Truth and Reconciliation Commission of South Africa 1999c: 323–24). One of its strongest recommendations was that:

> all personnel within the justice system (from clerks to judges) undergo intensive training in the values of the new South African Constitution and in the requirements of international law and standards, including the United Nations Basic Principles on the Independence of the Judiciary. Ongoing training should include sensitisation to human rights principles, including gender-specific abuse and appropriate responses. Care must be taken that the independence of judges is not compromised by any training process.
>
> (Truth and Reconciliation Commission of South Africa 1999c: 324)

There was a focus on juvenile offenders and a call for a more balanced composition of the judiciary. There was also a recognition of the informal court structure in South Africa. The Commission recommended that 'an urgent audit of these courts and their personnel be undertaken', that the practice of these courts of illegally assuming criminal jurisdiction be ended, that the Department of Justice monitor the administration of justice at this level, 'that these tribunals respect the rights established by the Constitution' and that they implement codes of practice (ibid: 327). There was also a cautionary warning about the potential reappearance of 'people's courts', established in the townships in the 1980s, partly in response to the perceived illegitimacy of the state-sanctioned court system, and which were in general repressive. It was recommended by the Commission that steps be taken to inhibit the reappearance of such 'people's courts', 'and that the Department of Justice should, as a matter of urgency, establish conflict resolution and mediation structures at the community level' (ibid).

Four factors indicated the importance of bringing faith communities into the Commission process, as outlined in the final report: the system of apartheid was regarded as stemming from the mission of the church; particular religious communities suffered under apartheid; South Africa's religious communities represented important sites of transformation, with victims, beneficiaries and perpetrators of apartheid often contained within the same community; and many within the religious communities themselves wished to 'remind themselves of their own obligation, testified to within their own traditions, to participate in social transformation and the national process of reconciliation' (Truth and Reconciliation Commission of South Africa 1999b: 59). Forty-one faith communities made submissions, with the notable exceptions being the Nederduitsch Hervormde Kerk and the Gereformeerde Kerk (although four theologians from this church made a submission in their personal capacity).

The faith hearings covered three main headings – faith communities as agents of oppression, as victims of oppression and as opponents of oppression. All the religious groups who appeared before the Commission acknowledged their complicity with apartheid (ibid: 65). The Report concluded:

> The failure by religious communities to give adequate expression to the ethical teaching of their respective traditions, all of which stand in direct contradiction to apartheid, contributed to a climate in which apartheid was able to survive. Religious communities need to accept moral and religious culpability for their failure as institutions to resist the impact of apartheid on the nation with sufficient rigour. The failure of the churches in this regard contributed not only to the survival of apartheid but also to the perpetuation of the myth, prevalent in certain circles, that apartheid was both a moral and Christian initiative in a hostile and ungodly world.
>
> (Truth and Reconciliation Commission of
> South Africa 1999b: 91)

It also concluded with a plea for 'other established religions to gain new understandings of traditional African religious symbols and beliefs', citing the 'reaffirmation of *ubuntu*', noted as 'humaneness', in the sense of 'people are people through other people' (ibid: 92).

The health hearings examined the complicity of health professionals with the apartheid system. At its end, 'health professionals who were named in submissions as having contravened ethics or acted unprofessionally' were 'referred to the appropriate disciplinary body': 'the Commission has neither the resources nor the time to conclude investigations to the point where individual findings can be made' (ibid: 155). The general findings were damning: from the Medical Association of South Africa failing to fulfil its stated aim of protecting the health of patients, to the former Government, in particular the Department of Health, failing to provide adequate health care facilities to black South Africans, to district surgeons, with few exceptions, failing to record complaints and evidence of torture and abuse, to members of the South African Medical Services, under the leadership of the Surgeon-General, being directly involved in the development of chemical and biological weapons (ibid: 155–57).

The inclusion of particular groups and institutions within the Commission truth-finding process is an important model for including institutions, not only individuals, within such a process. It is an attempt to investigate more fully the parameters and the components of such crime, and to establish accountability across such a spectrum. The process adopted by South Africa is an example of non-criminal institutional inclusion in addressing the crimes committed. Here, institutions were addressed in order to establish their role in the system of apartheid. As the Commission stated prior to the legal hearing:

> The purpose of the hearing is not to establish individual responsibility for human rights violations but to understand the role the legal system played in contributing to the violation and/or protection of human rights and to identify institutional changes required to prevent those abuses which occurred from happening again.
>
> (Truth and Reconciliation Commission of South Africa 1997a)

The parallel aim was thus to address the institutions themselves and how they may be transformed. This resulted in a number of recommendations in the final report. Yet the Commission had no inherent power to follow up its own recommendations. Nor is there any regulatory structure to ensure such follow-up. Its final recommendations were intended to be taken up by Parliament and the institutions themselves. This is not an indictment of the truth commission model as such. Such power could have been given to the Commission. The task of monitoring the state of South Africa has fallen to the Institute for Justice and Reconciliation. Established at the end of the truth commission as an independent research and policy body to continue work in building inclusive frameworks in South Africa and Africa in general, the Institute provides a yearly 'Transformation Audit' to assess the changes, challenges and efforts in addressing the structural legacies of apartheid in South Africa. Its patron, Archbishop Desmond Tutu, in their Annual Report of 2009, wrote:

> I am saddened that after all this time we are still waiting for an appropriate conclusion to the TRC [Truth and Reconciliation Commission] process. Government's lacklustre response to many aspects of the Commission's recommendations remains a source of deep disappointment, and beneficiaries of apartheid have also failed in adequately acknowledging the generosity of their victims' forgiveness.
>
> (Institute for Justice and Reconciliation 2009: 4)

The Commission is one of a number of mechanisms necessary to address the wrongs of the South African past. Its role was to establish a comprehensive 'post-mortem' of the apartheid regime. This is a crucial first step: an account that demonstrates both the broad spectrum of responsibility for apartheid, and the institutional parameters and the involvement of institutions. Further, its recommendations were to provide a working framework for the implementation of transformative institutional measures, recommendations put forward in acknowledgement of the role played by institutions and organizations during apartheid and aimed at preventing such abuses in the future. As noted by former Minister Mac Maharaj, 'Reconstruction and development and transformation requires that we restore to the people of South Africa what is theirs; that we build a South Africa that can honestly face up to its past and courageously face its future' (Maharaj 1997).

A new accountability for state crime

Law in its traditional prosecutorial form can only capture the institutional parameters so far. The bringing of heads of state, of ministers, of army commanders to trial gets us somewhat towards embracing the dimensions of state-sponsored murder and oppression. The investigation of institutions within a truth commission process also takes us along the road towards a multi-layered account of responsibility (it is, however, an account, not liability).

Criminal law has been innovative in dealing with institutions in state crime – from the grouping of ministers and heads of state in the Ottoman Courts-Martial for the Armenian genocide, to the grouping of individuals on trial and the principle of a 'common plan' for the crimes of the Nazi state at the International Military Tribunal at Nuremberg together with the criminalization of these organizations, the 'common plan' of the International Criminal Tribunal for Rwanda and the 'joint criminal enterprise' of the International Criminal Tribunal for the former Yugoslavia, and now with the principle of 'common purpose' on the books at the International Criminal Court.

Yet while criminal prosecutions importantly provide for individual accountability, they do not allow for institutional or state accountability. The exception here is the criminalization of institutions at the International Military Tribunal at Nuremberg. We have seen too that criminalization of institutions can be a risky path. Like lustration, it runs the danger of operating on an assumption of guilt and some level of collective responsibility. Further, as in the case of the German Wehrmacht, if institutions are not found to be criminal this can lead to the potentially false conclusions that they are in no need of transformation nor bear responsibility for the harm perpetrated.

Political-legal processes have also been innovative in developments in institutional accountability. The Truth and Reconciliation Commission of South Africa introduced the concept of institutional hearings which allowed for the documentation of a level of state and institutional accountability and out of which arose a set of recommendations for institutional change.

What we find in truth commission processes, however, is the establishment of an account of harm, not a finding of liability. We have no accountability as such. The question that must still be asked is how we can include *within* our legal proceedings a concept of state and institutional liability. This is the question asked by Hannah Arendt in the wake of the Eichmann trial. As she concluded, many aspects of the trial itself demonstrated 'the inadequacy of the prevailing legal system and of current juridical concepts to deal with the facts of administrative massacres organized by the state apparatus' (Arendt 1963: 294).

While we have developed new forms of legal institutions to address crimes committed by the state, most notably the truth commission, we are still grappling with addressing the full parameters of state crime. We have not developed new juridical concepts. We are still, largely, putting our hope in individualized legal mechanisms.

In the following section, I suggest a new juridical concept. The concept of 'civic liability' I put forward is a concept that may guide our approaches. The term civic is deliberately used to establish the depth of care owed by our institutions to the society that they function in. As one Deputy Prosecutor of the International Criminal Tribunal for Rwanda asked, 'where was the state, the army, the gendarmerie, the police? People who are supposed to protect the population'.

Civic liability draws on the duty of care owed by our core state and non-state institutions to society. It is configured as a way to bring the liability of institutions, both state and non-state, into an overarching framework of liability for state crime. State crime relies on the harnessing and assistance of core institutions both in order to perpetrate crimes on such a large and sustained scale and to make the crimes to an extent acceptable. State crimes against humanity are characterized, as Richard Vernon has put it, by the state using its resources to target rather than to protect its citizens: 'an abuse of state power involving a systematic inversion of the jurisdictional resources of the state' (Vernon 2002: 242).

The term 'civic liability' originates from this duty of institutions, state and non-state, to protect and nurture civil society, a duty failed during the perpetration of state crime. Institutions can fail in both an active and a passive manner: either as a core institution such as the police, the military and the executive that actively plans and participates in the crime, or possibly a less core institution such as the church or a national association that may be less active, but still supportive in a secondary manner of the crimes committed. Civic liability is an approach to address this failure of institutions and their complicity.

Civic liability. Considering institutional accountability

Civic liability derives from the fundamental responsibility owed by state and non-state institutions to the society in which they are located. Civil society depends for its well-being upon a framework of strong institutions. The abrogation of the responsibility of such institutions through their participation in the perpetration of gross violations of human rights means that they fail in their duty of care and assume a civic liability. The concept of civic liability is a way in which the institutions of the state – and the state itself – may be allocated responsibility. It distinguishes the liability of the institution from the liability of the individual. It is a way of demonstrating that liability for state crime does not lie solely with the individual. It also points to transformation of these organizations and institutions.

Civic liability offers a framework within which an investigation of how such offenses were committed and/or supported by these institutions can take place, and secures a process whereby reforms are explored and implemented. Additionally it may be possible, and desirable, to put certain key members of the organization or institution on trial for these crimes: clear cases are key strategists of the executive, the military and the police, or individuals within other less central institutions such as the church or the medical system for their own participation.

The web of responsibility for acts of genocide and state crime is broad. It can stretch as far as the states that supplied arms, to international bodies such as the United Nations who did little, to individuals who stood by. We are currently seeing moves to address corporate complicity for state crime – one of the first investigations carried out by the International Criminal Court highlighted the role of gold companies in the violence in Sudan. Further, the United Nations has established policy on human rights and transnational corporations, and there has been lobbying to create a United Kingdom Commission to regulate the role of British transnational companies in human rights violations. Genocide scholar Israel Charny has developed a matrix of criminal responsibility for genocide which extends to 'accomplices to genocide', including 'persons, institutions, companies, or governments who knowingly or negligently assist individuals, organizations, or government who are known murderers or potential murders to gain access to mega-weapons of destruction, or otherwise to organize and execute a plan of mass murders' (Charny 1994: 89). Such action may not warrant criminal liability, but it does have a place in any matrix of responsibility for state crime, and in our understanding of how state crime is perpetrated, the scaffolding and support necessary in order for it to be carried out.

Institutions of the state (the executive and the armed forces in particular), combined with the individuals responsible for them, obviously bear primary responsibility for the direct genesis and implementation of state crime. The institutional parameters of state crime can, however, include non-state institutions, such as churches and other religious institutions, professional organizations and businesses, all associations of civil society. A different level of responsibility may be attributed to such institutions of 'civil society', in their possible support and self-implementation of such state policy.

The support or 'toleration' of state policy by non-state institutions can be crucial in the perpetration of such crime. This was brought out clearly in the analysis of the support by non-state bodies of apartheid policy by the South

African Truth and Reconciliation Commission. The analysis of first-, second- and third-order involvement by businesses in maintaining apartheid South Africa, as outlined in the conclusions to the business hearings in the final report of the Commission, can be instructive here. First-order involvement was viewed as *direct* involvement with the state in formulating oppressive policies or practices, second-order was *knowledge* of the use to which services would be applied, and third-order was when business activities *benefited indirectly* from operating within the apartheid society with its racial segregation. A process of civic liability that first identifies the level of responsibility and then addresses it through transformation of that institution is of importance here.

It is not that institutions of civil society are always relied upon in the formulation and implementation of state crime. Yet, there is a substantial argument that such policy must resonate with significant institutions and sections of the population in order to be systematically applied. In regard to the genocide in Rwanda in 1994, it can be argued that the support of churches and business was crucial in the speed of killing. This is not to argue that all churches and all business were supportive, for there is clear evidence that they were not. In regard to Nazi Germany, it can be argued that the support of civil society was necessary in the gradual exclusion of Jews and other 'undesirables'. Otto Dov Kulka and Aron Rodrigue write of a 'passive complicity', implying, according to Hans Mommsen, that the prevailing passivity of the Germans with respect to the escalating persecution was a necessary precondition for the implementation of the 'Final Solution' (Mommsen 1991: 143). In an examination of the 'micro-politics' of Nazi Germany, Robert Gellately suggests that the division of the German people into Insiders and Outsiders, 'good citizens' and Jews, required a level of voluntary participation by German citizens (Gellately 1991).

A priest who gives a sermon in Rwanda supporting the killing of Tutsis, bears both personal responsibility and is an agent of institutional responsibility through his church organization. For the former, criminal liability may be allocated – for the latter civic liability. Institutions which carry out or more indirectly support genocidal policies do bear an important responsibility for state crime. While individuals may come and go, most institutions remain through changes of regime. It is therefore crucial that they be addressed as part of a matrix of accountability for state crime. The giving of an apology by a current state leader for crimes committed by previous executives is an example of this.

Civic liability can be broken down into three stages: firstly, the selection of key members of particular organizations and institutions for individual criminal liability; secondly, the transformation of institutions through the assumption of responsibility by institutions for their actions in an active manner; and thirdly, the external and internal monitoring of this. That is, institutions are not simply held passively responsible under law for the past; they are invited to manifest the virtue of taking active responsibility for a transformed, substantive rights-respecting future.

The acquitting of civic liability ties in with the rationale behind the acquitting of criminal liability. The purposes of establishing criminal liability can be seen to include the need for transparency (that it be clear what was done, and who was responsible), and potential reform (of that person and that society). These aims are particularly relevant in terms of institutional accountability, where such transparency and potential reform are both sought.

Civic liability may include some criminalization, if this begins a process of transformation and reform. The corporate model offers examples of successful criminalization of institutions in order to effect change. The criminalization of corporations has been shown to provide a catalyst for rethinking, reorganization and reform. For example, the case of Esso Italiana, an affiliate of Exxon, found guilty of bribery, resulted, according to Fisse and Braithwaite, in 'the most impressive compliance system we have seen for preventing financial crimes such as bribery'. This is, they write, 'a case study in which the outcome of uncovering the offenses was a substantial organizational reform ... where this reform was only in a minor way prompted by publicity over the offenses' (Fisse & Braithwaite 1983: 168–72). Criminalization of institutions cannot entirely be ruled out – the guiding principle is a holistic and multi-faceted approach. If criminalization achieves this, then it can be used as an important first step in institutional transformation.

Civic liability applies to both state and non-state institutions and organizations. However, whereas with state institutions, transformative practices can be imposed, this is more difficult with non-state institutions which may enjoy a special status or not have any kind of formal relationship with the state (the difference between a private security organization which needs to be registered with the state, and the church which does not). It is with these non-state institutions that a process of institutional hearings such as that employed by the South African Truth and Reconciliation Commission can be most effective: a state framework for the review of these institutions and their role, and the provision of recommendations for change. Further, as discussed above, that some criminalization is pursued as well. The final set of recommendations in the report of the Commission highlighted the importance of economic justice in achieving a strong and meaningful human rights culture in order to ensure no repetition of the past and called on the business community to implement particular changes. These investigative hearings contained an *expectation* of transformation.

Civic and criminal liability – institutional and individual – can make a powerful and effective combination. In cases of individual liability (for a church leader, a doctor or a lawyer, for example), law can reach behind the veil of potential absolution provided by their institution, and identify individuals in these institutions for criminal action. In the case of civic liability these enduring institutions can be addressed so that *sustained* change is possible. This requires unravelling the institutional responsibility of the state and civil institutions, and providing for the possibility of institutional transformation. As such, the *institutional dimensions* of state crime can be addressed.

It is necessary to acknowledge the different components of state crime and seek remedial paths that may encompass these layers. We can allow for a combination of accountabilities for which law can establish an important framework. What is sought is identifying the key players in a dually accountable and transformative manner, which, it is suggested, is a necessary combination for successfully addressing state crime. This requires an understanding of the different layers of responsibility, complicity and accountability. Being accurate about responsibility becomes important in institutional redress.

The importance of specifically addressing institutions is demonstrated by José Zalaquett, activist and lawyer during the Pinochet regime, who later served on the *Rettig Commission*, the Chilean National Commission on Truth and Reconciliation:

> from an ethical position, the ultimate purpose of dealing systematically with past human rights abuses is to put back in place a moral order that has broken down or has been severely undermined, or to build up a just political order if none existed in historical memory. Building or reconstructing a morally just order entails developing a political culture and setting in place values, institutions and policies that will guard against the repetition of the type of atrocities committed in the past. This has an assertive role in that certain values and institutions are affirmed. It also has a preventive role: one may not be able to ensure that these atrocities will never happen again, but at least one can create a system to act as a bulwark against their recurrence.
>
> (Zalaquett 1995: 45)

Conclusion

The law attempts to do a number of things in the wake of state crime: establish an account, judge, educate, allocate responsibility, and, subsequently, legal liability. Yet legal redress for state crime presently generally fails to address the crime in all its complexity and with regard to its particular features. In a newspaper article on the trial of Maurice Papon on charges of crimes against humanity, after Papon was found guilty of complicity in the transfer of nearly 1,600 Jews from Bourdeux to Paris from where they were transported to extermination camps, the following remark was made:

> the chief message to come out of it [the trial of Papon] has been the inadequacy of the legal system in trying to judge the past in this way.
>
> (Henning 1998: 5)

Law generally fails to acknowledge the institutional parameters of state crime and to allow for the possibility of a broad spectrum of responsibility. In so doing, it fails to build a space for diagnosis of institutional deficiencies, institutional transformation and restoration into the process. Importantly, it thus fails to build a basis for prevention and reconstruction.

Law cannot be a forum for the *full* explanation of what happened – nor should it be. A legal account cannot encompass all levels of responsibility, and of causation. What it can do is provide a forum both for the immediate 'specific' remedy for the offenses committed, and the stimulation of the later project of reconstruction, and continuing justice. In order for law to play this role, it needs to host a full, fair and transparent accounting of what has happened. In this manner, a holistic approach to state crime, one that both recognizes its parameters and establishes a process for a multi-layered justice, is achieved. Law thus provides a framework both for the attribution of backward-looking responsibility, as well as the stimulation of forward-looking active responsibility.

I have suggested in this chapter that the way forward for attribution of responsibility is through separating individual criminal liability and institutional liability through the use of the concept of civic liability for institutions. Civic liability provides the necessary framework for transformation of institutions to achieve lasting societal benefits, not achievable through individual criminal convictions alone.

A varied attribution of liability can provide a strong base for reconstruction rather than division. It entails a necessary awareness of the impact that legal decisions and legal and political-legal approaches will have on potential reconciliation and societal reconstruction, an issue more closely examined in the following chapter. In addition, the identification of a broader responsibility, and subsequently, liability, is crucial in providing an understanding of the structure of the killings, and providing political answers to what is a political act. Just as the definition of crime can provide greater understanding of such crime, so too does the allocation of different accountabilities. Such an approach – the identification of the state as the key actor, together with the institutions that collaborate and support, and what this means for issues of redress – provides us not only with a correct account of what happened, and why it happened, but an important foundation for restoration, the establishment of a society not bound by former divisions, and a basis for robust, future-oriented relations.

Notes

1 Thematic hearings were held by the CAVR on Political Imprisonment, Women and the Conflict, Famine and Forced Displacement, Massacres, Internal Political Conflict of 1974–76, Self-Determination and the International Community, and Children and the Conflict.

2 The Tribunal, however, does not clearly state what is a group, or what is an organization, although it does state that the two need to be distinguished in its discussion of the General Staff and High Command: 'No serious effort was made [by the Prosecution] to assert that they composed an "organization" in the sense of Article 9. The assertion is rather that they were a "group", which is a wider and more embracing term than organization' (International Military Tribunal 1947–49: 277). It could be argued that the reason that the SS, the Leadership Corps of the Nazi party, the Gestapo and SD were found to be criminal organizations was precisely because such organizations did not exist in the Allied countries – however, as organizations similar to the General Staff and High Command did exist outside of Germany (and almost certainly did commit war crimes), they could not be found to be criminal. In noting that the operational technique of the General Staff and High Command was the same as that of the Anglo-American Combined Chiefs of Staff, all that this is saying is that as such, they did not operate as a group. Thus, they could not be criminalized as a group. Yet, it does not admit the fact that they may have operated as a different kind of group and been utilized for common purposes. It is also unclear why the number of individuals in an organization is of importance. In the conclusions of the Tribunal with regard to the Reich Cabinet, it was stated that 'Where an organization with a large membership is used for such purposes, a declaration [of criminality] obviates the necessity of inquiring as to its criminal character in the later trial of members who are accused of participating through membership in its criminal purposes and thus saves much time and trouble'. The small number of persons (17) on trial who were former members of the Reich Cabinet led the Tribunal to the conclusion that 'there is no such advantage in the case of a small group like the Reich Cabinet'. It can be asked then as to the purpose of declaring these organizations to be criminal, other than ease of judgement in later individual cases. It can also be questioned as to whether this means that members can be tried for the sole purpose of being a member of such organization, aside from proving individual criminal liability. With the conscious removal from the designated SS group of administrative staff (typists, etc.), this would seem to be the case.

3 Article 6, *London Agreement* of 8 August 1945: nothing in this Agreement shall prejudice the jurisdiction or the powers of any national or occupation court established or to be established in any Allied territory or in Germany for the trial of war criminals.

4 Article 10, *Charter of the International Military Tribunal*: in cases where a group or organization is declared criminal by the Tribunal, the competent national authority of any Signatory shall have the right to bring individuals to trial for membership therein before national, military or occupation courts. In any such case the criminal nature of the group or organization is considered proved and shall not be questioned.

5 Article 11, *Charter of the International Military Tribunal*: any person convicted by the Tribunal may be charged before a national, military or occupation court, referred to in Article 10 of this Charter, with a crime other than of membership in a criminal group or organization and such court may, after convicting him, impose upon him punishment independent of and additional to the punishment

imposed by the Tribunal for participation in the criminal activities of such group
or organization.

6 Each occupying authority, within its Zone of occupation:

> (a) shall have the right to cause persons within such Zone suspected of having
> committed a crime, including those charged with [sic] crime by one of the
> United Nations, to be arrested and shall take under control the property, real
> and personal, owned or controlled by the said persons, pending decisions as
> to its eventual disposition.
>
> (Control Council Law No. 10, Article III (1)(a))

Chapter 5

Bringing us all together

Law, reconstruction and reconciliation

Along with the increasing number of legal proceedings established in the wake of state crime, we can also identify an increasingly prominent call for reconciliation through legal channels. This is not put forward as a possible byproduct of international criminal trials or truth commissions, but a stated goal of these legal proceedings, a legal objective, found in statutes, preambles and resolutions.

The Security Council resolution that created the International Criminal Tribunal for Rwanda declared that prosecutions would contribute to 'the process of national reconciliation and to the restoration and maintenance of peace' (Statute of the International Criminal Tribunal for Rwanda 1994). The United Nations agreement on trials of the Khmer Rouge notes the 'pursuit of justice and national reconciliation' (Draft Agreement 2003). The mandate of the Truth and Reconciliation Commission in Sierra Leone states as an objective to 'promote healing and reconciliation and to prevent a repetition of the violations and abuses suffered' (Truth and Reconciliation Commission Act 2000). Desmond Tutu, in his introductory statements at the 'Mandela Football Club' human rights violation hearings at the Truth and Reconciliation Commission of South Africa said, 'We seek again, may I emphasize, the truth, not for purposes of prosecution, but for the purpose of seeking to re-integrate people into our society' (Truth and Reconciliation Commission of South Africa 1998).

There are increasing expectations that law will reconstruct in the wake of state crime, in particular, that law will reconcile. While a 'bringing together' can be important in the wake of state crime, this chapter considers what makes law a transformative actor and what reconciliation, and a broader reconstruction, may be dependent upon. It considers when and how legal processes stimulate or harness broader societal processes, and when this transformative space is opened and when it is blocked. In so doing it examines the relationship between law, a broader institutional reconstruction, and deeper societal change.

Legal processes do not necessarily stimulate processes of reconciliation. Law does not always provide the necessary constitutive space, nor is reconciliation always a feasible aim. This chapter examines what can make law a constitutive actor and how law may provide a basis for a societal reconstruction and reconciliation. It begins by outlining this new role for reconciliation in law. It continues with a discussion of how law may impact on broader reconstruction in the wake of state crime, the relationship between a deeper reconciliation and a broader societal reconstruction. I consider further the implications of a focus on individual reconciliation on accountability for state crime, and the necessity of a recognition of the state as key perpetrator. The chapter concludes with a consideration of the factors that determine when law may be a constitutive actor in the wake of state crime, discussing the type of state crime addressed, the way in which the harm was ended, and the legal institutional approach taken. I show that the institutional design of legal processes and the path taken by a government in the wake of such crime do impact on societal reconstruction. However, this does not mean that legal proceedings *create* societal reconstruction or reconciliation. At best they establish spaces that open up these possibilities.

The new call for reconciliation and reconstruction

The call for reconciliation and reconstruction in the wake of state crime is fairly new. We heard no call for reconciliation in the wake of the Holocaust and the crimes of Nazi Germany, for example, but have heard it prominently in the wake of the genocide in Rwanda. And while this could be dismissed as a practical measure (Rwandans still need to live together, Jews and Germans, on the whole, did not – although Romani and Europeans did), this does not fully explain this call, or its implications. If we do look at the conflicts and consider whether this need to live together plays a role in the push for reconciliation, we can see that it does not always.

Reconciliation as an objective and a companion to addressing state crime seems to have entered legal discourse in the early 1990s. The first mention of reconciliation in legal and political-legal proceedings designed to establish accountability for state crime can be found at the Chilean National Truth and Reconciliation Commission held in 1990 to investigate the systematic human rights abuses under Augusto Pinochet's military rule. The Commission clearly states in its mandate that one of its aims is to '... bring about the reconciliation of all Chileans' (Chilean National Commission on Truth and Reconciliation 1990: Article 1). In the early 1980s, the truth commission established in 1983 by Argentine President Raúl Alfonsín to investigate the forced 'disappearances' of Argentina's 'Dirty War' had no mention of reconciliation (Argentine National Commission on the Disappeared 1984).

At the same time, we also see the use of reconciliation as a justification for the granting of amnesties. In 1989, five years after its truth commission, the Argentine Presidential Pardons were enacted, to 'create the conditions necessary for permanent national reconciliation' (Argentine Presidential

Pardons 1989). A year later, we saw Amnesty and Reconciliation legislation passed in Nicaragua due to the 'need for an authentic national reconciliation to facilitate peace and internal stability, and the reconstruction of the country' (Law on General Amnesty and National Reconciliation 1990). We can then observe numerous examples, from the response to apartheid South Africa with its national Truth and Reconciliation Commission and amnesty legislation, to the genocide in Rwanda, and to the crimes of the Khmer Rouge in Cambodia.

Reconciliation increasingly is seen as a core component of any post-conflict legal redress. It is presumed that a certain relationship exists between reconciliation and law, that law can create conditions for reconciliation. The expectation, for example, of the Security Council resolution establishing the International Criminal Tribunal for Rwanda was that law would occupy a central place in the reconciliation process in Rwanda. The expectation was that law would have a role to play in societal transformation, in the restoration and reconstruction of communities, and in the reconciliation of societies divided by conflict and harm.

The Truth and Reconciliation Commission of South Africa also supported such an expectation, in fact was based on this: the final clause of the Interim Constitution of 1993 stated that 'The pursuit of national unity, the well-being of all South African citizens and peace require reconciliation between the people of South Africa and the reconstruction of society' (Constitution of the Republic of South Africa 1993). It was an expectation inherent in the mandate for the East Timor Commission for Reception, Truth and Reconciliation. It is a perspective, now common, that suggests that legal proceedings initiated in the wake of regime transformation and gross harm perpetrated by states can provide a broad working framework beyond the actual focus of trials or particular legislation, and that their role can go beyond investigation, prosecution and punishment, towards reconciliation and social reconstruction.

Although law can initiate and stimulate a broader societal transformation process in the wake of state crime, it does not always play this role. The impact of law and the functions played by legal process in each case may be very different. Law does not always function in a broadly constitutive manner in all situations of transition. The 'reconstructive' element of law may not always be found.

Law, reconstruction and reconciliation

In the wake of violent conflict, particularly conflict directed at a particular group, as in the case of genocide, there is generally not only societal division, but institutional fragility as well. The perpetration of state crime entails the harnessing, transformation and sometimes destruction of state institutions. The destruction in 1994 of the legal profession (including many of the 'law-bearers') in Rwanda, for example, meant that the rebuilding of the institution of the law became a primary task for the country, particularly when the decision was made that law would play a central role in the wake of the genocide. It also meant that the potential for another 're-fashioning' existed – as can be seen by the fact that no Hutu judges were appointed. In post-apartheid South Africa institutional fragility can be interpreted in part as the need to build a supportive institutional framework for the majority of South Africans: that is, a set of institutions geared, not to their separation and oppression, but to their constitutional well-being. It is another 'institutional re-fashioning' that is required in terms of the establishment of new institutions, and the transformation of existing ones. It is an institutional task directly related to the societal: where housing is built, and for whom (in a society in which formerly there was institutional segregation) will, for example, impact greatly on any societal reconstruction.

In the wake of the Second World War, as discussed in Chapter 3, 'emergency legislation' passed by the Allies included measures for providing adequate housing, for rationing food, gas and electricity, for currency reform, for reviving the Federal character of Germany, as well as for replacing former legal institutions. Denazification legislation meant both the 'purging' of former Nazi officials and the restructuring of the public service. Denazification, as Krawinkel points out, also meant the blocking and control of property of prominent Nazis, which, in given cases, was reserved for the restitution and rehabilitation of persecuted people (Krawinkel 1949: 250). These were all measures aimed at broad reconstruction.

Reconstruction in the wake of state crime can be both societal and institutional. Institutional reconstruction is to be found on a number of levels: physical reconstruction (of infrastructure), a reshaping of institutions, of the state and civil society, as discussed in the previous chapter, and economic reconstruction. Societal reconstruction also contains a number of dimensions: the establishment of ways of living together, as well as dimensions of reconciliation, healing and forgiveness. We can identify reconstruction thus as broad institutional and state reconstruction, and deep interpersonal or intra-societal reconstruction (which may be understood as reconciliation).

Broad reconstruction is the structural transformation of state and institutional structures and frameworks. Institutional transformation is also part of a process of acquitting civic liability, as discussed in Chapter 4. Deep reconstruction refers to interpersonal and intra-societal reconstruction, including reconciliation. Reconstruction can thus be understood as occurring at both the institutional and the intra-societal level. These are the two areas upon which legal redress has a chance to impact. They are, critically, interconnected, the achievement of broad reconstruction of state and other institutions supporting deep reconstruction at a societal and interpersonal level, that may include reconciliation.

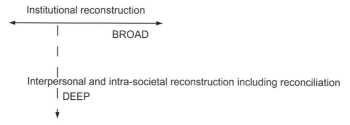

Figure 5.1 Broad and deep reconstruction in the wake of genocide and state crime

In legal redress for state crime, we may see deep reconstruction attempted without concurrent broad institutional reconstruction, yet we also see instances where the two are integrally connected. The incumbent African National Congress government argued for the necessity of institutional change to achieve societal reconstruction, in particular reconciliation. Hence, the institutional hearings of the Truth and Reconciliation Commission of South Africa out of which comprehensive recommendations came for change in both state and non-state institutions and structures that had been integral to apartheid. This necessary connection between reconciliation and institutional change was noted by former South African President Thabo Mbeki:

> given the history of our country, true reconciliation can only take place if we succeed in our objective of social transformation. Reconciliation and transformation should be viewed as an interdependent part of one unique process of building a society.
>
> (Krog 1998: 111)

Yet the story of Peter and John hovered over the proceedings, a story told by Reverend Mxolisi Mpambani at a public forum on reconciliation. Peter, who stole a bicycle from John, then later came and said 'let's talk about reconciliation'. John asked, 'what about my bicycle?' And Peter said, 'let us forget about the bicycle, let us talk about reconciliation'. That there seemed to be too little change, too little restoration, yet so much expected of black South Africans, is a common theme in the wake of state crime.

Reconciliation without rights, without institutional change, runs the risk of being short lived. It is critical that the particular harm perpetrated, and its causes, are addressed. That is, that a broader reconstruction is attempted. This is critical both for redress and any future prevention. It means a turning inside out of institutions, as discussed in Chapter 4, and an investigation into the deeper causes of the state crime. Importantly, it means that the state acknowledges, and addresses, the harm.

Reconciliation cannot remain solely at the personal level, between perpetrator and victim. In order to be lasting and effective, reconciliation must contain some level of institutional change as well as recognize the many levels of the conflict – local, national, regional, international – and the many groups and institutions within the civil society that have been affected. One of the difficulties of the reconciliation process in Australia, for example, is that it has relied on the personal, with little to no structural or institutional change. Only with the 2008 government apology to the stolen generations was there an acknowledgement at the state level of harm perpetrated that could frame any reconciliation. Yet here, still, no subsequent redress was forthcoming. With the exception of the state of Victoria, with its following of the recommendations of the Royal Commission into Aboriginal Deaths in Custody that advocated a level of institutional change, there has been no consistent programme of addressing the legacy of state crime. Reconciliation in Australia has become a process not based in legal accountability.

Reconciliation as relationship misses the necessary structural and institutional dimension (justice, rights, law) that is an important factor in its sustainability. Without institutional change, or legal accountability, it can be questioned how enduring the processes of reconciliation at the societal level can be. And this is the key point: reconciliation requires a structural and institutional dimension for its sustainability. It is not that reconciliation cannot occur without justice – on a personal or communal level it may do – but rather that in its public dimension (the kind spoken about in preambles to legal proceedings such as in Rwanda for example) reconciliation is dependent upon a framework of rights and justice; a framework, ultimately, of institutional reconstruction.

At the South African truth commission institutional hearings into business, various strategies for redress and as a contribution to reconstruction were suggested. These included social responsibility investment programmes, support for non-governmental organizations, and improved employment equity programmes. They also included proposals such as the cancellation of all apartheid debt, the introduction of a 'wealth tax', and the establishment by business of a reparations fund. As the final report noted, an alarming gap between rich and poor exists in South Africa, one aggravated by the fact that wealth and poverty are very largely defined in racial terms (Truth and Reconciliation Commission of South Africa 1999b: 16). The final set of recommendations of the Commission highlighted the importance of economic justice in achieving a strong and meaningful human rights culture in order to ensure no repetition of the past.

Institutional change is commonly understood to be a factor in genocide prevention. Leo Kuper, for example, in the context of mass killings in Uganda, relates how at a conference in 1987 sponsored by International Alert and Makerere University, recommendations to the President emphasized the need for a political solution to promote national integration, including strong representation of minorities at the centre of government. It was also recommended that economic institutions should be designed to develop a national integrated economy, redressing regional and other imbalances (Kuper 1992: 152). Elsewhere, we see in the seesawing in power between Hutu and Tutsi in Burundi and Rwanda the need to reform institutions. Here, Kuper observes that the response to the massacres of Tutsi in Burundi in 1982 was to institutionalize Tutsi superiority, with most of the key institutions, including the army, becoming almost totally Tutsi (ibid: 155). Institutional change thus incorporates the level of structural and political transformation.

The report of the Organization of African Unity that investigated the 1994 Rwandan genocide stated:

> Apologies alone are not adequate. In the name of both justice and accountability, reparations are owed to Rwanda by actors in the international community for their roles before, during and since the genocide. ... funds paid as reparations should be devoted to urgently needed infrastructure developments and social service improvements in Rwanda.
> (Organization of African Unity 2000)

Reconstruction can be physical as well as institutional and societal. In the case of Rwanda, by July 1994, an estimated 800,000 Rwandans had been killed. Two million had fled, mainly to refugee camps. Infrastructure, buildings, supplies were laid waste, much destroyed as a conscious policy by the interim government when it fled Kigali. What was moveable had been taken by the interim government – this included all the Central Bank foreign currency reserves as well as large amounts of Rwandese francs (Prunier 1995: 306). Rwanda was a country destroyed. It was dealing with the great influx of Tutsi refugees who were flooding into the country, and the severe outbreak of cholera in the refugee camps on its borders that claimed an estimated 30,000 lives. The cholera epidemic had the international community erroneously and unhelpfully calling this a 'second genocide'. Similarly, in post-Second World War Germany, much of the country was in ruins.

Law has an important role in enabling reconstruction. At the level of political and institutional change, law can play a role in facilitating broader processes of reconstruction. The banning of the Nazi party in Germany in the aftermath of the Second World War was a signal as to what kind of public speech was allowed in the new state. Further, the change in January 2000 to Germany's citizenship legislation that shifts the requirements for citizenship from descent to origin of birth is an important framework for any 'coming together' within Germany. The impact will be less on its Jewish citizens, but one hopes more for those of Turkish origin.

So too the South African constitution enacted in the wake of apartheid, that recognized its past and set to provide for its future, and in so doing set out a blueprint for a new South Africa that would, among other things, 'Heal the divisions of the past and establish a society based on democratic values, social justice and fundamental human rights' (Constitution of the Republic of South Africa 1996, Preamble).

Considering the causes of state crime, and working to address them through institutional and societal reconstruction, has become an important focus in redress for state crime. Rama Mani, in a study of the meaning of post-conflict justice, notes the complexity of justice needs post-conflict, particularly in low-income societies, and argues that the underlying causes of conflict, the structural and systemic injustices such as political and economic discrimination and inequalities of distribution, have not been addressed by national and international post-conflict practitioners (Mani 2002). J.P. Lederach has identified the importance of socio-economic justice to peace (Lederach 1999). Addressing the causes, providing a broad institutional response to state crime, can be critical to reconciliation.

If reconciliation is to be enduring, then this must be framed by institutional change, which includes law. This can take the form of the establishment or restoration of rights, the creation of new types of institutions and new types of governance and processes of restitution. Such institutional reconstruction provides a necessary public dimension to societal reconstruction. Reconciliation has a public dimension to it that healing does not necessarily have. The paths of healing and reconciliation have the same beginning – acknowledgement of harm and the establishment of a record of this harm – but the path of healing, for individuals, communities and nations, is a different but connected one. As Claudia Braude writes in regard to the murder of Ruth First in South Africa, without knowledge of the true circumstances behind First's murder, and the establishment of a national memory, personal healing is impossible (Braude 1996: 51). It is this public dimension, public acknowledgement, that can facilitate enduring reconciliation. Without acknowledgement, a broader and sustained reconciliation is impossible too.

Even so, institutional reconstruction is a necessary, but not a sufficient, condition for processes of reconciliation. These processes are locally contingent, and cannot be thought to be wholly determined by legal decision-making or legal processes. What makes reconciliation enduring is conditional both on the institutional structure and on local factors. For example, the centrality of religion in South Africa, in particular Christianity, meant that the design of the Truth and Reconciliation Commission with its emphasis on confession and confrontation, as well as the language used (healing and forgiveness were central terms) was both in the main acceptable and effective in opening up channels of communication between South Africans. The design and language of the Commission may not have the same impact elsewhere. Without the strong presence of Chairperson Archbishop Desmond Tutu and his particular manner in guiding and framing the process in terms of the language of healing and forgiveness, open hearings may have resulted, not in a bringing together of the nation, but in stigmatization and isolation for those offenders who came before the Commission. Rather, what we saw was what John Braithwaite has termed a shaming 'terminated by repentance and forgiveness' rather than a 'shaming that permanently ruptures social bonds' (Braithwaite 2000: 118). This is largely what the Commission seems to have achieved, largely avoiding the shame of stigmatization.

Yet reconciliation cannot replace accountability, either for individual perpetrators, or indeed, for the state: there is a duty in the wake of state crime to 'make good'. This extreme disquiet over the inclusion of reconciliation in discussions of justice and accountability was articulated powerfully by Ntsiki Biko, the widow of Steve Biko, at the start of the truth commission process:

> I have long been waiting for justice to come. I did announce this after the inquest, that I needed the case to be reopened so that we could get the actual truth. Nobody has ever been able to explain to me what this Commission is all about, and all that I know is that at the end of it we will have to forgive these people. But how can you forgive without proper justice having been done? It's very difficult for me to go again and listen to the lies that I listened to in 1978 during the inquest. ... What guarantee have I that the perpetrators are going to tell the truth now? They will tell whatever lies so that they get amnesty. To me it is an insult [to be asked to go before the Commission] because all that is needed is to have the perpetrators taken to a proper court of justice ... I doubt very much whether they can convince me that this Truth Commission is going to bring us reconciling: one would think of reconciling after justice, but justice must be done first.
>
> (Brittain 1996)

The focus on individual reconciliation

Reconciliation has been defined by one commentator as meaning at its core the restoration of relationships, the rebuilding of trust, and the overcoming of animosity (Gobodo-Madikizela 1998). It can occur at the national, the communal, and the personal levels, taking the form of a reckoning of communities, of nations, or a bringing together of persons. Yet while the goal of reconciliation put forward in law may be termed 'national reconciliation' (for example, the International Criminal Tribunal for Rwanda is to 'contribute to the process of national reconciliation'), it is at the level of interpersonal reconciliation that reconciliation initiatives are mostly focused. This focus on individual reconciliation, however, may actually hinder attempts to achieve institutional and societal transformation through legal means.

Reconciliation in legal redress for state crime has been focused at the level of individuals – individual perpetrators and individual victims. These are personal reconciliations to support the 'national reconciliation' story, the individual statements of remorse and forgiveness that featured so strongly at the Truth and Reconciliation Commission of South Africa, or the often forced comings together at the Rwandan gacaca hearings where prisoners publicly state their crimes and deliver apologies in the community in which they lived and perpetrated their crimes. Face-to-face meetings that have become the core of post-conflict proceedings for state crime.

The South African Truth and Reconciliation Commission, did, in its use of public forums and institutional hearings, move away from the criminal justice model of individual perpetrators and individual victims. The institutional hearings, together with the Final Report, gave a clear sense of apartheid as state crime. Bringing South Africans together was the dominant motive of the truth commission. In this it was quite clear. Yet in its focus on individual reconciliation it remained very much an individual model, with a focus on individual victims and individual perpetrators. And while, as discussed earlier in the book, we must of course not ignore the culpability of individuals for state crime, this raises real issues for our approach to these crimes of the state.

State crime is not reducible to individual crime. Gacaca meetings in Rwanda that focus on individuals returning to communities, that do not look at the structural and institutional genesis of the genocide, but rather only its individual elements, do not necessarily address this. While clearly there was a pragmatic aspect to gacaca (a way of solving the problem of the many *genocidaires* in prison), much was placed on the gacaca process, that 'this will bring Rwandans together'. So too the Community Reconciliation Procedures required under the East Timor Commission for Reception, Truth and Reconciliation, drawing on traditional customary dispute resolution practices of 'nahe biti'. While communally located, they failed to incorporate the broader processes that facilitated the state crime. These former customary legal procedures ('agacaca' and 'nahe biti') were utilized as vehicles of reconciliation to address the violations committed. Yet these processes were established to deal with community disputes, not state-orchestrated violence.

The push for reconciliation as individual reconciliation has the potential to misrepresent the key actors in the perpetration of these state crimes. In the push for a mostly individual reconciliation, and with reconciliation as flagship for these proceedings, we see a mischaracterization of these state crimes. The institutional dimensions of the harm are not recognized, the genesis of perpetration not identified and redressed. What we are left with is a view of state crime as based on individual hatreds, or 'warring tribes', rather than organized and institutionalized state-perpetrated crime that requires a recognition of this for any proper redress. These crimes are ones committed by individuals of course, however committed within the framework of the policy of the nation-state, that has harnessed the institutions of the state to carry out this policy.

In the use of a mainly individual reconciliation as a vehicle for a broader national reconciliation, we see a different characterization of the violence, one that focuses on individual perpetrators and individual victims, rather than on the institutional parameters and state-directed nature of state crime. This has implications for our understanding of state crime, and for the possibilities of law to create spaces for reconstruction. The focus on individuals does not necessarily allow the space and the framework for an enduring reconciliation.

Law's limitations in achieving reconciliation and reconstruction

The recognition of the state as responsible for mass harm is core to enduring frameworks of reconstruction. So too a process of institutional change in the wake of state crime. The ability of law to achieve reconciliation and reconstruction in state crime further hinges on a number of factors that influence the way in which law can be and is used. If we take the whole range of legal processes together, we can isolate two outcomes, both of which arise out of legal processes for state crime and provide crucial support for any project of transformation (societal and institutional). These are:

- Official acknowledgement of the harm perpetrated
- Production of a statement of the facts of the harm and an attempt made to establish a common story of events.

These are both important 'building blocks' needed for any broader reconstructive role law may play. They are the basis for two possible further outcomes:

- A framework for societal debate
- A 'foundational moment' for the society.

In seeking to establish accountability, law provides official acknowledgement of the offenses committed. On a first, pragmatic level, this provides a statement of the facts of what has happened. On a broader 'constitutive' level, this official acknowledgement and statement of facts can provide a framework and baseline for societal debate, and thus potentially become a 'foundational moment' for a society. In acknowledging and defining the mass harm, law can change perceptions. It can mean a moment of change, of a break between the 'old' and the 'new'. The acknowledgement can be critical for victims. As Kerstin McCourt has outlined, in relation to the Rwandan national criminal process:

Despite the fact that the [monetary] awards never materialized, victims continued to engage with the criminal trial process, which indicates that it was not only the potential monetary gain that motivated them but also the process itself.

(McCourt 2009: 281)

Yet law does not always move on from these 'building blocks'. As we saw in Chapter 3, moving from official acknowledgement and statement of facts to societal debate and a 'foundational moment' is dependent on the purposes the legal processes are employed for, and the extent to which they are a form of nation-building for the incumbent government – they may be designed as a foundational moment for the state but not its citizenry. We saw this in the case of Ethiopia, a trial that went on for 12 years, and was aimed at elimination of a political foe. While the hearings were important for many survivors, others commented:

We all know what happened. There are no surprises. Some relatives of victims may have a chance through these proceedings to find out some more, to find out some details, to gain a fuller understanding of the way in which their son, brother, mother, father was killed, tortured, 'disappeared'. But we knew about this regime, and we know about this regime. It has gone on too long.

(Personal communication 1998)

The manner in which the trials were conducted, and public debate censored, meant that they failed to reach out broadly to the society in the way that, for example, the open Truth and Reconciliation Commission hearings in South Africa did.

There are no guarantees that the combination of official acknowledgement and statement of facts will mean acceptance of the perpetration of harm and this 'new reality'. The political sphere can marginalize any impact law may have. This impact can be still-born – for example, with the rise of the Kemalist government and the demise of the Sultan, the findings of the Ottoman state's Courts-Martial in the wake of the Armenian genocide were placed outside the public sphere and consciously transformed into another message of Turkish martyrdom rather than institutionalized harm against the Armenian people by the Ottoman state. The marginalization and transformation of these legal proceedings meant that they played no role in reconstruction, apart from the reconstruction of the nationalist Turkish party.

Law that is victim-initiated has even less chance of stimulating a foundational moment. The 1992 Australian High Court *Mabo* decision, brought by Torres Strait Islander Eddie Mabo and others, was remarkable in the extent to which it did create a shift in perception in Australia. The finding by the court that the Australian continent was not 'terra nullius' (empty land) at the time of colonization created a new public framework. Yet it was still not completely accepted, in part due to the lack of political will to follow the lead of the Australian High Court and the lack of any institutional change, as well as other factors.

As Udesthra Naidoo wrote:

> We believed that the truth would dispel the web of lies, myths and stereotypes that sustain racial antagonisms. We believed that the truth would lead to reconciliation, which we understood in fairly vague terms, as an era of racial harmony. To an extent, we were right. Arguably, we could point to an increased awareness of social injustice, past and present. But it is impossible to ignore the existence of a wide array of other responses ranging from indifference and excuses right through to a rise in racism, in light of which our initial optimism was a little ill-founded, if not naive.
>
> (Naidoo 1998: 133)

What marks the use of law for redress in Australia is that victims have of necessity, due to the absence of state-initiated proceedings, brought these cases. One case, initiated by members of the Aboriginal Tent Embassy, asked that the court recognize the continuation of genocide in Australia due to the imminent introduction of legislation that would further limit rights to land by Aboriginal Australians. While the case did not succeed, it did elicit a critical recognition from the judge, which was the first of its kind in Australia: 'There is ample evidence to satisfy me that acts of genocide were committed during the colonisation of Australia' (Supreme Court of the ACT 1998). To have this stated in law is an important moment. The case, however, has had no broader public impact. This was one of a series of cases that have been brought by Aboriginal Australians to force some recognition of the multiple harms, including genocide, that have been perpetrated, and that continue.

While we can say something about unsuccessful cases not having a wider impact, more critically we see the importance of 'living law', that is, that the normative orders in a society must be receptive to the official law. When they stand too far outside it, when there are competing societal orderings, then they may fail, as Sally Falk Moore showed with her examination of different societal microcosms: '[when] new laws [are] thrust upon ongoing social arrangements in which there are complexes of binding obligations already in existence. The social arrangements are often effectively stronger than the new laws' (Moore 1973: 723). In Australia, these 'social arrangements' may be described as the ongoing structural racism and the foundation myth of 'terra nullius' that has been necessary to justify the legitimacy of the nation state, and an inability to countenance, as those Australian parliamentarians who ratified the Genocide Convention in 1949, the fact of genocide in Australia: that 'the horrible crime of genocide is unthinkable in Australia' (Hansard 1949, in Tatz 2003: 67).

Law can be a reference point for the society and an important basis for the future. Law can provide official acknowledgement – yet the extent to which this may translate into a foundational moment, into real change and recognition, is dependent upon a number of factors that determine the potential constitutive impact of law on state crime.

They include, firstly, who brings the legal proceedings. Proceedings brought by the state have more chance of success that those brought by victims. Secondly, the extent to which, as discussed, the findings concur with that society's 'living law' or 'laws'. There has to be some connection to current normative orders, not too far a leap. Thirdly, the type of state crime being addressed. This is bearing in mind the distinctions from Chapter 1, between state destruction of a group (genocide), state systematic killing and state systematic subjugation, as different types of state crime. They also include how the crime was ended – through internal or external defeat, or through negotiation. Finally, they include the approach taken to the use of law and the nature of the legal process – a more individual approach to the state crime, or one that examines the harm as perpetrated 'in the name of the state' and which takes a broader approach, locating responsibility with the state and its institutions, together with key individuals. These last three will now be discusssed in greater depth.

The effect of the type of state crime

State crimes, ranging from state destruction of a group (state murder which includes genocide) to state subjugation (which includes apartheid and other forms of systematic state repression), have different rationales and different subject peoples. This changes both what is possible through law, and what law must consider in order to address it effectively. What this means is that different contexts of harm present different issues for legal proceedings – and different possibilities in terms of reconciliation and reconstruction.

The harm in Ethiopia under Mengistu and the harm in Cambodia under Pol Pot, like that during the Holocaust, the Armenian genocide, the former Yugoslavia, Rwanda and South Africa, can very broadly be conceived as politically motivated crime. Like our other situations of state crime, these were crimes committed for the purposes of state-building, to consolidate or create a state in a particular image. As such, they were nation-building projects, of horrific dimensions.

One difference, however, in the harm perpetrated is that whereas in the Holocaust, the Armenian genocide, the former Yugoslavia, Rwanda and South Africa the victims were primarily of a particular ethnic, racial, or religious group, in Ethiopia under Mengistu and in Cambodia under Pol Pot and the Khmer Rouge they were primarily not. In Germany, the Ottoman state, the former Yugoslavia, Rwanda and South Africa, divisions between the perpetrator and victim groups had existed prior to the harm (not necessarily well drawn and not necessarily accepted by the victims – many Jews in

Germany saw themselves as German not Jewish). In Ethiopia and Cambodia (with the exception of the genocide of the Cham Muslim), such divisions were not so easily distinguishable.

These different historical relationships in state crime can mean that a very different process is required by law, if legal process is to impact on any future reconstruction. With acts that are dominantly politically motivated (such as those in Ethiopia, and Cambodia in part), the change of the ruler and regime can mean the end of the harm and the end of the particular victim–perpetrator relationship. State crime which involves ethnic, racial or religious motivation (but which, importantly, cannot be solely attributed to this), such as those of the Holocaust, the Armenian genocide, the former Yugoslavia, Rwanda and South Africa, can mean that the change of the ruler and regime signal the end of that particular harm – but not the end of that particular relationship. Addressing this determines the constitutive impact of law.

A further distinction may be made between genocide and other forms of state crime. It is rare that survivors of genocide remain in the country. This is clear if we compare apartheid South Africa and Mengistu's Ethiopia with the Ottoman state, National Socialist Germany and the former Yugoslavia. Rwanda is mostly an exception here. It is important, however, to note this in terms of the role law may or may not play. It could be argued that for law to play a constitutive or intra-societal role, it is necessary that this be achieved at the primary 'site' of harm, which includes participation by the spectrum of victim and perpetrator communities. In many situations this is just not possible.

When survivors and perpetrators no longer live together, other forms of reconstruction may be played out. In the case of the Holocaust, a different level of intra-societal reconstruction occurred, that between the State of Israel and the former West Germany. This reconstruction between the two communities occurred at a fairly abstract political level. It occurred in part through the former West Germany giving a sum of money to Israel by way of restitution, as well as in the knowledge that some of the main perpetrators had been brought to trial. In the future, it is possible that Bosnia-Herzegovina and Serbia-Montenegro could be reconciled through sharing some sovereignty again as members of the European Union.

Further, a conclusion may be drawn from our cases that law has played a constitutive role only in situations which are not genocide, or in situations where the genocide or other forms of systematic state killing are not addressed immediately. When legal redress occurs immediately post-genocide, it does not play this role. When a people has been almost destroyed, reconciliation immediately in the wake of this is at best premature.

The effect of the manner of cessation of the conflict

The manner of cessation of the conflict is a critical factor in the constitutive impact of legal proceedings for state crime. A distinction may be drawn between legal proceedings convened in the wake of negotiated transitions, and legal proceedings convened in the wake of non-negotiated transitions. That is, between conflicts ended through negotiation, and conflicts ended through force, that is, military overthrow. Additionally with conflicts ended by military overthrow, we can distinguish between whether this was by a national or international force. Negotiated transitions are usually internal.

Examples of non-negotiated transitions include the Armenian genocide (which ceased with the defeat of the Ottoman state), the Holocaust (which ceased with the defeat of Germany), and the genocide in Rwanda (which ceased with the defeat of the Hutu government by the Tutsi exile army). In all these cases, the genocide ended only when there was an armed victory against the perpetrators. Into this category of non-negotiated transition can be added a number of situations of both systematic oppression and state murder by a state: Cambodia under Pol Pot (ceased with the defeat of the Khmer Rouge by Vietnam), and the former Yugoslavia (ceased with the defeat by NATO forces). We can add too the situation of systematic oppression of Ethiopia under the military dictatorship of Mengistu and the Dergue (ceased with the defeat of Mengistu by the Ethiopian People's Revolutionary Democratic Front and the Ethiopian People's Liberation Front).

Within the category of harm ended through negotiation can be placed other forms of state crime, in particular state oppression. We can include here most of the former military regimes in South America, most of the former communist states and South Africa under apartheid. These were negotiated and essentially non-violent transitions. The cessation of harm meant the beginning of a new type of governance.

Legal proceedings are contingent upon a change of regime. If it is an internal decision that the harm ends yet the regime stays the same, it is seldom that we see legal redress (we can see this in the case of China's 'Cultural Revolution' or Stalin's crimes). This is particularly evident in the case of harm against indigenous peoples. There is generally no 'change of regime' with indigenous state crime. By the time the crimes are actually redressed, if ever, they fall within the general framework of 'the past', or 'the difficult past', and are addressed in conjunction with other wrongs. In Australia, this translates into the various legacies of state crime, such as the higher prison incarceration rate of indigenous Australians. Another example is Indonesia where there has been no redress for the killing by the Indonesian state of an estimated 600,000 alleged Communists in 1965–66. In such cases, it falls to the victim community to bring charges, with less confidence of success and which are less likely to play a central role, compared with legal proceedings convened by governments. For this reason, the Australian *Mabo* judgement, in a case brought by the indigenous community, establishing that Australia was not terra nullius (empty land) when colonized, is noteworthy in its impact, in providing a public reference point. These distinctions demonstrate that a general rule does not hold for the impact of legal proceedings in post-conflict situations.

Examples of external defeat

When the defeat is by an external player, the main legal redress will be primarily external or externally run. Examples here include the International Military Tribunal at Nuremberg and the International Criminal Tribunal for the former Yugoslavia. When state crime has been addressed by law in any serious way, this has been done by outsiders, generally outside the bounds of the nation-state (that is, in the international arena), and by criminal trial and no other legal mechanism. The exception here is the denazification process in the American zone in the wake of the Second World War.

All sustained 'rule of law' legal redress for state crime has been external, with limited internal mechanisms deployed. The exception to this is the recently convened joint United Nations–Cambodia 'Extraordinary Chambers in the Courts of Cambodia'. When law sits outside the nation-state, the result has, generally, been fourfold: the society is generally not witness to the proceedings and fails to participate in any meaningful way; the group of people affected is relatively small; the use of the criminal trial as the only tool means that law plays a fairly limited role; and there may be a lack of 'societal ownership' of the proceedings. As Michael Ignatieff emphasizes, there are limits to the healing that outsiders can bring (Ignatieff 1998: 7).

This is not to argue that legal proceedings that are externally run play no constitutive role at all, rather, it is to argue that it is not a *truly* constitutive role. In post-War (West) Germany, law was a tool of accountability, with the new Constitution providing probably a foundational moment, not a framework for reconciliation but rather for institutional reconstruction. However, legal process with regard to the crimes committed by the Nazi regime was in the hands of the Allies. It was only in the 1960s that German courts began dealing more systematically with the crimes committed, and it was arguably only with the end to a statute of limitations that the scope of the crimes committed during the Second World War was further absorbed by German society.

The legal proceedings in the Hague for the conflict in former Yugoslavia (the International Criminal Tribunal for former Yugoslavia and the case brought by Bosnia-Herzegovina to the International Court of Justice) play a broader global role without this being either a deeply societal or constitutive role. Yet they were and are too far away, and operate without sufficient local legitimacy to play a locally constitutive role. Efforts at reconciliation, connected with the return of refugees to Bosnia-Herzegovina for example, must thus operate without the benefit of a legal structure which both details the history of the conflict and provides a framework which may help in supporting the bringing together again of neighbours and communities. As has been documented, the physical return of refugees is not enough for sustainable return – it must be backed up by political, legal and humanitarian initiatives if reconciliation is to be achieved, initiatives which would fare much better in conjunction with an accountability process (Englbrecht 2001). The failed Bosnian Truth and Reconciliation Commission could have gone some way towards establishing such a process, if local political support could have been found.

Thus, while it could be argued that the Rwandan and Yugoslav Tribunals have functioned as a foundational moment for the international community, in terms of reinforcing an international normative code (which was crucial for the momentum towards the permanent International Criminal Court), it cannot as yet be argued that they provide a foundational moment in the countries they are addressing. The minimal impact of the international legal proceedings for Rwanda and the former Yugoslavia on daily life there, and in fact the hostility towards these Tribunals, illustrates this. Initiatives such as those suggested by the International Crisis Group that the Hague Tribunal should relocate as a 'moveable feast' around the states of the former Yugoslavia could have gone some way towards redressing this, as could that suggested by former chief prosecutor for the International Criminal Tribunal for Rwanda, Louise Arbour, to hold some trials in Rwanda itself, rather than solely in Arusha.

The international stage is just too far away to play a central role in societal reconstruction. In the situations in which the harm has ceased through external force, legal process employed in the wake of the defeat did not play and has not played an overtly constitutive role.

Examples of internal defeat

If the harm is ended through internal defeat, that is, if the 'victor' gains control of the country, then any subsequent legal proceedings will be an extension of this control. Legal process is then used primarily as a tool of consolidation and of power and retribution, in a new version of nation-building.

In looking at examples of internal defeat, we must also consider the additional factor that political control is often the aim of the defeat. The overthrow of the Nazi regime in Germany by the Allies sought not control but defeat of the regime. So too the defeat of the Ottoman state in the First World War, and the defeat of Serbian forces by NATO. This is substantially different to the internal defeat of Rwanda and Ethiopia. Both Ethiopia and Rwanda were overthrown by forces seeking control of the country, comprised of nationals of that country, or who saw themselves (as in the case of the Tutsi Rwandan Patriotic Front in exile in Uganda, many of whom had been exiled from Rwanda in their early years, or who had been born outside Rwanda) as nationals of that country. The overthrow of the Khmer Rouge in Cambodia can be placed somewhere in between – a neighbour, Vietnam, who found it politically more expedient to seize control of the Cambodian state rather than risk further incursions.

In the case of Rwanda, although the military successes of the Rwandan Patriotic Front put an end to the genocide, reports demonstrate that their main interest was in the undisputed control of Rwanda, not the saving of Tutsi lives. That their primary goal was control of the country is reflected in reports that in July 1994, when FAR (the Armed Forces of Rwanda, the Hutu-dominated Rwandan Army) was in retreat, yet the killings had not stopped, the RPF (the Rwandan Patriotic Front) kept advancing, in order to create absolute control over the country. As Human Rights Watch reported, they refused offers of American help, even though this would have stopped the killing (Des Forges 1999). Further reports of massacres carried out in their passage through Rwanda confirm this (for example that commissioned by the United Nations High Commissioner for Refugees, concluded in September 1994),[1] as do later massacres in internal refugee camps (including that at Kibeho).[2]

A similar scenario can be observed in the overthrow of the Mengistu regime by the Ethiopian People's Revolutionary Democratic Front and the Ethiopian People's Liberation Front, whose primary objective was overthrow of the regime. Cambodia can also be included in this category. Although the overthrow of the Pol Pot regime by Vietnam was external, Vietnam did seek the military conquest of Cambodia – and subsequently put in its own government, the Vietnamese-backed Heng Samrin regime. The regional relationship of Cambodia and Vietnam could classify the overthrow as closer to 'internal'. Little effort was spent on bringing to justice those most responsible for the crimes committed, apart from the show trial of Pol Pot and Ieng Sary. The line between the old and the new regime was drawn by highlighting the horror stories of the Pol Pot era at public gatherings; however, as noted in Chapter 4, it was not unusual for some of the people who carried out such orders to be seated in the audience or even on the podium with the victim recounting the story (Shawcross 1984: 359).

Examples of negotiated transitions

The negotiated transition presents some different issues to the non-negotiated transition (where internal or external force is used to end a conflict). The securing of a broad base of acceptance of the new state of affairs can mean a path bordering on amnesia is taken, or it can form the basis for an inclusionary institutional approach. South Africa is an example of the latter. The post-communist transition in East-Central Europe lies somewhere in between.

It is in a negotiated transition, in which the base is inclusion, not exclusion, that the possibility for a deep societal role for law is greater. Of the cases discussed, South Africa is the clearest example of this. The transition from a National Party-led system of apartheid to an African National Congress-led South Africa was a negotiated one, between African National Congress leaders and the ruling party. Yet, as Łoś and Zybertowicz have shown in their analysis of post-communist Poland, this is not to argue that a negotiated transition will always result in accountability. In the case of Poland, they conclude:

> change introduced through negotiated agreement between the old regime's elite and the opposition elite creates a fertile ground for 'crime at the top'. A revolution based on 'a gentlemen's agreement and a hand-shake' has lulled vigilance and disarmed the opposition forces. It has led to a willful underestimation of the formidable apparatus of the totalitarian police state and its potential forms of disintegration and survival.
>
> (Łoś & Zybertowicz 1999: 299)

The lustration procedures in the former communist countries such as the Czech Republic and Poland present a different approach to that used in South Africa. Lustration functions at the level of individual penalization, operating as a dialogue between the state and the individual. Although the process stimulated vigorous societal debate in some countries (for example in then Czechoslovakia), it did not consciously involve a broader section of the population, it did not seek to address those who may have been the most responsible for abuses committed, nor did it address the crimes committed in a holistic manner. Its function, similar to the function of the criminal trials in Rwanda and Ethiopia, appears to be a measure of elimination – basically, that those who formerly held high positions in the communist regimes should not hold public office. Yet those formerly in official public positions, who may now work in the private sector, were immune from any penalization. Thus many of the most culpable, the higher political elites, in avoiding the public sphere, could thus avoid public scrutiny. The result is that many of these old *nomenklatura* now operate in (and influence) the private sphere (see Zybertowicz 1995, 1993). Similarly, the access given to Secret Service files (for example, in the former East Germany) is also individually oriented. It is an individual, not a national process.

In contrast, the Truth and Reconciliation Commission of South Africa has been a nationwide public process, or at least one that consciously attempted to be so. The Commission defined apartheid as state crime. It identified the individual and the institutional actors, and was designed with these para-meters in mind. The combination of individual human rights, violations hearings and institutional hearings was recognition that to look at one or the other in isolation was neither to gain the full story, nor to apportion responsi-bility accurately. The combination worked in that not only could individual stories be located within institutional perspectives, but also the parameters of the crime as a political crime could be recognized and analyzed as such.

Mahmood Mamdani commented that 'the power of the [Truth and Reconciliation] Commission is really to define the terms, to set the terms of a social debate', and in this sense is quite different from the International Tribunals for former Yugoslavia and Rwanda – although he argued that the

Commission missed this opportunity in not facing up to the 'banal reality' of apartheid – the reality of Pass Laws, forced removals, Bantu education, and the reality of racialized poverty alongside racialized wealth (Mamdani 1998).

No matter how much South Africans may try to ignore it or argue vehemently against it, the Commission has been a part of the fabric of the lives of South Africans and became a reference point around which the past and the future could be discussed and debated. It was created as a public forum, a structure within which 'ordinary people' could confront their place, their role and the harm they either experienced, committed or observed, within the apartheid regime. Many South Africans may have needed to have nothing to do with the Commission – they may be neither victim nor perpetrator – yet it may have changed the reference points of their lives in a way in which the change of government did not. Governmental change can be explained as a political exercise, put down to politics and regime change. The Truth and Reconciliation Commission, however, forced many people, mainly white South Africans, to engage with the reality of apartheid in a way in which they had never previously been forced to do. It forced many South Africans to confront their place in this system.

Thus the process became something much more than a legal process. As the journalist Antjie Krog wrote, in respect to the process of amnesty within the Truth and Reconciliation Commission, it became the only forum where South Africans can say, 'We may not have committed a human rights abuse, but we want to say that what we did – or didn't do – was wrong and that we're sorry' (Krog 1998: 121–22). She relates a story of six black youths walking into the Commission's offices in Cape Town, shortly before midnight on Saturday, 10 May 1997, the final deadline for amnesty applications. They filled out the forms and took the oath. Their application read: 'Amnesty for Apathy' (ibid).

In the main case studies analyzed above (the Armenian genocide, the Holocaust, Cambodia, Ethiopia, South Africa, Rwanda and the former Yugoslavia) and those brought into the discussion (post-communist and post-military regime countries), a distinction can be drawn between the types of legal proceedings and their impact (state, institutional and societal) felt by societies when the end of harm is negotiated, and the types of legal proceedings and their impact when the harm is ended through force.

In all of these cases law appears to play a constitutive or intra-societal role only in negotiated transitions. As discussed, it may play a role in punishment and accountability in situations of internal or external defeat, but when the conflict ends through violence, law takes some time (if ever) to play a constitutive role. We see that reconciliation and reconstruction through law is a vain hope in the former Yugoslavia at this point in time, with its division into separate states. It took years for Cambodia to address the state crime of the Khmer Rouge and for law to begin to play a constitutive role.

If the harm is ended through internal defeat, that is, if the 'victor' gains control of the country, then the legal proceedings can be an extension of this control. We saw this illustrated in Chapter 3 and it is clear in both Rwanda and Ethiopia. Law has a greater chance of playing a constitutive role in the wake of negotiated transitions, than when the transition is imposed or violently achieved.

Negotiated transition has the possibility to provide something different. It is clear that while the Truth and Reconciliation Commission of South Africa provided the space within which a formal accounting of the past could take place, it also stimulated processes outside of this framework, creating spaces for further societal debate both in and outside the Commission framework. The success of South Africa's Commission is that in its being a public, inclusive and holistic process, it has the potential to be an enduring process. This is something that processes of lustration in the post-communist countries, or even individual war crimes trials, cannot claim. The South African process also points to a crucial factor in the societal impact of legal and political-legal proceedings – the connection between the chosen legal institutional approach and political will. Political will and institutional design clearly influence the possibilities of law to facilitate societal reconstruction in the wake of state crime.

It is the new government that chooses the legal process taken. New states choose what their imagined future will look like together with what they can, politically, do. Law here is used as a tool again in governing. Of course this can be chosen for them as well – as in the case of East Timor where the dominant models were imposed by the international community.

The 'state crime' legal institutional approach

The institutional design and legal process chosen can have an impact on the potential for societal reconstruction. This can be dependent on what the mandate for the legal process is – what does it hear, who does it hear? Are all harms heard, how far back does the mandate go? Does the legal and political-legal approach taken characterize the harm broadly as 'state crime', or does the approach identify the perpetrators solely as individuals or communities? In this next section I discuss the broad institutional approach taken in legal redress for mass harm, suggesting that a 'state crime' approach has the most chance of stimulating processes of societal reconstruction. Building into the legal process the investigation of such crime as *state crime* allows communities and societies to develop their own formative and constitutive structures and spaces for reconstruction.

If a purely individual approach to legal redress is taken, the effect can be the closing of channels, and the limitation of any foundational moment for that society. An approach that locates responsibility purely at the individual, or communal, level will freeze identities. In the context of Rwanda, the Hutu will remain killer and the Tutsi victim. A more holistic approach, that recognizes the institutional dimension of the crime, has a greater chance of contributing to societal reconstruction. The constitution of the society through legal proceedings for the purposes of societal reconstruction and possible reconciliation appears to be absent in Rwanda and Ethiopia. The purpose of the legal process, as suggested earlier, is the further consolidation of control: this is its constitutive function. It could be termed a backwards looking foundational moment. This is in contrast to the South African Truth and Reconciliation Commission, an institution designed to address both individual and institutional responsibility, and that takes a 'state crime' approach.

In the approach taken by the Rwandan national legal proceedings, there is no space, for example, for Hutus who saved Tutsis, or for Hutus who were themselves targeted. In the Rwandan national legal proceedings, there is no process at the official level which might allow for an explanation other than the Hutu perpetration of violence against Tutsi victims. Mahmood Mamdani notes that the state language in Rwanda, the language of state officials and also of others, divides the population of Rwanda into five categories: returnees, refugees, victims, survivors and perpetrators. As he writes, 'to be a Hutu in contemporary Rwanda is to be presumed a *perpetrator*' (Mamdani 2001: 266–67). There is no category for those who rescued and those who saved (Mamdani 1996: 22–23).

While some Hutus may have taken advantage of the climate to 'settle old scores', the legal approach taken does not allow for the institutional parameters of the genocide and its orchestrated and planned nature, and the harnessing of media and churches to be recognized. There is no room for an explanation of the broader dimensions to the genocide, its state-orchestrated nature. While legislation (such as that which bans ethnic and racial identity on identity cards) and public institutions (such as the Rwandan National Unity and Reconciliation Commission) to support a 'coming together' of Rwandans has been introduced, the population is said to be more divided than ever. Although this can be expected in the wake of a genocide, and indeed it can be questioned, as discussed earlier, whether there can be deep reconciliation immediately in the wake of such crime and in fact whether it is reasonable to expect this, the approach taken by the Rwandan government does not appear at this stage to encourage nor stimulate societal reconstruction. The approach taken through law has been one that fosters division.

In this political context, the statement in the preamble to the Organic Law No. 08/96 of 30 August 1996 which established the trial process, that ' … in order to achieve reconciliation and justice in Rwanda, it is essential that the culture of impunity be eradicated forever', has not been realized. Measures such as trials held outside on hilltops or parading those without files intended to be released from jails through communes, can also be seen as efforts to prevent further bloodshed (revenge killings), not efforts at greater public participation to achieve reconciliation.[3] The decision by the government to resurrect customary law and formally establish gacaca tribunals to try accused in the second and third categories of the national genocide legislation, can in this light be viewed as a strategy to move quickly through the then estimated 122,000 persons still in Rwanda's jails on genocide charges, rather than a means of Rwandans 'coming together'.

The use of legal proceedings for limited purposes can similarly be observed in the Dergue trials in Ethiopia. The 1992 proclamation establishing the Office of the Special Prosecutor stated in its preamble 'it is in the interest of a just historical obligation to record for posterity the brutal offences [and] the embezzlement of property perpetrated against the people of Ethiopia and to educate the people and make them aware of these offences in order to prevent the recurrence of such a system of government' (Proclamation No 22/1992). It is a historical record the government is keeping a very tight rein on, as evidenced by the political appointment of judges and dismissal of defence counsel.

In the context of Rwanda, Mamdani comments that in 1995, less than one year after the genocide, a growing consensus in Rwanda involved two propositions. The first was that the number legally responsible for genocide and the number that one can politically afford to hold responsible are not the same. Within this observation, Mamdani makes a crucial point: that the answer to the question, 'who planned the genocide', cannot *begin* with an identification of individuals. The brief response to this question, he notes, must be 'the state power'. Only then will the responsibility for the genocide be political, not ethnic (Mamdani 1996: 20). Mamdani appears to make this as a reconciliation point – that in order to find a political basis for the reunification of the population, one must seek political, not purely individual, answers. His second observation is that justice must seek to identify those who sought to divide the population into two – killers and victims – and isolate those who did not. Importantly, he draws attention to the significant group who refused to participate or dared to shelter Tutsi people; that public attention must thus be brought to this group and a general amnesty given to the rest (ibid). He relates a conversation with the head of the Rwandan Army Political Group, who said: 'If you can bring to trial those who planned the genocide, then the question of the peasant who caught people on the hills is political. We can overlook that' (ibid). Clearly though, this wisdom did not prevail – as the over 100,000 persons who ended up in jail on charges of genocide attests.

An approach taken that highlights and encompasses the institutional dimensions of state crime, that investigates it as crimes perpetrated by states – that is, as acts that contain an institutional and political dimension distinguishable from individual murder or individual acts of harm – can have a different impact to one highlighting only individual (or communal) responsibility. This is in addition to individual responsibility, which, as Chapter 4 showed, is part of any holistic addressing of state crime. What is suggested, however, is that whereas the location of responsibility purely at the individual level will not stimulate societal reconstruction, the inclusion of responsibility at the political and institutional level may.

In Chapter 4 I suggested a distinction between *criminal* liability for key leaders and *civic* liability for key institutions, both state and non-state. Civic

Table 5.1 Institutional approach to state crime: assessment and action

Process	Action
Establishing causation	Post-mortem: Untangle web, understand structure of crime
Establishing responsibility	Identify key players: Individuals and institutions
Establishing liability	Prosecute key individuals
Transformation	Acquit civic liability: Reorganize and transform key institutions
Reconciliation and reconstruction	Initiate processes of 'coming together' Initiate processes of broader reconstruction

liability was put forward as a way to conceptualize institutional non-individual accountability as a core component of state crime. What this means in practical terms is an approach which both addresses all the components of the crime and provides a structure for transformation.

A two-phase process to achieve this can be identified:

(1) The immediate project of legal remedy. This is the establishment of causation, responsibility and potential liability. It includes in its approach both the recognition of the parameters of a state crime, and significant addressing of key perpetrators and remedies for victims for the offenses committed, including the establishment of a framework for institutional reorganization and transformation. It is here that we find civic liability for institutional redress together with individual liability.

(2) The ongoing forward-looking project of transformation (societal and institutional) and the assumption of responsibility for redress for what has occurred. This second stage includes an emphasis on broader societal and state reconstruction, and may include reconciliation.

We can summarize this process in Table 5.1.

Table 5.1 shows the clear and necessary links between the projects of immediate legal remedy and societal transformation. Civic liability is one important link between the two phases. It establishes a framework for transformation and allocates responsibility within a legal process to institutions. It is a way of demonstrating that liability for state crime does not lie with the individual alone.

Conclusion

This chapter has shown that law can function on three important levels in relation to societal reconstruction and reconciliation: as a vehicle for personal or communal knowledge, as a potential base for wider societal understanding, and as a vehicle and catalyst for institutional change. It is this last that is key in considering the relationship between a broader institutional reconstruction and a deeper societal change. Most legal proceedings provide official acknowledgement of the harm perpetrated and a statement of the facts of this harm. The extent to which this is a complex, nuanced account, however, varies significantly.

Achieving a framework for societal debate and a 'foundational moment' for the society is less easily attainable. The case studies have shown us that the channels that facilitate the move from official acknowledgement and statement of the facts to institutional reconstruction and intra-societal reconstruction and reconciliation are dependent upon a number of factors. These shape whether the constitutive role played by law is deep or shallow. These factors include who initiates the proceedings, the particular type of state crime addressed, the manner of cessation of the conflict, and the legal institutional approach taken. The case studies have also shown that different contexts result in different levels of reconstruction and reconciliation – for example, the reconciliation processes between the former West Germany and the State of Israel compared with the reconciliation processes in South Africa.

It cannot be assumed that in all situations law can be expected to play a role beyond accountability, that a role beyond accountability will even be possible. Addressing the parameters of state crimes, as shown in Chapter 4, is critical to a broader accountability. But even this may not lead to a broader reconstruction or reconciliation. This chapter has suggested that the role played by legal proceedings does differ, according to the type of state crime addressed, and according to the approach taken to the legal proceedings. The case studies have shown that building into the legal process the investigation of certain crimes as *state crimes* allows communities and societies to develop their own formative structures and spaces for reconstruction. These may be developed and acted upon outside of law, but can be fuelled by law and legal political acts which themselves will come to be seen as foundational moments.

Harm by the state must be acknowledged as such. This provides a key foundation for any further reconstruction. Without concurrent institutional and structural change, however, without a broader political and social reconstruction, any intra-societal reconstruction may be hollow. What becomes fundamental is a holistic redress that considers the range of causes of the state crime, and then sets up the possibility of institutional change.

Addressing the particular legacies and causes of state crime, providing a level of institutional change that will frame any societal reconstruction, is critical in addressing state crime, if enduring reconstruction is to be found. In this, it is crucial that the particular differences between state crime are recognized – different types of harm, different approaches to using law, different causes and different endings.

Some general principles can be observed from the case studies. These can be read as hypotheses to guide future research on new cases of state crime:

- When the harm is forcibly ended by an external power, the proceedings convened will generally be externally convened, have limited reconstructive potential, yet be a reliable vehicle for discovering a set of facts of what has occurred (the Nuremberg and Yugoslav scenario).

- When the harm is forcibly ended internally, any legal proceedings convened will most likely be an extension of control, and have limited reconstructive potential (the Rwanda and Ethiopia scenario).
- Negotiated transition offers the greatest hope for an approach that will most stimulate processes of reconstruction (the South Africa scenario), yet there is the danger that policies of reconciliation may overshadow policies of accountability.
- If law takes a purely individual approach, then broader reconstruction and reconciliation is less likely.
- An approach which frames the acts committed as 'state crime' will most likely stimulate processes of reconstruction (the South Africa scenario).
- Reconciliation is something that can be achieved independently of law – but is not sustainable without institutional support and transformation and without the public acknowledgement by legal processes (the South Africa scenario).

Finally, the opening of a transformative space is dependent upon political will, which in turn can be gathered generally from the circumstances of the cessation of harm, as can be observed in the cases of Cambodia, Rwanda and Ethiopia, in which there has been a blockage of law as a conduit to further reconstruction. However, even when political will favours a non-retributive approach (as in the case of the International Criminal Tribunal for the former Yugoslavia or the International Criminal Tribunal for Rwanda), the functioning of legal process at a distance means a failure in terms of any immediate societal reconstruction.

The most crucial role law must play is in establishing these possibilities, institutional and societal reconstruction and reconciliation. That is, constituting monitored, accountable fora which may enable it. We must be cautious in our expectations that victims engage in reconciliation in the wake of state crime. In this, the feat of the South African truth commission is extraordinary, in that it was able to provide a framework for reconstruction and a space for reconciliation. While not all took it up, some did, and it is up to the South African government now to build on its recommendations for change.

Enduring reconciliation may not occur in the first instance, even with the structural institutional dimension contributed to by legal process. The temporal dimensions of reconciliation are different to those of other processes such as accountability. It may not occur in the first generation, nor even in the second generation – it may never fully occur. All law can do is attempt to stimulate this process, providing a framework through a full accountability. What the state can do is to push for structural harmony – not for love, but for co-existence, ways of 'living together'. The final report of the Truth and Reconciliation Commission of South Africa was clear on this. If groups are to continue living together it is an important question for new governments to ask how divides will be healed, and thus, how reconciliation may come about. If, on the other hand, they wish to use these divides to their own political advantage (as can be seen in Rwanda and in the former Yugoslavia in part), the question of reconciliation will only be a rhetorical one.

Law's relationship to reconstruction is rather like its relation to reconciliation: the law constitutes spaces for reconstruction and reconciliation that are just and accountable rather than pursuing reconstruction and reconciliation as legal objectives. In so doing, law as formal and state-authorized has the potential to stimulate and to frame the normative sphere, and create conditions through which societies may find ways of living together. We should not expect reconciliation in the wake of state crime. However, we can consider ways in which the use of law may create a basis of rights, reparation and acknowledgement that will create a strong reparative and inclusionary basis for a society. This can firstly be through bringing to account both individuals and institutions complicit in state crime, and secondly, through considering ways in which law may be used to create and reshape new institutional arrangements in the wake of mass harm. In so doing, law may provide a way both to reconstitute in the wake of mass harm and provide an institutional framework for prevention.

Notes

1 In an investigation into the Rwandan Patriotic Front (RPF), commissioned by the United Nations High Commissioner for Refugees, undertaken by a senior US Government official, Robert Gersony, it was concluded that the RPF killed an estimated 30,000 civilians in their approach to Kigali. The inquiry, concluded in September 1994, was suppressed by the former United Nations Secretary-General Boutros-Boutros Ghali, although the findings had already been presented to members of the Rwandan Government by officials of the United Nations High Commissioner for Refugees. These conclusions were later confirmed by Gérard Prunier, who testified at the Belgium Senate Inquiry into the Rwandan genocide that *'je crois aujourd'hui que ce chiffre est une sous-estimation'* (I believe today that this figure is an undervaluation): Compte Rendu Analytique des Auditions, *Commission d'enquête parlementaire concernant les événtments du Rwanda. Bruxelles* (Senat de Belgique 1997: 717). I am grateful to Fiona Terry for her translation of this.
2 An independent International Commission of Inquiry (established in Kigali on 3 May 1995) into the killings at the Kibeho camp for internally displaced persons in April 1995 did confirm the killings, however it concluded 'there is no evidence to suggest that the operation was intended to eliminate a certain category of people, especially those belonging to one ethnic group' (Brisset-Foucault 1995: 7).
3 Trials held 'on the hills' were a form of legal proceeding occasionally chosen by judges, within the Rwandan criminal trial process. To encourage the acceptance of sentences, judges literally held the trials outside, on the hilltops, so that people of that commune would witness the proceedings.

Chapter 6

Law and the constitution of state crime and genocide

In conclusion, this book considers the connections between law in perpetration, law in redress and law in prevention. It considers the constitutive effect of law and what this may mean for the place of law in society and in relation to the state.

Years ago I attended a commemoration for the genocide of the Armenians, at Chatswood Town Hall in Sydney, Australia. It held many similarities to the numerous Holocaust commemorations I had attended over the years – the same solemnity, and dignity, the telling of the stories, the reciting of prose, the same gravity. A coming together of a community to remember and to mourn.

One thing was achingly different, however – and this was a palpable absence of any recognition. For the killing of 1.2 million Armenians by the Ottoman state during the First World War, there was, and still is, no official recognition. This extends to the lack of recognition of the other Christian minorities, the Assyrians and Pontiac Greeks, also murdered by the Ottoman state. This crime of genocide has not been named as such. Rather, modern-day Turkey has spuriously engaged in a system of denial, supported by most of the world. It is only recently that some countries have recognized the genocide perpetrated by the Ottoman state, with Parliaments and Heads of States acknowledging this state crime. This is despite the killings being recognized as genocide by international scholars, despite the existence of numerous eyewitness accounts, and despite the Ottoman state, and the Allies, initially declaring it as a crime to be punished and Turkey establishing its own Courts-Martial to try the perpetrators.

I in fact was taught nothing about the genocide of the Armenians while studying history at school, and it was only when I did a subject at university in my political science studies, *The Politics of Genocide*, that examined both the genocide of the Armenians and the Holocaust, taught by Professor Colin Tatz, that I learned about this genocide. There is in fact more official denialist literature available produced by Turkey and persons and institutions supported by Turkey than scholarship on the genocide.

It is in this context that the recognition by the Australian government of the harms committed by the Australian state against the Stolen Generations, the Aboriginal children taken by the state from their parents, elicited an enormous sense of relief. The apology given at the beginning of 2008 in the Federal Parliament by both the Prime Minister and the Leader of the Opposition was a key moment. Listened to by millions on large screens and in small halls around the country, it was both a cathartic relief for many Australians to hear the words said, and a critical recognition for many victims and survivors in the indigenous community. For those of us who were initially sceptical about the apology (and I was one of them), seeing it as political expedient and empty words, it was humbling to hear the responses from those affected, and to be reminded how crucial such recognition – and apology – can be. Comments such as 'be like a whole new day for us' and 'bring a whole lot of healing' reminded me of the power and necessity of acknowledgement, crucially official and state acknowledgement.

The lack of such official acknowledgement can be devastating to survivors. This I saw at the commemoration of the genocide against the Armenians at that town hall in Chatswood years ago, and heard in the stories of survivors. I heard it recently again in a community forum on genocide, in which Assyrian community members spoke. In commemorating, these communities must not only honour and mourn their dead, but convince the world that it in fact happened. The indigenous community in Australia has had to do the same in relation to its stolen children. And must still do in relation to the many crimes of dispossession and genocide committed in the name of establishing a British colony and a new nation.

Official acknowledgement can create a space for mourning. It is crucial for victims. It is also crucial for the state. Official acknowledgement creates a remembrance that is critical for a nation and its future. It is critical that state crime be brought into the history of a nation, be publicly acknowledged, and be forged into its institutions.

But it is generally not enough. This is where the partnership with law becomes so important. Law both rests on acknowledgement, and creates it. The decision to use law to address state crime is of necessity based on official acknowledgement of the perpetration of the crime. Being taken up by law, however, moves it from being possibly empty political statements, to having urgency, and consequence. It also moves acknowledgement into the realm of justice.

It is just for survivors that there be recognition of what was done to them. This is the minimum that they ask. It is why there was the imperative to record and remember during the Holocaust, with the words of scholar Simon Dubnow: 'Yidn, shreibt un ferschreibt' ('Jews, write and record'). It is why at the end of the war the Jewish communities established their own 'Historical Commissions' in the Displaced Persons camps in Germany, to gather documentary evidence both of the world that was lost and of what had been perpetrated. To do justice requires at minimum the use of law. This does not mean that law will result in justice. We have seen survivors argue that the use of law does not result in justice, a broader justice that includes health, employment and security. What the law does may not even be what survivors want. What it does, at best, however, is implant itself in the institutional memory of the state, and in so doing provide a basis for prevention. And, critically, provide a level of recognition for the survivors.

In addition to recognition, it is the systematic and accurate accounting by law – the determination of responsibility and allocation of liability, both criminal and civic – that is core. Law creates legacies. It is incumbent then that the story get told in its entirety. Thus, we need to be cautious of the overt focus on individual reconciliation in legal proceedings for state crime – that this may tell a different story, one based on 'individual hatreds' rather than the more complete story of state-organized perpetration of mass harm. We must be alert to a broader accountability, one that includes institutions as well as individuals.

What we are dealing with is state crime, state-organized harm of the individuals within its control. The key challenge to law is to address these crimes as crimes of state. This, as I have discussed in the book, throws up particular issues of redress and complicity that law must deal with. These are crimes perpetrated 'in the name of the state', to fulfil state policy and to violently fashion a state or state to be in a particular and terrible image. This means the perpetration of systematic exclusions and destructions of individuals and groups within its realm.

How law acknowledges is critical. How it portrays the acts perpetrated. How it attributes responsibility. In acknowledging the role of the state or emerging state, and in recognizing the involvement of institutions, it has the potential to reconstitute. Law's addressing of state crime can play a powerful role in the constitution of this crime. In being taken up by law, there is recognition and acknowledgement of the harm perpetrated. How it is constituted through law, however, can have wider implications for the life of that society. The recognition of state crime as crimes perpetrated by the state is critical in acknowledging the kind of harm perpetrated. Further, it is critical in enabling law's reconstructive potential.

Addressing the dimensions of state crime means considering how to 'redo' the exclusions perpetrated, to consider new institutional arrangements and new ways of living together in the new state. Any reconciliation that ensues is dependent on a framework of broad institutional change to support this, and to make it sustainable. This can include new constitutions, new citizenship legislation, new institutional arrangements for political representation, and legislation that allows for an equality of inclusion and access. It is a process both focused at official law but one too that must work with the unofficial normative orders, the 'living law' of that society. When law during the perpetration of state crime impacts on and delineates who is citizen, then it is critical that law after addresses this as well. These are ideological crimes of exclusion, on who is considered citizen and worthy of protection – how then to include becomes fundamental.

Addressing the parameters of state crime also means considering how to bring the institutions, both state and non-state, that are harnessed by the state and who collaborate with the state, into a process of legal redress. There has been some innovation in this, with the concept of a 'common plan' devised at Nuremberg, or 'common purpose' as now used at the permanent International Criminal Court. What we need to think further about, as I suggested in Chapter 4, is how to bring the state and its institutions into the process of accountability. This, I suggested, means moving beyond (although not excluding) individual liability to institutional liability, through to what I term civic liability. While it may include some criminalization of institutions, it is focused on a transformation and a bringing to account institutions of the state and of civil society who abrogated their responsibility to protect. It is a way of bringing the institutions into a process of accountability and liability that becomes a comprehensive one, and may focus us thereby both on redress as well as prevention. As noted by the Truth and Reconciliation Commission of South Africa prior to the hearings into the role of the law and the legal establishment in apartheid, 'to identify institutional changes required to prevent those abuses which occurred from happening again' (Truth and Reconciliation Commission of South Africa 1997a).

Without access to its institutions or significant resources, state crime could not be of this magnitude. State responsibility is acquitted through institutional responsibility – through the transforming of institutions. It is through these crimes being *state* directed that they send an official message of inclusion and exclusion. It is only in addressing the institutions afterwards within the framework of the state that we will be able to move from exclusion to inclusion.

Law must focus on accountability first. It establishes causation, attributes responsibility and then liability. This initial specific redress is critical to any broader societal redress. Yet with this done, it can be a springboard to other processes, to a broader acknowledgement and transformation. The concept of civic liability can be used to achieve transformation of institutions to achieve societal reconstruction. It is in this ongoing forward-looking project of transformation (societal and institutional) together with the immediate project of legal remedy that lasting redress for state crime may be found.

Law plays a particular role during state crime, as collaborator and companion to the state. It establishes the new state, and is used as a partner in nation-building. It is the state in the perpetration of state crime that assumes power, under cover of law, over life and death. As Arnold Toynbee wrote in his account of the genocide of the Armenians:

[This] genocide was carried out under the cloak of legality by cold-blooded governmental action. These were not mass-murders committed spontaneously by mobs of private people …

(Dadrian 1996: 421)

The state does not relinquish this power easily – as we saw in Chapter 2 in the case of Johann Meisslein, who in being accused of ordering two Jewish women to be killed, was found guilty of *Amtsanmaßung*, assuming powers one did not have. Yet it makes law companion in this, in establishing the conditions which make this possible. And, as in the case of the genocide by the Ottoman state, forming legislation to cover it. This is both the formal legislation of exclusion in South Africa and in Nazi Germany, and the space of difference they establish, yet also the informal laws that are created that made Meisslein's foreman believe that being told to take someone away meant to kill them.

The fact of law operating in such conditions makes it collaborator. It may still operate as a forum for alternate voices at times, as the use of political trials by activists in apartheid South Africa demonstrated. As Fullard noted, 'the courtroom became the last remaining space in which banned organizations could articulate their views' (Fullard 2004: 342). Yet it was also by definition a partial justice. As Nelson Mandela pointed out in his 1962 trial in Pretoria, 'a judiciary controlled entirely by whites and enforcing laws enacted by a white parliament in which we have no representation' cannot mean any equality before the law (Mandela 1986: 135).

Yet that law can operate as a space for injustice to be voiced (if not necessarily heard) during state crime means that it has the possibility to continue this way. Further, that while law is partner in creating the nation, it stops short of partnering in extermination or killings, allows it to maintain some legitimacy. Law is able to occupy a space between the past and the present. In appearing to continue in some kind of tradition, whether a deep legal one of Germany where laws of exclusion were introduced, or a more informal legal ordering as in Cambodia where the Khmer Rouge took over the role of the 'wise men', its use demonstrates a kind of continuity that makes the terror less remarked upon. In so doing it can provide too a continuity in the wake of state crime. For these reasons, we see law still appealed to in the wake of state crime. Law that so often stood by, or was a companion to the state crime, is the vehicle now used to administer redress.

Importantly, law can create a record. The Turkish Courts-Martial did this. In its hearing of eyewitness testimony and its gathering of documentation, together with the judgements of the estimated twenty-four trials held, an institutional record has been created. It is a record that has been made inaccessible to most scholars, but it is one that exists. We see similar records in the trials for the genocide in Rwanda and for the war in the former Yugoslavia, as too the trials of Mengistu and the Dergue in Ethiopia. Through witness and victim testimony, together with a piecing together of the evidence to create a picture of what has been perpetrated, we see important records maintained.

Records established by law during state crime can be of importance as well. Priscilla Hayner has noted that *Brasil: Nunca Maís*, the independent report authored by the Archbishop of São Paulo and the World Council of Churches on the human rights violations carried out during military rule in Brazil, in particular their policy of torture, relied on the evidence of official court documents which included prisoners' complaints of abuse, photocopied in secret by the investigators (Hayner 1994: 652). Further, in Chile, *Comisión Nacional para la Verdad y Reconciliación*, the government commission established to investigate abuses resulting in death or disappearance over the previous seventeen years of military rule, relied on legal records to provide its initial evidence. Hayner suggests that due to a strong legal tradition in Chile, the vast majority of cases of disappearances were taken to court during the years of military rule, leaving detailed records (ibid: 621). These records were given to the Commission and provided important evidence. While the court system in Chile under military rule rarely provided justice, it was still able to provide a detailed record of the abuses committed, even if those abuses had not been properly addressed by the courts.

Decisions around state crime are contentious and contested. It is rare that a state initiates proceedings for state crime, and this is almost always dependent on a change of regime. Legal proceedings for state crime define the state. They have at their core a judgement on how a state treats its citizens. States can have every reason to counter it (we see this with victim-initiated legal proceedings in Australia), so these foundational moments can be brief. The history of the genocide of the Armenians and other Christian minorities is contentious because it defines the Ottoman state as a genocidal state. It redefines the self-image of the nation. New legislation was introduced to overturn the decisions of the Courts-Martial that had found otherwise, and perpetrators found guilty were transformed into 'national martyrs'. The law here has not become part of the institutionalized history of the state as its findings were so quickly and comprehensively overturned.

Law during state crime is a partner in nation-building. In the use of law after, we see a similar role for law. What we see in national legal processes for state crime is the use of law as a tool of governance of the new regime. It is used to signal its mandate and its approach. This may be in a weak or strong manner. For example, in the case of Cambodia, in the direct aftermath of the killings, genocide and dispossession of the Cambodian people and particular groups by the Khmer Rouge, the Vietnamese installed government used the *in absentia* trial of Pol Pot and Ieng Sary in a number of ways. It installed their authority to the Cambodian people. It drew a clear line between the old regime of the Khmer Rouge and the new one of the Vietnamese. It signalled to the Khmer Rouge that they were now on the political periphery.

Yet while the trials clearly spelt out the nature of the crimes committed, and did establish a record to an audience of Khmer as well as internationally, this is where it stopped. There were few prosecutions of Khmer Rouge cadre, and in fact they were largely incorporated within the structure of the state. The 1979 Tribunal, and the later local trial of Pol Pot, can be seen to be important in terms of their role of 'cutting down' the 'big men' of the Khmer Rouge. This can be seen as a weak form of legal redress, although clearly playing a particular normative role at that moment. Stronger redress was to come much later, with the current joint United Nations-Cambodia criminal tribunal, and it is too early to say how sustained this will be. While there has been a strong push for a Tribunal, both by international and national non-governmental organizations and by Cambodians, victims have also used their own ways to address the harm perpetrated against them, harnessing a kind of 'living law' that was of necessity separate to the inaction of the state and the international community.

In Rwanda, there has been a constant and sustained national legal redress since the genocide was ended through the invasion of the Rwandan Patriotic Front, the Tutsi exile army. This is in contrast to the use of law during the genocide, yet the local nature of the trials accords with the local use of law prior to the genocide. The numbers of victims who have been turning up to criminal trials demonstrates the importance of local proceedings for victims. The gacaca proceedings are less clear. There have been reports of coercion for attendance, and of former victims afraid to speak against the 'reintegration' of former perpetrators into the community, due to a government push for 'reconciliation' (see Aghion 2002, 2009). There have also been reports of people being afraid to testify at the hearings in support of Hutus due to the new genocide denial legislation (Human Rights Watch 2008). Yet there have also been reports that they have achieved a sense of solidarity for victims (Clark 2010).

Law has been used as a clear tool of governance by the Rwandan state. While clearly a difficult task in the wake of a country destroyed, complicated by lack of resources, the process has it seems, missed an opportunity to use the legal process to establish the broad parameters of the genocide, rather focusing on the many individual perpetrators responsible for the killings. The local nature, both through the many local criminal courts utilized as well as the gacaca meetings, means that they are close to communities in which survivors live. This has been important it seems for public accountability, and victim participation. Yet the state-directed nature of the genocide it seems has been less highlighted.

In Ethiopia, we see a use of law similar to its use in perpetration. Like the Special Proclamations brought in under Mengistu, the trials clearly signalled the new regime. While clearly necessary, as a tool of accountability for the systematic and enduring atrocities of the Mengistu regime, the heavy handedness with which they were overseen meant that the trials failed to be a public and inclusive process. They appear to have been used as a clear tool of governance, with limited access by most Ethiopians, and control on the reporting of the trials. Yet their marginalization too by the international community was disappointing, as they had the potential to be an important set of trials for a state crime.

The first wave of post-war Germany proceedings were established in the direct aftermath of the crimes committed by the Nazi regime. Their aim was specifically to punish the perpetrators, to separate out 'Germans' and 'perpetrators' and to establish a new foundation for (ultimately West) Germany. These included the International Military Tribunal at Nuremberg, the war crimes trials held in the different Allies' zones, and the denazification procedures. They also included specific 'crisis' legislation such as currency reform. There has been a deep use of law, that continues today. What has been marked about the response is the dominant and immediate focus on perpetrator redress. Victim redress came later. What we have seen less of is a broader, more societal redress. For example, it is only fairly recently that Germany changed its citizenship legislation to grant German citizenship to those born in Germany, not just those of 'German descent' (and even this remains limited). It has meant that a discriminatory attitude has persisted to those defined as 'non-Germans' such as those born in Turkey or of Turkish descent. While legislation such as Holocaust denial or anti-Nazi legislation has been important, its 'forward looking' nature has been limited in its being focused on the past rather than what may be taken out of it more broadly: that is, who is perceived to be German.

Law has been peripheral to the states of the former Yugoslavia. It has either failed them again, like the International Court of Justice judgement that found Serbia not responsible for the genocide at Srebrenica (although importantly, naming it genocide) or been too far away to make an impact. Local legal responses have been slow to eventuate.

The generation of a local legal process through the Ottoman parliamentary system demonstrated the continued importance of law. That the Courts-Martial could arise though existing local processes showed the centrality of law. Despite being used as companion during the genocide, it was called upon again to provide redress, albeit short-lived.

South Africa shied away from direct perpetrator redress, rather fashioning an institution that included both victim redress as well as a more societal redress. Its impact was clearly greater on the latter, but in its setting out of the apartheid regime and in its amnesty provision for perpetrators, it included both, with a process for the 'bringing to account' of institutions that had collaborated with and supported the apartheid state.

What is important in legal redress for state crime is that these legal processes are integrated into the systems of the society on which they focus. What we see in the wake of state crime are legal processes introduced 'on top of' existing institutions. For example, new truth commissions or new criminal tribunals. While these can be important in establishing an overt foundational moment, in clearly marking the space between the past and the present, their separateness can also mean a lack of integration into the everyday frameworks of the state. This can be a problem for prevention, when addressing genocide and other forms of state crime 'sits outside' the usual processes of the state and its citizenry. In the same way, as Fraenkel has noted (1941: 87), that those classified as Jewish in Nazi Germany were subject, with the introduction of the 1935 Nuremberg laws, to the 'exceptional' laws (the *Ausnahmegesetze*) as well as to the general Aryan Laws of 1933, redress in the wake of state crime takes the form of 'exceptional' laws as well. These are little integrated, and introduced on top of existing legislation and institutions. We see only later, for example with the merging of the Human Rights Chamber of the Dayton Agreement in Bosnia-Herzegovina into the Constitutional Court, that some integration may occur.

What the law makes possible can be seen both during state crime and in its aftermath. The utilization of law during the perpetration of harm makes possible the acceptance of the greater crimes committed that occur outside of law. The use of law in redress for state crime is a statement of official acknowledgement that can be a foundational moment and form a basis for reconciliation and further reconstruction. The accountability process, both individual and institutional, can provide a basis for implementation of particular institutional reforms that may provide a basis of prevention. We can also identify its limits. For example, as discussed in Chapter 5, reconciliation as a goal of law may do a disservice to law's broader mission of accountability – yet the use of law for redress may facilitate processes of reconciliation. When law has the ability to constitute can be seen in the legal institutional approach taken. That is, whether the crime is addressed as 'state crime' and thus provides a space for a reconstitution. Does the legal institutional path taken block any 'coming together', or facilitate it? This too, as shown in Chapter 5, is dependent on who establishes the legal processes, where they are located, the type of harm addressed and what their goals are.

Law is companion, collaborator and bystander. Law can also be preventer. We can see these four different roles for law. These are differently activated both during the perpetration of state crime, and after, in attempts at redress. Prevention, however, as we have seen, requires a full accountability, and institutional change.

Law participates, law fails to protect, law makes the crime 'allowable'. Yet law is a site of justice too. We can see here the connections between law in perpetration, law in redress and law in prevention. An examination of the relationship between genocide, state crime and law reveals the fundamental dichotomy within law itself, simply that between law as facilitator of harm, and law as facilitator of redress. Law can both enfranchise and disenfranchise, be a tool of empowerment as well as of exclusion.

Law partners the state in acknowledging its citizens in the wake of state crime, and in determining who is citizen and who is not during state crime. It collaborates in their exclusion, yet is still looked to as a space for justice.

The final report of the South African Truth and Reconciliation Commission included these words from writer Mtutuzeli Matshoba, born in Soweto, and written in the wake of the 1976 uprisings:

> *For neither am I a man in the eyes of the law,*
> *Nor am I a man in the eyes of my fellow man.*
>
> Mtutuzeli Matshoba, *Call Me Not a Man*,
> Ravan Press 1979, p. 18

It is in the perpetration of state crime, and the role that law plays in contributing to its 'allowability', in creating a legitimate space in which it may be possible and accepted, that we see the power of law to exclude, to horrific extent. Yet it is in the process of addressing state crime, in accountability and in redress, that we may see its possibilities – as a framework for a reconstruction and a re-imagining that may, we hope, provide a bulwark against repetition. That law still is seen as a site of justice continues to surprise, yet it is that law maintains this space that gives us hope.

Bibliography

Abel, R.L. (1995) *Politics By Other Means. Law in the Struggle Against Apartheid, 1980–1994*, New York and London: Routledge.

Aghion, A. (2009) *My Neighbour, My Killer*. Videorecording. Gacaca Productions. New York: Anne Aghion.

——(2002) *Gacaca: Living Together Again in Rwanda?* Videorecording. New York: First Run/Icarus Films.

Agreement between the United Nations and the Royal Government of Cambodia Concerning the Prosecution under Cambodian Law of Crimes Committed During the Period of Democratic Kampuchea (2003) Extraordinary Chambers in the Courts of Cambodia/Legal Documents/Agreements, Phnom Penh 6 June. Online. Available HTTP: www.eccc.gov.kh/english/agreement.list.aspx

Agreement for the Prosecution and Punishment of Major War Criminals of the European Axis (1945) 82 U.N.T.S. 279, signed at London, 8 August 1945, entry into force 8 August 1945.

Ahmed, Z. (1996) 'The Case of Bangladesh: Bringing to Trial the Perpetrators of the 1971 Genocide', in A. Jongman (ed.) *Contemporary Genocides: Causes, Cases, Consequences*, Leiden: PIOOM.

Alvarez, A. (2009) *Genocidal Crimes*, London: Routledge.

Amnesty International (2007) *Ethiopia – Amnesty International Report 2007: Human Rights in Federal Democratic Republic of Ethiopia*. Online. Available HTTP: www.amnesty.org/en/region/ethiopia/report-2007

Application of the Convention on the Prevention and Punishment of the Crime of Genocide (2007) Judgment, Bosnia and Herzegovina v. Serbia and Montenegro, ICJ Reports, 91, 26 February.

Application of the Convention on the Prevention and Punishment of the Crime of Genocide (1994) Memorial of the Government of The Republic of Bosnia and Herzegovina, ICJ Reports, 15 April.

Application of the Convention on the Prevention and Punishment of the Crime of Genocide (1993) Order of Court, Memorial of the Government of The Republic of Bosnia and Herzegovina, ICJ Reports, 8 April.

Arad, Y., Gutman, Y. and Margaliot, A. (eds) (1981) *Documents on the Holocaust. Selected Sources on the Destruction of the Jews of Germany and Austria, Poland, and the Soviet Union*, Jerusalem: Yad Vashem.

Arendt, H. [1954] (1994) 'Understanding and Politics (The Difficulties of Understanding)', in H. Arendt (ed.) *Essays in Understanding 1930–1954*, New York:
Harcourt Brace & Company.
——(1963) *Eichmann in Jerusalem: A Report on the Banality of Evil*, Harmondsworth,
England: Penguin Books.
——(1951, 2nd ed 1959) *The Origins of Totalitarianism*, New York: Meridian Books.
Argentine National Commission on the Disappeared (1984) 'Nunca Más: The Report
of the Argentine National Commission on the Disappeared', in N.J. Kritz (ed.)
(1995) *Transitional Justice: How Emerging Democracies Reckon with Former
Regimes: Laws, Rulings, and Reports*, Washington, D.C.: United States Institute of
Peace.
Argentine Presidential Pardons Decree (1989) Argentina, 1002/89.
Ashforth, A. (1990) *The Politics of Official Discourse in Twentieth-Century South
Africa*, New York: Oxford University Press.
Astourian, S. (1992) 'Genocidal Process: Reflections on the Armeno-Turkish Polar-
ization', in R.G. Hovannisian (ed.) *The Armenian Genocide. History, Politics,
Ethics*, New York: St Martin's Press.
Avocats sans Frontieres (1998) *Annual Report*. On file with author.
*Azanian Peoples Organisation (AZAPO) and Others v. The President of the Republic
of South Africa and Others* (1996) South African Constitutional Court, CCT 17/96,
25 July 1996.
Balint, J. (2008) 'Dealing with International Crimes: Towards a Model of Account-
ability and Justice', in A. Smeulers and R. Haveman (eds) *Supranational Criminology:
Towards a Criminology of International Crimes*, Antwerp: Intersentia.
——(1996) 'Conflict, Conflict Victimization, and Legal Redress, 1945–96', *Law and
Contemporary Problems*, 59: 231–47.
Balint, R. (2010) 'The Ties that Bind: Australia, Hungary, and the Case of Károly
Zentai', *Patterns of Prejudice*, 44: 281–303.
Barak, G. (1994) 'Crime, Criminology, and Human Rights: Toward an Under-
standing of State Criminality', in G. Barak (ed.) *Varieties of Criminology. Readings
from a Dynamic Discipline*, Connecticut: Praeger.
——(1991) 'Toward a Criminology of State Criminality', in G. Barak (ed.) *Crimes by
the Capitalist State. An Introduction to State Criminality*, Albany: State University
of New York Press.
Barnett, A. (1983) 'Democratic Kampuchea: A Highly Centralized Dictatorship', in
D.P. Chandler and B. Kiernan (eds) *Revolution and its Aftermath in Kampuchea:
Eight Essays*, Monograph Series No 25, New Jersey: Yale University Southeast
Asia Studies.
Bassiouni, M.C. (2003) *Introduction to International Criminal Law*, Ardsley, New
York: Transnational Publishers.
——(1996) 'The Commission of Experts Established Pursuant to Security Council
Resolution 780: Investigating Violations of International Humanitarian Law in the
Former Yugoslavia', Occasional Paper No 2, International Human Rights Law
Institute, DePaul University College of Law.
Bauer, Y. (1989) *Jewish Reactions to the Holocaust*, Tel Aviv: MOD Books.
Bauman, Z. (1989) *Modernity and the Holocaust*, Cambridge and Oxford: Polity Press.
Becker, E. (1986) *When the War was Over. Cambodia's Revolution and the Voices of
its People*, New York: Simon & Schuster.

Bennett, T.W. (2004) *Customary Law in South Africa*, The Hague: Kluwer.

Berlin, I. (1991) *The Crooked Timber of Humanity. Chapters in the History of Ideas*, London: John Murray.

Boraine, A. (2000) 'Truth and Reconciliation in South Africa. The Third Way', in R.I. Rotberg and D. Thompson (eds) *Truth v. Justice. The Morality of Truth Commissions*, Princeton and Oxford: Princeton University Press.

Boua, C., Kiernan, B. and Barnett, A. (1980) 'Bureaucracy of Death', *New Statesman*, 99: 674.

Braham, R. (1996) 'Hungary', in D. Wyman (ed.) *The World Reacts to the Holocaust*, London: John Hopkins University Press.

Braithwaite, J. (2000) 'Repentance Rituals and Restorative Justice', *The Journal of Political Philosophy*, 8: 115–31.

Braude, C. (1996) 'The Archbishop, the Private Detective and the Angel of History: The Production of South African Public Memory and the Truth and Reconciliation Commission', *Current Writing*, 8: 39–65.

Brietzke, P. (1982) *Law, Development, and the Ethiopian Revolution*, Lewisburg: Bucknell University Press.

Brisset-Foucault, M. (1995) Report of the Independent International Commission of Inquiry on the Events at Kibeho April 1995, Kigali, 18 May.

Brittain, J. (1996) 'Interview with Ntsiki Biko', *Index on Censorship*, 5.

Burman, S. and Schärf, W. (1990) 'Creating People's Justice: Street Committees and People's Courts in a South African City', *Law & Society Review*, 24: 693–744.

Buscher, Frank M. (1989) *The U.S. War Crimes Trial Program in Germany, 1946–1955*, New York: Greenwood Press.

Bushnell, P.T., Shlapentokh, V., Vanderpool, C.K. and Sundram, J. (1991) 'State Organized Terror: Tragedy of the Modern State', in P.T. Bushnell, V. Shlapentokh, C.K. Vanderpool and J. Sundram (eds) *State Organized Terror. The Case of Violent Internal Repression*, Colorado: Westview Press.

Caldwell, P. (1994) 'National Socialism and Constitutional Law: Carl Schmitt, Otto Koellreutter, and the Debate over the Nature of the Nazi State', *Cardozo Law Review*, 16: 399–427.

Carney, T. (1989) 'The Organization of Power', in K.D. Jackson (ed.) *Cambodia 1975–1978. Rendezvous with Death*, New Jersey: Princeton University Press.

Case Concerning Johann Meisslein (1943) Court of the Command Centre of the Area of Proskurow, Military Judgment, F.K.183.

Chambliss, W.J. (1989) 'State-Organized Crime – The American Society of Criminology, 1988 Presidential Address', *Criminology*, 27: 183–208.

Chandler, D.P. (1991) *The Tragedy of Cambodian History*, New Haven and London: Yale University Press.

Chandler, D. (1992) *A History of Cambodia*, 2nd edn, Boulder: Westview Press.

Chandler, D., Kiernan, B. and Boua, C. (trans. and eds) (1988) *Pol Pot Plans the Future. Confidential Leadership Documents from Democratic Kampuchea, 1976–1977*, Monograph Series 33, New Haven: Yale University Southeast Asia Studies.

Chanock, M. (2001) *The Making of South African Legal Culture 1902–1936: Fear, Favour and Prejudice*, Cambridge: Cambridge University Press.

Charny, I.W. (1994) 'Toward a Generic Definition of Genocide', in G. Andreopoulos (ed.) *Genocide: Conceptual and Historical Dimensions*, Philadelphia: University of Pennsylvania Press.

Charny, I.W. with Rapaport, C. (1982) *How Can we Commit the Unthinkable? Genocide: The Human Cancer*, Boulder: Westview Press.

Charter of the International Military Tribunal (1945) Annexed to the London Agreement for the Prosecution and Punishment of the Major War Criminals of the European Axis, London, signed 8 August 1945.

Chhang, Y. (2007) 'The Thief of History – Cambodia and the Special Court', *International Journal of Transitional Justice*, 1: 157–72.

Chilean National Commission on Truth and Reconciliation (1990) *Supreme Decree No. 355*, Santiago: United States Institute of Peace Library, 25 April. Online. Available HTTP: www.usip.org/library/tc/doc/reports/chile/chile_1993_decree.html

Clark, P. (2010) *The Gacaca Courts, Post-Genocide Justice and Reconciliation in Rwanda: Justice without Lawyers*, Cambridge and New York: Cambridge University Press.

Cohen, L. (1993) *Broken Bonds. The Disintegration of Yugoslavia*, Boulder: Westview Press.

Cohen, S. (1995) 'State Crimes of Previous Regimes: Knowledge, Accountability and the Policing of the Past', *Law and Social Inquiry* 20: 7–50.

Constitution of Democratic Kampuchea (1976) trans. Raul Jennar, entry into force 5 January 1976. Online. Available HTTP: www.dccam.org/Archives/Documents/DK_Policy/DK_Policy_DK_Constitution.htm

Constitution of the Republic of South Africa (1996) Act 200, entry into force 4 February 1997. Online. Available HTTP: www.info.gov.za/documents/constitution/1996/index.htm

Constitution of the Republic of South Africa (1993) Act 200, entry into force 27 April 1994. Online. Available HTTP: www.info.gov.za/documents/constitution/93cons.htm

Convention on the Non-Applicability of Statutory Limitations to War Crimes and Crimes against Humanity (1970) U.N. G.A. Res. 2391, 754 U.N.T.S. 73, entry into force November 1970.

Convention on the Prevention and Punishment of the Crime of Genocide (1948) U.N. GA Res. 96, 78 U.N.T.S. 277, entry into force 1 January 1951.

Corder, H. (2004) 'Judicial Authority in a Changing South Africa', *Legal Studies*, 24: 253–74.

——(1998) 'The Law and Change in South Africa', paper presented at Hidden Structures of Law workshop, International Institute for the Sociology of Law, Oñati.

——(1984) *Judges at Work: The Role and Attitudes of the South African Appellate Judiciary 1910–1950*, Cape Town: Juta & Co Ltd.

Cotic, D. (1996) 'Introduction', in R. Clark and M. Sann (eds) *The Prosecution of International Crimes*, New Brunswick: Transaction Publishers.

Crawford, J. (1998) *Special Rapporteur First Report on State Responsibility, Addendum*, International Law Commission Fiftieth Session, A/CN.4/490/Add.3.

Creation of the Commission on Truth and Reconciliation (Chile) (1990) Supreme Decree No. 355. Santiago, 25 April 1990, Online. Available HTTP: www.usip.org/library/tc/doc/reports/chile/chile_1993_decree.html (accessed 17 September 2004).

Cunneen, C. (2008) 'State Crime, The Colonial Question and Indigenous Peoples', in Smeulers, A. and Haveman, R. (eds) *Supranational Criminology: Towards a Criminology of International Crimes*, Antwerp: Intersentia.

Czarnota, A. (2001) 'Law as Mnemosyne and as Lethe: Quasi-Judicial Institutions and Collective Memories', in E. Christodoulidis and S. Veitch (eds) *Lethes's Law. Justice, Law and Ethics in Reconciliation*, Oxford: Hart Publishing.

Dadrian, V.N. (1997a) 'The Turkish Military Tribunal's Prosecution of the Authors of the Armenian Genocide: Four Major Court-Martial Series', *Holocaust and Genocide Studies*, 11: 28–59.

——(1997b) *The History of the Armenian Genocide. Ethnic Conflict from the Balkans to Anatolia to the Caucasus*, 3rd edn, Oxford: Berghahn Books.

——(1996) *German Responsibility in the Armenian Genocide: A Review of the Historical Evidence of German Complicity*, Watertown, Massachusetts: Blue Crane Books.

——(1994a) 'The Documentation of the World War I Armenian Massacres in the Proceedings of the Turkish Military Tribunal', *Journal of Political and Military Sociology*, 22: 97–131.

——(1994b) 'The Secret Young-Turk Ittihadist Conference and the Decision for the World War I Genocide of the Armenians', *Journal of Political and Military Sociology*, 22: 173–201.

——(1993) 'The Role of the Special Organisation in the Armenian Genocide during the First World War', in P. Panayi (ed.) *Minorities in Wartime. National and Racial Groupings in Europe, North America and Australia during the Two World Wars*, Oxford: Berg.

——(1986) 'The Role of Turkish Physicians in the World War I Genocide of Ottoman Armenians', *Holocaust and Genocide Studies*, 1: 10–46.

Dallaire, R. (1994) Fax sent on 11 January 1994, from General Dallaire (UNAMIR) to Major-General Baril (DPKO, UN), with the subject heading: 'Request for Protection for Informant'. Online. Available HTTP: www.gwu.edu/~nsarchiv/NSAEBB/NSAEBB53/index.html

Dawidowicz, L. (1975; 2nd edn 1990) *The War against the Jews 1933–45*, New York: Penguin.

D'Costa, B. and Hossein, S. (2010) 'Redress for Sexual Violence before the International Crimes Tribunal in Bangladesh: Lessons from History, and Hopes for the Future', *Criminal Law Forum*, 21: 331–59.

Decree for the Protection of Volk and State ('Reichstag Fire Decree') (1933) *Reichsgesetzblatt*, 1, February 28.

De Nike, H., Quigley, J. and Robinson, K. (eds) (2000) *Genocide in Cambodia: Documents from the Trial of Pol Pot and Ieng Sary*, Philadelphia: University of Pennsylvania Press.

Des Forges, A. (1999) *'Leave None to Tell the Story': Genocide in Rwanda*, New York: Human Rights Watch.

——(1995) 'The Ideology of Genocide', *Issue: A Journal of Opinion*, XXIII/2: 44–47.

Donovan, D. (1993) 'Cambodia: Building a Legal System from Scratch', *The International Lawyer*, 27: 445–54.

Draft Agreement between the United Nations and the Royal Government of Cambodia Concerning the Prosecution under Cambodian Law of Crimes Committed during the Period of Democratic Kampuchea (2003) Entry into force 17 March 2003. Online. Available HTTP: www.yale.edu/cgp/Cambodia%20Draft%20Agreement%2017-03-03.doc

Draft Articles on Responsibility of States for Internationally Wrongful Acts (2001) International Law Commission, A/56/10, in *Report of the International Law*

Commission on the Work of its Fifty-third Session, Official Records of the General Assembly, U.N. Doc. A/56/10, New York: United Nations.

Drost, P. (1959a) *Book I. Humanicide. International Governmental Crime against Individual Human Rights*, Leyden: A. W. Sythoff.

——(1959b) *Book II. Genocide. United Nations Legislation on International Criminal Law*, Leyden: A. W. Sythoff.

Dunlop N. and Thayer, N. (1999) 'Duch Confesses', *Far Eastern Economic Review*, 162: 18–23.

Dyzenhaus, D. (1998) *Judging the Judges, Judging Ourselves. Truth, Reconciliation and the Apartheid Legal Order*, Oxford: Hart Publishing.

——(1991) *Hard Cases in Wicked Legal Systems. South African Law in the Perspective of Legal Philosophy*, Oxford: Clarendon Press.

Ehrlich, E. (1913) *Gründlegung der Soziologie des Rechts*, München: Duncker & Humblot; trans. Walter L. Moll (1936) *Fundamental Principles of the Sociology of Law*, Massachusetts: Harvard University Press.

Eisenbruch, M. (2007) 'The Uses and Abuses of Culture: Cultural Competence in Post-Mass-Crime Peace-Building in Cambodia', in B. Pouligny, S. Chesterman and A. Schnabel (eds) *After Mass Crime: Rebuilding States and Communities*, Tokyo: United Nations Press.

Elgesem, F. and Girmachew, A.A. (2009) 'The Rights of the Accused. A Human Rights Appraisal', in K. Tronvoll, C. Schaefer and A.A. Girmachew (eds) *The Ethiopian Red Terror Trials. Transitional Justice Challenged*, Woodbridge, Suffolk; Rochester, New York: James Currey.

Ellis, Mark S. (1997) 'Purging the Past: The Current State of Lustration Laws in the Former Communist Bloc', *Law and Contemporary Problems*, 59 (4): 181–96.

Ellmann, S. (1992) *In a Time of Trouble: Law and Liberty in South Africa's State of Emergency*, Oxford: Clarendon Press.

Englbrecht, W. (2001) 'Bosnia and Herzegovina – No Future without Reconciliation', *Forced Migration*, 11: 18–21.

Etcheson, C. (2005) *After the Killing Fields: Lessons from the Cambodian Genocide*, Westport: Praeger Publishers.

Fawthrop, T. and Jarvis, H. (2005) *Getting Away with Genocide? Elusive Justice and the Khmer Rouge Tribunal*, Sydney: UNSW Press.

Federal Republic of Germany Nationality Law (1999) *Federal Law Gazette* 1, 1618, entry into force 1 January 2000.

Fein, H. (1990) 'Genocide: A Sociological Perspective', *Current Sociology*, 38: 1–101.

——(1979) *Accounting for Genocide. National Responses and Jewish Victimization during the Holocaust*, New York: The Free Press.

——(1978) 'A Formula for Genocide: Comparison of the Turkish Genocide (1915) and the German Holocaust (1939–45)', in R.F. Tomasson (ed.) *Comparative Studies in Sociology. An Annual Compilation of Research*, I, Connecticut: Jai Press.

Ferstman, C.J. (1997) 'Domestic Trials for Genocide and Crimes against Humanity: The Case of Rwanda', *Radic*, 9: 857–77.

Fisiy, C.F. (1998) 'Of Journeys and Border Crossings: Return of Refugees, Identity, and Reconstruction in Rwanda', *African Studies Review*, 41: 17–28.

Fisse, B. and Braithwaite, J. (1993) *Corporations, Crime and Accountability*, Sydney: Cambridge University Press.

——(1983) *The Impact of Publicity on Corporate Offenders*, Albany: State University of New York Press.

Fontaine, C. (1998) 'U.N. Team Offered Full Support in Prosecuting Khmer Rouge', *CNN Interactive Report*. Online. Available HTTP: www.encyclopedia.com/doc/1P1–19414949.html

Fraenkel, E. (1941) *The Dual State. A Contribution to the Theory of Dictatorship*, New York: Oxford University Press.

Fullard, F. (2004) 'State Repression in the 1960s', in South African Democracy Education Trust, *The Road to Democracy in South Africa: 1960–70*, Johannesburg: Zebra Press.

Ganguly, S. (1995) 'Wars without End: The Indo-Pakistani Conflict', *ANNALS AAPSS*, 167–78.

Gellately, R. (1991) '"A Monstrous Uneasiness": Citizen Participation and Persecution of the Jews in Germany', in P. Hayes (ed.) *Lessons and Legacies. The Meaning of the Holocaust in a Changing World*, Evanston, Illinois: Northwestern University Press.

General Framework Agreement for Peace in Bosnia and Herzegovina 'Dayton Peace Agreement' (1995) Online. Available HTTP: www.ohr.int/dpa/default.asp?content_id=380

Girmachew, A.A. (2006) 'Apology and Trials: The Case of the Red Terror Trials in Ethiopia', *African Human Rights Law Journal*, 6: 64–84.

Gobodo-Madikizela, P. (1998) 'Transforming Society Through Reconciliation: Myth or Reality?', presented at Truth and Reconciliation Commission Public Discussion, Cape Town, 12 March.

Goldenberg, S. (1972) 'Crimes against Humanity – 1945–70', *The Western Ontario Law Review*, 11: 1–55.

Goldstone, R. (2000) *For Humanity. Reflections of a War Crimes Investigator*, New Haven & London: Yale University.

Gow, J. (1997) *Triumph of the Lack of Will. International Diplomacy and the Yugoslav War*, London: Hurst & Company.

Grabosky, P.N. (1989) *Wayward Governance. Illegality and its Control in the Public Sector*, Australian Institute of Criminology.

Green, P. and Ward, T. (2004) *State Crime: Governments, Violence and Corruption*, London: Pluto.

Gurr, T.R. (1988) 'War, Revolution and the Growth of the Coercive State', *Comparative Political Studies*, 21: 45–65.

Gutman, I. (ed.) (1990) *Encyclopedia of the Holocaust: Volume 1*, New York: Macmillan.

Haile-Mariam, Y. (1999) 'The Quest for Justice and Reconciliation: The International Criminal Tribunal for Rwanda and the Ethiopian High Court', *Hastings International and Comparative Law Review*, 22: 667–745.

Hajari, N. (1997) 'End of the Line: Looking to Rehabilitate Their Image, Cambodia's Khmer Rouge Put the Dreaded Pol Pot on Trial in the Presence of Two Western Journalists', *Time (Asia)*, 150.

Hannum, H. (1989) 'International Law and Cambodian Genocide: The Sounds of Silence', *Human Rights Quarterly*, 11: 82–138.

Harff, B. and Gurr, T.R. (1989) 'Victims of the State: Genocides, Politicides and Group Repression since 1945', *International Review of Victimology*, 1: 23–41.

Harris, D. (2004) *Cases and Materials on International Law*, 6th edn, London: Sweet & Maxwell.

Hawk, D. (1988) 'The Cambodian Genocide', in I. Charny (ed.) *Genocide. A Critical Bibliographic Review*, New York: Facts on File Publications.

——(1987) *Internet on the Holocaust and Genocide*, Issue 8, Jerusalem: Institute of the International Conference on the Holocaust and Genocide.

Hayner, Priscilla B. (2001) *Unspeakable Truths. Confronting State Terror and Atrocity*, New York and London: Routledge.

——(1994) 'Fifteen Truth Commissions – 1974 to 1994: A Comparative Study', *Human Rights Quarterly*, 16: 597–655.

Henning, Christopher (1998) 'A Fear in Provence', *The Sydney Morning Herald*, April 4, p. 5.

Hillesum, E. (1986) *Letters from Westerbork*, trans. Arnold J. Pomerans, New York: Pantheon Books.

Hinton, A.L. (1998) 'Why Did You Kill? The Cambodian Genocide and the Dark Face of Face and Honor', *The Journal of Asian Studies*, 57: 93–122.

Horowitz, I. (1989) 'Counting Bodies: the Dismal Science of Authorized Terror', *Patterns of Prejudice*, 23: 4–15.

——(1976) *Genocide, State Power and Mass Murder*, New Jersey: Transaction Books.

Höss, A. (1992) 'The Trial of Perpetrators by the Turkish Military Tribunals: The Case of Yozgat', in R. G. Hovannisian (ed.) *The Armenian Genocide. History, Politics, Ethics*, New York: St Martin's Press.

Hovannisian, R.G. (1986) 'The Historical Dimensions of the Armenian Question, 1978–1923', in R.G. Hovannisian (ed.), *The Armenian Genocide in Perspective*, New Brunswick and London: Transaction Publishers.

Human Rights Chamber for Bosnia and Herzegovina (2003) 2002 Annual Report. Online. Available HTTP: www.hrc.ba/ENGLISH/annual_report/2002/annual_report.htm

Human Rights Chamber for Bosnia and Herzegovina (1999) 1999 Annual Report. Online. Available HTTP: www.hrc.ba/ENGLISH/annual_report/1999/cases_1999.htm

Human Rights Watch (2008) *Rwanda Events of 2008*. Online. Available HTTP: www.hrw.org/en/node/79182

——(2001) *World Report 2001*. Online. Available HTTP: www.hrw.org/wr2k1/africa/southafrica.html

——(1999a) *Ethiopian Dictator Mengistu Haile Mariam*. Online. Available HTTP: www.hrw.org/node/82112

——(1999b) *Leave None to Tell the Story. Genocide in Rwanda*. Online. Available HTTP: www.hrw.org/reports/1999/rwanda/

Ignatieff, M. (1998) *The Warriors's Honour. Ethnic War and the Modern Conscience*, London: Chatto & Windus.

Institute for Justice and Reconciliation (2009) *Annual Report* Online. Available HTTP: www.ijr.org.za/2009-annual-report.pdf

Integrated Regional Information Network for Central and Eastern Africa (1999) *Update No. 687*, IRIN-CEA, 7 June. Online. Available HTTP: www.rdrwanda.org/Rwanda/infos/IRIN07061999.html

Interim Report of the Commission of Experts Established Pursuant to Security Council Resolution 780 (1992) UN Doc. S/25274, 27 May.

International Commission of Jurists (1988) *South Africa: Human Rights and the Rule of Law*, G. Bindman (ed.) London and New York: Pinter Publishers.

International Commission of Jurists (1960) *South Africa and the Rule of Law*, Geneva.

International Conference on Military Trials (1945) *Minutes of Conference Session of July 2, 1945*, London. Online. Available HTTP: www.avalon.law.yale.edu/imt/jack20.asp

International Covenants on Human Rights (1979a) *Letter Dated 17 September 1979 from the Permanent Representative of the Socialist Republic of Vietnam to the United Nations Addressed to the Secretary-General, U.N. Doc.A/34/491*, New York: United Nations.

——(1979b) *Letter Dated 4 October 1979 from the Permanent Representative of the Socialist Republic of Vietnam to the United Nations Addressed to the Secretary-General*, U.N. Doc.A/C.3/34/1, New York: United Nations.

International Crimes (Tribunals) Act 1973 (People's Republic of Bangladesh) No. XIX, 20 July.

International Military Tribunal (1947–49) *Trial of the Major War Criminals before the International Military Tribunal, Nuremberg, 14 November 1945–1 October 1946*, Volumes 1-42: Nuremberg, Germany.

Islamic Community in Bosnia and Herzegovina v. The Republika Srpska (1999) Human Rights Chamber for Bosnia and Herzegovina, CH/96/29.

Jackson, K.D. (1989) 'The Ideology of Total Revolution', in K.D. Jackson (ed.) *Cambodia 1975–1978. Rendezvous with Death*, New Jersey: Princeton University Press.

Jahan, R. (1995) 'Genocide in Bangladesh', in S. Totten, W. Parsons and I. Charny (eds) *Genocide in the Twentieth Century: Critical Essays and Eyewitness Accounts*, New York: Garland Publishers.

Jaspers, K. and Augstein, R. (1966) 'The Criminal State and German Responsibility: A Dialogue', *Commentary*, trans. Werner J. Dannhauser, 41: 33–39.

Jelin, E. (1994) 'The Politics of Memory: The Human Rights Movement and the Construction of Democracy in Argentina', *Latin American Perspectives*, 81: 38–58.

Karekezi, U.A., Nshimiyimana, A. and Mutamba, B. (2004) 'Localizing Justice: Gacaca Courts in Post-Genocide Rwanda', in E. Stover and H.M. Weinstein (eds) *My Neighbor, My Enemy. Justice and Community in the Aftermath of Mass Atrocity*, Cambridge: Cambridge University Press.

Karstedt, S. (1998) 'Coming to Terms with the Past in Germany after 1945 and 1989: Public Judgments on Procedures and Justice', *Law & Policy*, 20: 15–56.

Kauzlarich, D. (1995) 'A Criminology of the Nuclear State', *Humanity and Society*, 19: 37–57.

Kauzlarich, D. and Kramer, R.C. (1998) *Crimes of the American Nuclear State. At Home and Abroad*, Boston: Northeastern University Press.

——(1993) 'State-Corporate Crime in the US Nuclear Weapons Production Complex', *The Journal of Human Justice*, 5: 4–28.

Kauzlarich, D., Kramer, R.C. and Smith, B. (1992) 'Toward the Study of Governmental Crime: Nuclear Weapons, Foreign Intervention, and International Law', *Humanity & Society*, 16: 543–63.

Kazarian, H.K. (1971) 'Turkey Tries its Chief Criminals: Indictment and Sentence Passed Down by Military Court of 1919', *The Armenian Review*, 24: 3–26.

Kent, L. (2010) '*Justica Seidauk Mai* (Justice is yet to come): Rethinking the Dynamics of Transitional Justice in East Timor', unpublished thesis, University of Melbourne.
——(2004) 'Unfulfilled Expectations: Community Views on CAVR's Community Reconciliation Process', *Judicial System Monitoring Programme*, August 2004. Online. Available HTTP: www.jsmp.minihub.org/new/otherreports.htm

Kiernan, B. (1996) *The Pol Pot Regime: Race, Power and Genocide in Cambodia under the Khmer Rouge 1975–79*, New Haven: Yale University Press.

Kirchheimer, O. (1961) *Political Justice. The Use of Legal Procedure for Political Ends*, New Jersey: Princeton University Press.
——(1940) 'Criminal Law in National Socialist Germany', trans. Anke Grosskopf and William E. Scheuermann, in W.E. Scheuerman, (ed.) *The Rule of Law under Siege. Selected Essays of Franz L. Neumann and Otto Kirchheimer*, Berkeley: University of California Press.
——[1935] (1996) 'State Structure and Law in the Third Reich', trans. Anke Grosskopf and William E. Scheuermann, in W.E. Scheuerman (ed.) *The Rule of Law under Siege. Selected Essays of Franz L. Neumann and Otto Kirchheimer*, Berkeley: University of California Press.

Klinghoffer, A. (1998) 'Parameters of Genocide', in Klinghoffer, A. (ed.) *The International Dimension of Genocide in Rwanda*, New York: New York University Press.

Koch, H.W. (1989) *In the Name of the Volk. Political Justice in Hitler's Germany*, London: I.B. Tauris & Co. Ltd.

Krawinkel, H. (1949) 'Law in the British Zone of Germany', *Current Legal Problems*, 2: 245–57.

Krog, A. (1998) *Country of My Skull*, South Africa: Random House.

Kuper, L. (1992) 'Reflections on the Prevention of Genocide', in H. Fein (ed.) *Genocide Watch*, New Haven: Yale University Press.
——(1981) *Genocide. Its Political Use in the Twentieth Century*, New Haven and London: Yale University Press.

Kwiet, K. (2000) 'Judenmord als Amtsanmaßung. Das Feldurteil vom 12. März gegen Johann Meißlein', *Dachauer Hefte*, 16: 125–35.

Lambourne, W. (2004) 'Post-Conflict Peacebuilding: Meeting Human Needs for Justice and Reconciliation', *Peace, Conflict and Development*, 4: 1–24.

Laplante, Lisa J. (2008) 'Transitional Justice and Peace Building: Diagnosing and Addressing the Socioeconomic Roots of Violence through a Human Rights Framework', *The International Journal of Transitional Justice*, 2: 331–55.

Law No. 81 on General Amnesty and National Reconciliation (1990) Nicaragua, in N.J. Kritz (ed.) (1995) *Transitional Justice: How Emerging Democracies Reckon with Former Regimes: Laws, Rulings, and Reports*. Washington, D.C.: United States Institute of Peace.

Law on the Establishment of the Extraordinary Chambers in the Courts of Cambodia for the Prosecution of Crimes Committed during the Period of Democratic Kampuchea, with Inclusion of Amendments as Promulgated on 27 October 2004 (NS/RKM/1004/006) (2004). Online. Available HTTP: www.eccc.gov.kh/english/law.list.aspx

Lederach, J.P. (1999) 'The Challenge of the 21st Century: Justpeace', in *People Building Peace: 35 Inspiring Stories from Around the World*, Utrecht: European Centre for Conflict Resolution.

Lemarchand, R. (1995) 'Rwanda: The Rationality of Genocide', *Issue: A Journal of Opinion*, XXIII/2: 8–11.

Lemkin, R. (1944) *Axis Rule in Occupied Europe. Laws of Occupation. Analysis of Government. Proposals for Redress*, Washington: Carnegie Endowment for International Peace.

Lévai, E. (1969) 'The War Crimes Trials Relating to Hungary', in R.L. Braham (ed.) *Hungarian Jewish Studies II*, New York: World Federation of Hungarian Jews.

Lewy, G. (1964) 'Pius XII, the Jews, and the German Catholic Church', *Commentary*, 37: 23–35.

Lifton, R. (1986) *The Nazi Doctors. Medical Killing and the Psychology of Genocide*, London: Macmillan.

Lopez, G.A. (1984) 'A Scheme for the Analysis of Government as Terrorist', in M. Stohl and G.A. Lopez (eds) *The State as Terrorist. The Dynamics of Governmental Violence and Repression*, Connecticut: Greenwood Press.

Łoś, M. and Zybertowicz, A. (2000) *Privatizing the Police State: The Case of Poland*, Basingstoke: Macmillan.

——(1999) 'Is Revolution a Solution? State Crime in Communist and Post-Communist Poland (1980–95)', in M. Krygier and A. Czarnota (eds) *The Rule of Law after Communism*, Dartmouth: Aldershot.

Mabbett, I. and Chandler, D. (1995) *The Khmers*, Oxford and Cambridge: Basil Blackwell.

Macdonald, D. (1957) *The Responsibility of Peoples and Other Essays in Political Criticism*, London: Victor Gollancz Ltd.

McCourt, K. (2009) 'Judicial Defenders', *International Journal of Transitional Justice*, 3: 272–83.

Maharaj, M. (1997) 'Justice or Reconciliation. The Situation in South Africa Today', presented at the Justice or Reconciliation Conference, Chicago, 25 April.

Maley, W. (1997) 'The United Nations and Ethnic Conflict Management: Lessons from the Disintegration of Yugoslavia', *Nationalities Papers*, 25: 559–74.

Mam, K. (2008) 'Legal Justice Lessens Anger of Villagers', Cambodia Tribunal Monitor, 17 October 2008. Online. Available HTTP: www.cambodiatribunal.org

Mamdani, M. (2001) *When Victims Become Killers. Colonialism, Nativism, and the Genocide in Rwanda*, New Jersey: Princeton University Press.

——(2000) 'The Truth According to the TRC', in I. Amadiume and A. An-Na'im (eds) *The Politics of Memory: Truth, Healing and Social Justice*, London: Zed Books.

——(1998) *Truth and Reconciliation Commission Public Discussion: 'Transforming Society Through Reconciliation: Myth or Reality?'*, Cape Town, 12 March 1998. Online. Available HTTP: www.truth.org.za

——(1996) 'From Conquest to Consent as the Basis of State Formation: Reflections on Rwanda', *New Left Review*, 216: 3–36.

Mandela, N. (1986) *The Struggle is my Life*. His speeches and writings brought together with historical documents and accounts of Mandela in prison by fellow-prisoners, London: International Defence and Aid Fund for Southern Africa.

Mani, R. (2002) *Beyond Retribution. Seeking Justice in the Shadows of War*, Cambridge: Polity Press.

Marks, S.P. (1999) 'Elusive Justice for Victims of the Khmer Rouge', *Journal of International Affairs*, 52 (2): 691–718.

Marks, S. (1994) 'The New Cambodian Constitution: From Civil War to a Fragile Democracy', *Columbia Human Rights Law Review*, 26: 45–110.

Mathews, A. (1986) *Freedom, State Security and the Rule of Law. Dilemmas of the Apartheid Society*, Cape Town: Juta & Co.

McDonald, G. (1998) 'The Eleventh Annual Waldemar A. Solf Lecture: The Changing Nature of the Laws of War', *Military Law Review*, 156: 30–51.

McMillan, N. (2008) 'Coming to Terms: Responding to the Rwandan Genocide', unpublished thesis, University of Melbourne.

Meierhenrich, J. (2008) *The Legacies of Law. Long-Run Consequences of Legal Development in South Africa, 1652–2000*, Cambridge: Cambridge University Press.

Melson, R. (1986) 'Provocation or Nationalism: A Critical Inquiry into the Armenian Genocide of 1915', in R.G. Hovannisian (ed.) *The Armenian Genocide in Perspective*, New Brunswick and London: Transaction Publishers.

Melvern, L. (2000) *A People Betrayed. The Role of the West in Rwanda's Genocide*, London and New York: Zed Books.

Mexico Peace Agreements (1991) Provisions Creating the Commission on Truth (El Salvador), Mexico City, April 27, 1991. United States Institute of Peace Library. Online. Available HTTP: www.usip.org/library/tc/doc/charters/tc_elsalvador.html

Miller, R.M. (1995) *Nazi Justiz. Law of the Holocaust*, London: Praeger.

Minister of the Interior v. Lockhat (1961) South African Court of Appeal, (2) SA 587 (A).

Mommsen, H. (1991) 'The Reaction of the German Population to the Anti-Jewish Persecution and the Holocaust', in P. Hayes (ed.) *Lessons and Legacies. The Meaning of the Holocaust in a Changing World*, Evanston, Illinois: Northwestern University Press.

Moore, S.F. (1973) 'Law and Social Change: The Semi-Autonomous Social Field as an Appropriate Field of Study', *Law & Society Review*, 7: 719–46.

Morgenthau, H. (1918) *Ambassador Morgenthau's Story*, New York: Gomidas Institute.

Moscow Declaration on German Atrocities of 30 October 1943. Appendix I, *The Charter and Judgment of the Nürnberg Tribunal. History and Analysis*. Memorandum submitted by the Secretary-General. (United Nations-General Assembly, International Law Commission, Lake Success, New York, 1949.)

Müller, I. (1991) *Hitler's Justice: The Courts of the Third Reich*, trans. Deborah Lucas Schneider, Cambridge, Massachusetts: Harvard University Press.

Naidoo, U. (1998) 'The Truth Hurts: Psychoanalytic Speculations on Racism', *Melbourne Journal of Politics*, 25: 133–48.

National Service of Gacaca Jurisdictions, *Organic Law*. Online. Available HTTP: www.inkiko-gacaca.gov.rw/En/EnLaw.htm

Nazis and Nazi Collaborators (Punishment) Law, 5710-1950 (1950) Entry into force 1 August 1950. Published in Sefer Ha-Chukkim No. 57 of the 26th Av, 5711 (9 August 1950). p. 281. Online. Available HTTP: www.mfa.gov.il/MFA/MFAArchive/1950_1959/Nazis+and+Nazi+Collaborators+-Punishment-+Law-+571.htm

Nicaragua: Law on General Amnesty and National Reconciliation (1990) Law No. 81 1990, excerpts in N. Kritz (ed.) (1995) *Transitional Justice: How Emerging Democracies Reckon with Former Regimes: Laws, Rulings, and Reports*, Washington D.C.: United States Institute of Peace.

Ntsebexa, D.B. (2000) 'The Uses of Truth Commissions. Lessons for the World', in R.I. Rotberg and D. Thompson (eds) *Truth v. Justice. The Morality of Truth Commissions*, Princeton and Oxford: Princeton University Press.

Omar, D. (1995) 'Statement as Minister of Justice of South Africa'. Online. Available HTTP: www.justice.gov.za/trc/legal/justice.htm

——(1990) 'An Overview of State Lawlessness in South Africa', in D. Hanson and D. van Zyl Smit (eds) *Towards Justice? Crime and State Control in South Africa*, Cape Town: Oxford University Press.

Organic Law of 30 August 1996 on the organization of prosecutions for offences constituting the crime of genocide or crimes against humanity committed since 1 October 1990, Law No. 8/96 (1996) *Official Gazette of the Republic of Rwanda*, 17: 14–26.

Organization of African Unity (2000) *Rwanda: The Preventable Genocide.* The Report of the International Panel of Emment Personalities to Investigate the 1994 Genocide in Rwanda and the Surrounding Events, Addis Ababa: Organization of African Unity.

Penal Code of the Empire of Ethiopia (1957) Proclamation No. 414/2004, Addis Ababa, 5 May 1958.

People's Revolutionary Tribunal. Held in Phnom Penh for the Trial of the Crime of Genocide Committed by the Pol Pot-Ieng Sary Clique (1979) Ministry of Information, Press and Cultural Affairs of the People's Republic of Kampuchea, Phnom Penh, August 1979. Manuscripts (English Translation).

Permanent Representative of Rwanda (1994) *Statement Dated 28 September 1994 on the Question of Refugees and Security in Rwanda* (1994) annex to *Letter Dated 28 September from the Permanent Representative of Rwanda to the United Nations Addressed to the President of the Security Council*, U.N. Security Council, U.N. Doc. S/1994/1115.

Philips, D. (2008) 'From People's Charter to Freedom Charter: Violent and Non-violent Democratic Struggle in Britain and South Africa', *London Grip*. Online. Available HTTP: www.londongrip.com/LondonGrip/SouthAfrica_FreedomCharter_David_Philips.html

Phillips, R. (1949) 'Introduction', in Phillips, R. (ed.) *Trial of Josef Kramer and Forty-Four Others (The Belsen Trial)*, London: William Hodge and Company, Limited.

Podgórecki, A. (1996) 'Totalitarian Law: Basic Concepts and Issues', in A. Podgórecki and V. Olgiati (eds) *Totalitarian and Post-Totalitarian Law*, Aldershot: Dartmouth Publishing Company Ltd.

Ponchaud, F. (1978) *Cambodia Year Zero*, trans. Nancy Amphoux, London: Allen Lane.

Potsdam Agreement (1945) The Berlin (Potsdam) Conference, July 17–August 2 1945. Protocol of the Proceedings, August l, 1945. Online. Available HTTP: http://avalon.law.yale.edu/20th_century/decade17.asp?

Preliminary Report of the Independent Commission of Experts established in accordance with Security Council Resolution 935 (1994) UNSC, UN Doc. S/1994/1125 (1994) Annex.

Pritchard, S. (1998) 'The Stolen Generations and Reparations', *University of New South Wales Law Journal*, 21 (1): 259–67.

Proclamation Establishing the Office of the Special Prosecutor (1992) Proclamation No 22/1992, Addis Ababa 8 August 1992.

Proclamation to Provide for the Establishment of a National Revolutionary Operations Command (1977) Proclamation No 129 of 1977, Addis Ababa, 27 August 1977.

Promotion of National Unity and Reconciliation Act (1995) Act 34, entry into force 26 July 1995. Online. Available HTTP: www.info.gov.za/documents

The Prosecutor v Duško Tadić (1997) Trial Chamber Opinion and Judgment, International Criminal Tribunal for the former Yugoslavia, IT-94-1-T.

The Prosecutor v. Jean Kambanda (1998) International Criminal Tribunal for Rwanda, ICTR 97-23-S.

The Prosecutor v. Jean-Paul Akayesu (1998) International Criminal Tribunal for Rwanda, ICTR-96-4-T.

The Prosecutor v. Slobodan Milošević (2002) International Criminal Tribunal for the Former Yugoslavia, IT-02-54.

Prunier, G. (1995) *The Rwanda Crisis. History of a Genocide*, New York: Columbia University Press.

Radio Free Europe/ Radio Liberty (2000) *Balkan Report*, 4, 31 October.

Ratner, S. and Abrams, J.S. (1997) *Accountability for Human Rights Atrocities in International Law. Beyond the Nuremberg Legacy*, Oxford: Clarendon Press.

Report of the Group of Experts for Cambodia Established Pursuant to General Assembly Resolution 52/135 (1999) Online. Available HTTP: www.unakrt-online. org/04_documents.htm

Report of the Special Rapporteur of the Commission on Human Rights on the Situation of Human Rights in Rwanda (1995) UN Doc. A/50/709-S/1995/915, 2 November.

Revolutionary Flags (1976), Special Issue, Sept-Oct 1976, trans. Kem Sos and Timothy Carney, in K.D. Jackson (ed.) *Cambodia 1975–1978. Rendezvous with Death*, New Jersey: Princeton University Press.

Robinson, N. (1960) *The Genocide Convention: A Commentary*, New York: Institute of Jewish Affairs, World Jewish Congress.

Roht-Arriaza, N. (2004) 'Reparations Decisions and Dilemmas', *Hastings International & Comparative Law Review*, 27 (1): 157–219.

Rosenthal, J. (1985) 'Legal and Political Considerations of the United States' Ratification of the Genocide Convention', *Antioch Law Journal*, 3: 117–44.

Ross, J.I. (1995) 'Controlling State Crime: Toward an Integrated Structural Model', in J.I. Ross (ed.) *Controlling State Crime. An Introduction*, London: Garland Publishing.

Rückerl, A. (1979) *The Investigation of Nazi Crimes 1945–1978, A Documentation*, Heidelberg: C.F. Müller.

Rummel, R.J. (1994) *Death by Government*, New Brunswick: Transaction Publishers.

Sachs, A. (1970) *South Africa: The Violence of Apartheid*, London: International Defence and Aid Fund.

Sarat, A. and Kearns, T.R. (eds) (1993) *Law in Everyday Life*, Ann Arbor: The University of Michigan Press.

Schabas, W. (2008) 'State Policy as an Element of International Crimes', *Journal of Criminal Law & Criminology*, 98: 953–82.

Schmid, A.P. (1991) 'Repression, State Terrorism, and Genocide: Conceptual Clarifications', in P.T. Bushnell, V. Shlapentokh, C.K. Vanderpool and J. Sundram (eds) *State Organized Terror. The Case of Violent Internal Repression*, Colorado: Westview Press.

Schwelb, E. (1946) 'Crimes against Humanity', *The British Year Book of International Law*, 23: 178–226.

Senat de Belgique, Commission d'enquête parlementaire concernant les événtments du Rwanda (1997) *Compte Rendu Analytique des Auditions*, Bruxelles, 1–75 COM-R.

Shawcross, W. (1984) *The Quality of Mercy. Cambodia, Holocaust and Modern Conscience*, New York: Simon and Schuster.

Shklar, J. (1964) *Legalism*, Cambridge: Harvard University Press.

Siklová, J. (1999) 'Lustration or the Czech Way of Screening', in M. Krygier and A. Czarnota (eds) *The Rule of Law after Communism*, Dartmouth: Aldershot.

Smeulers, A. and R. Haveman (eds) *Supranational Criminology: Towards A Criminology of International Crimes*, Antwerp: Intersentia.

Special Penal Code Proclamation (1977) *Negarit Gazeta*, Proclamation No. 110 of 1977, Addis Ababa, 11 February 1977.

Special Penal Code Proclamation (1974) *Negarit Gazeta*, Proclamation No. 8 of 1974, Addis Ababa, 16 November 1974.

Spinedi, M. (1989) 'International Crimes of State: The Legislative History', in J. H. Weiler, A. Cassese and M. Spinedi (eds) *International Crimes of State. A Critical Analysis of the ILC's Draft Article 19 on State Responsibility*, Berlin: Walter de Gruyter.

Stanton, G. (1993) 'The Khmer Rouge Genocide and International Law', in B. Kiernan (ed.) *Genocide and Democracy in Cambodia*, New Haven: Yale University Southeast Asia Studies.

Statute of the International Criminal Tribunal for Rwanda (1994) S.C. Res. 955, U.N. DOC. S/RES/955, New York: United Nations.

Statute of the International Tribunal for the Former Yugoslavia (1993) S.C. Res. 827, U.N. Doc. S/RES/827, New York: United Nations.

Stohl, M. (1984) 'International Dimensions of State Terrorism', in M. Stohl and G.A. Lopez (eds) *The State as Terrorist. The Dynamics of Governmental Violence and Repression*, Connecticut: Greenwood Press.

Stohl, M. and Lopez, G.A. (1984) 'Introduction', in M. Stohl and G.A. Lopez (eds) *The State as Terrorist. The Dynamics of Governmental Violence and Repression*, Connecticut: Greenwood Press.

Stolleis, M. (1998) *The Law under the Swastika. Studies on Legal History in Nazi Germany*, trans. Thomas Dunlop, London: The University of Chicago Press.

Supreme Court of the ACT (1998), In the matter of an application for a writ of mandamus directed to Philip R. Thompson Ex parte Wadjularbinna Nulyarimma, Isobel Coe, Billy Craigie and Robbie Thorpe (Applicants), Tom Trevorrow, Irene Watson, Kevin Buzzacott and Michael J. Anderson (Intervenors), ACTSC 409, 18 December 1998.

Tan, L.H. (1979) 'Cambodia's Total Revolution', *Index on Censorship*, 8: 3–10.

Tatz, C. (2003) *With Intent to Destroy*, New York: Verso.

Terry, F. (2002) *Condemned to Repeat? The Paradox of Humanitarian Action*, New York: Cornell University Press.

Thayer, N. (1997a) 'Brother Number Zero', *Far Eastern Economic Review*, 160: 14–18.

——(1997b) 'Pol Pot Unmasked', *Far Eastern Economic Review*, 160: 19–20.

Thompson, J.L.P. and Quets, G.A. (1990) 'Genocide and Social Conflict: A Partial Theory and Comparison', *Research in Social Movements, Conflict and Change*, 12: 245–66.

Tilly, T. (1985) 'War Making and State Making as Organized Crime', in P.B. Evans, D. Rueschemeyer and T. Skocpol (eds) *Bringing the State Back in*, New York: Cambridge University Press.

Timor-Leste Commission for Reception, Truth and Reconciliation (2005) *Chega! Report of the Timor-Leste Commission for Reception, Truth and Reconciliation*, Dili. Online. Available HTTP: www.cavr-timorleste.org/en/chegaReport.htm

Treaty of Peace with Hungary (1947) *The American Journal of International Law*, 42, 4, Supplement: Official Documents: 225–51.

Treaty of Sèvres (1920) *The Treaties of Peace 1919–1923 Vol. II*, New York: Carnegie Endowment for International Peace.

Trial of Pakistani Prisoners of War, Interim Protection Order of 13 July 1973 [1973] ICJ Reports 1973.

Trial of Pakistani Prisoners of War, Interim Protection Order of 15 December 1973 [1973] ICJ Reports 1973.

Trials of War Criminals before the Nuremberg Military Tribunals under Control Council Law No. 10 (1949–53) Volumes 1–15, Washington D.C: U.S. Government Printing Office.

Tribunal Memorandum of Understanding Between the United Nations and the Royal Government of Cambodia (2000) *Phnom Penh Post*, 9, 27 October – 9 November. Online. Available HTTP: www.yale.edu/cgp/

Triffterer, O. (1986) 'Prosecution of States for Crimes of State', in M.C. Bassiouni (ed.) *International Criminal Law: Vol III (Enforcement)*, New York: Transnational Publishers.

Tronvoll, K., Schaefer, C. and Girmachew A.A. (eds) (2009) *The Ethiopian Red Terror Trials: Transitional Justice Challenged*, Woodbridge, Suffolk; Rochester, New York: James Currey.

Truth and Reconciliation Commission Act (2000) *Supplement to the Sierra Leone Gazette*, CXXXI, 9, 10 February. United States Institute of Peace Library. Online. Available HTTP: www.usip.org/library/tc.doc/charters/tc_sierra_leone_02102000.html

Truth and Reconciliation Commission of South Africa (2003) *Truth and Reconciliation Commission of South Africa Report*, vol. 6, London: MacMillan Reference.

——(1999a) *Truth and Reconciliation Commission of South Africa Report*, vol. 1, London: MacMillan Reference.

——(1999b) *Truth and Reconciliation Commission of South Africa Report*, vol. 4, London: MacMillan Reference.

——(1999c) *Truth and Reconciliation Commission of South Africa Report*, vol. 5, London: MacMillan Reference.

——(1998) Mandela United Football Club Hearings, Johannesburg, 24 November–4 December 1997 and 28–29 January 1998. Online. Available HTTP: www.truth.org.za/special/index.htm

Truth and Reconciliation Commission of South Africa Press Release (1997a) *Statement: Legal Submission*, 22 October.

——(1997b) *Special TRC Legal Hearing*, 19 October.

Tutorow, N.E. (1986) *War Crimes, War Criminals, and War Crimes Trials. An Annotated Bibliography and Source Book*, New York: Greenwood Press.

Twining, W. (2000) *Globalisation and Legal Theory*, London: Butterworths.

United Nations (1999) *Cambodia Should not be Accused of Practising 'Culture of Impunity', Delegation Tells Human Rights Committee*, U.N. Doc. HR/CT/99/11, New York: United Nations.

United Nations Department of Public Information (1996) *The United Nations and Rwanda 1993–1996* with an introduction by Boutros Boutros-Ghali, New York: United Nations.

United Nations Security Council Resolution 955 (1994) S/RES/955, 8 November. Online. Available HTTP: www.un.org/Docs/scres/1994/scres94.html

United Nations Security Council Resolution 1534 (2004) S/RES/1534, 26 March. Online. Available HTTP: www.un.org/Docs/sc/unsc_resolutions04.html

Vernon, R. (2002) 'What is Crime against Humanity?', *The Journal of Political Philosophy,* 10 (3): 231–49.

Wagner, M. (1998) 'All the *Bourgmestre's* Men: Making Sense of Genocide in Rwanda', *Africa Today,* 45 (1): 25–36.

Wenig, J. (1997) 'Enforcing the Lessons of History: Israel Judges the Holocaust', in T. McCormack and G. Simpson (eds) *The Law of War Crimes. National and International Approaches,* The Hague: Kluwer Law International.

White, J.B. (1985) *Heracles' Bow. Essays on the Rhetoric and Poetics of the Law,* Madison: The University of Wisconsin Press.

Willis, J.F. (1982) *Prologue to Nuremberg: The Politics and Diplomacy of Punishing War Criminals of the First World War,* Connecticut: Greenwood Press.

Witness Statement. Report on Orphans Relief Centre (1979) *People's Revolutionary Tribunal Held in Phnom Penh for the Trial of the Genocide Crime of the Pol Pot-Ieng Sary Clique,* Doc. No. 2.4.04, August 1979.

Wolfe, P. (1994) 'Nation and MiscegeNation: Discursive Continuity in the Post-Mabo Era', *Social Analysis,* 36: 93–131.

Yacoubian, G.S. (1997) 'Underestimating the Magnitude of International Crime: Implications of Genocidal Behavior for the Discipline of Criminology', *Injustice Studies,* 1: 1.

Yalta Agreement (1945) Online. Available HTTP: www.h-net.org/~hst306/documents/ YALTA.html

Zalaquett, J. (1995) 'Chile', in A. Boraine and J. Levy (eds) *The Healing of a Nation?,* Cape Town: Justice in Transition.

Zybertowicz, A. 'Institutional background for the post-Nomenklatura networks in Poland', paper presented at Hidden Structures of Law workshop, International Institute for the Sociology of Law, Oñati, May 1995, with reference to Zyberto-wicz, A. (1993) *W Uscisku Sluzb Tajnych (In Secret Services' Embrace),* Warsaw: Antyk.

Index